Happy 50th Birthday
Pete...

Love
Val & Georgia

STORIES OF SERVICE

Valley Veterans
Remember World War II

compiled by
Janice Stevens

Craven Street Books
Fresno, CA

STORIES OF SERVICE
Valley Veterans Remember World War II
by Janice Stevens

Cover design: James Goold
Book design: Carla Green, Studio C Graphics

135798642
ISBN: 978-1-933502-08-3
printed in U.S.

Library of Congress Cataloging-in-Publication Data
  Stories of service : Valley veterans remember World War II /
compiled by Janice Stevens.
      p. cm.
  Includes index.
  ISBN 978-1-933502-08-3 (hardcover : alk. paper)
  1. World War, 1939-1945—Personal narratives, American.
  2. World War, 1939-1945—Veterans—California--San Joaquin Valley Region—
Biography.
  3. United States—Armed Forces—Military life.
  4. Veterans—California—San Joaquin Valley—Biography.
  5. San Joaquin Valley (Calif.)—Biography.
  I. Stevens, Janice (Janice Mae), 1944- II. Title.

D810.V42U677 2007
940.54'817948--dc22   2007019624

Craven Street Books
Linden Publishing Inc.
2006 S. Mary
Fresno, CA 93721
www.lindenpub.com
800-345-4447

Veterans pictured on the front cover, left to right, top to bottom:
Juan Cedilla, Helen Caraway, Jose Salazar, Sr., Jesse Woodward, Jr.,
Chris Christensen, Leonard Frame, Penny Mirigian-Emerzian, Raymond Lee,
Dorothy Dormandy, George Middleton, John Costello, Robert Brummer.
Front flap: Robert Owens. Back cover: Victor Smith.

ACKNOWLEDGMENTS

With deep appreciation, I want to thank the veterans who served in World War II for their sacrifices in the fight for our freedom. I especially want to thank those who shared their stories for this work.

Special thanks must go to the people below, whose generous efforts contributed greatly to the completion of this book:

Brandon Wright, California Coordinator for the Stories of Service Project, a project of the Digital Clubhouse Network, operated in the Central Valley by the Center for Multicultural Cooperation.

The staff at Clovis Adult Education

The Board of Directors for the Clovis Memorial District

John Ballinger

Aileen Bos and Gene Bos

Patsy Champ

Nina Coon

Rachel B. Frauenholz

Debbie Hernandez

Nancy and Robert Huey

Pat Hunter

Barbara Majors

Kent Sorsky of Linden Publishing

Richard Sorsky of Linden Publishing

Monica Stevens

Al Verret

Kilulu von Prince

Tom Wright

Stan Wells

Deep appreciation is extended to the veterans and their families for providing photos and documents to accompany their stories.

TABLE OF CONTENTS

THE PACIFIC THEATER

FOREWORD

Not long after I started the Stories of Service Project here in the valley, I heard about a group of veterans that met each week to share their military experiences. I contacted their instructor, Janice Stevens, and asked if I could meet with her to discuss our working together to interview the veterans. We are both passionate about preserving living history, and there was a natural symmetry between my project—working with high school students, adult mentors, and veterans to create DVDs of their stories—and her project of compiling the veterans' stories into a book. So she invited me to her classes and was instrumental in helping me recruit veterans for my own project.

> "There is no snow in the South Pacific, and the Vietnam War took place after World War II. During WW II there was no Air Force, they called it the Army Air Corps. And for heaven's sake be careful who you call a soldier—they just might be a marine...."

When we first started to train young people to interview and produce digital videos about veterans through the Stories of Service Project, I had no idea that I would be giving the above advice. But to the latest generation, living in the 21st Century, WW II was several lifetimes ago and could have taken place on another planet. Home cooked meals, barn dances, and big band have been replaced by Super Value Meals, MySpace, and hip hop. Many of these student interviewers were first generation Americans who had grown up with English as their second language. You can imagine how well the initial conversation went as WW II veterans, some of whom have limited hearing, tried their best to interpret the first few oral history interview questions asked by teenagers with accents exaggerated by nervousness!

But these veterans, many of whom had never told their closest loved ones about the war, made themselves vulnerable by going back over sixty years and relaying their own personal experiences. As the barriers came down and the initial nervousness wore off, connections were made and the learning started to take place. This happened in Janice's class, and it happened for the youths in my project, as well.

These volunteers learned someone's exact location and reaction when they heard the ghastly news of December 7, 1941. They learned about C-rations and boot camp. They learned about the freezing cold, the deafening boom of artillery, the loss of friends, and the utter inhumanity of war. They listened to what it means to someone to be an American—the hopes, the values, and the deepest beliefs that someone was willing to die for. They learned to wait patiently as memories were reflected upon, some of joy, some of horror, and some of courage—from so many years ago. They learned to pause when the tears came: tears of love for friends made, tears of sadness for friends lost, and tears of guilt for the incomprehensible luck of their own survival. They learned that the elderly person being interviewed was once not much older than they are, and that they have a lot more in common than they thought.

When we first began our interviews a few short years ago, we could not find enough volunteers to assist with the constant rush of veterans ready to finally share their stories. Here, in the twilight of their lives, they willingly stepped forward to pass on a lifetime of experiences and knowledge as only they can. But now, even though we have only scratched the surface, the phone rings much less often, and we are coming to terms with the fact that it will ring less and less with each passing month and year. The veterans of this generation are like the white buffalo, and when the last one passes from our midst, there shall never be another, and somehow, it won't quite be the same.

I am proud that the youth and adult volunteers from the Stories of Service Project were able to contribute some of the stories in Janice's wonderful book (the rest coming from her memoir-writing class). I believe that the many volunteers who helped bring forth and compile the stories contained in this book came out of the process with a new perspective that will last a lifetime. They now know there isn't snow in the South Pacific, and they know that not everyone in the U.S. Armed Forces likes to be referred to as a soldier. But it goes deeper than that. The stories they have been entrusted with will inspire and sustain them in their own everyday lives. They will go forward with a new perspective and sense of confidence as they face the challenges of the 21st Century. I know this is the case for me, and as you read the following collection of memories of so many who were ready to sacrifice so much, it is my hope for you as well.

Brandon Wright, *California Coordinator*
The Stories of Service Project
www.stories-of-service.org
A project of the Digital Clubhouse Network
Operated in the Central Valley by the
Center for Multicultural Cooperation

INTRODUCTION

In early 2002, the Clovis Memorial District, a veterans' organization in Clovis, California, approached Clovis Adult Education to request an instructor to teach a class in preserving the histories of those who served in the military as a permanent tribute and legacy of their service. Barbara Majors, Learning Director and coordinator of the Older Adult Program for Clovis Adult Education, asked me if I would like to be involved. Having taught memoir-writing classes for the past fifteen years, I saw the veterans' class as another focused extension of memoir writing and was elated and honored to be asked.

The class was advertised in the C.A.E. catalog, and on a Monday morning in March of 2002, eight veterans and I met for the first time in a small room at the Clovis Memorial District. We sat in a circle and each veteran introduced himself. At first, they were reluctant to share very much, but were pleased nonetheless that someone believed their story needed to be preserved. Nancy Huey came to that first meeting and offered to tape record each session to create a permanent record of the oral histories presented. Shortly thereafter Al Verret came forward to offer his services to videotape and photograph the veterans and the memorabilia they brought in to show.

It wasn't long before the class had grown to more than twenty, which required a move to the Clovis Memorial District's much-larger "Freedom Room." Aileen Bos, accompanying her husband Gene one morning, offered to take attendance and notes of each session. More people volunteered: Gene made the coffee; Stan Lee set up the tables; Aileen passed around a treat; and others helped out to cover the duties of a volunteer who wasn't able to attend each time.

The veterans formed friendships and on Mondays, wishing to prolong the camaraderie of the morning, frequented restaurants in the Clovis area. Parties and field trips reinforced the friendships gleaned from the class. From that small beginning, the class grew to averaging more than forty people.

Little did I know how deeply affected I would be by the stories of sacrifice related by the veterans of this terrible war. Over and over each Monday morning I would hear, "Freedom isn't free," as one veteran after another described the life-changing events of his or her service.

The detail in their remembrances was sometimes chilling, and it became evident that these experiences haunted them. Some veterans would come to share their story only once. The telling might be a dry recitation of service as if read off a discharge paper, or it could be a deeply painful story of comrades losing life and limb. Some would relate very specific details—still fresh in their mind—of the terrain, the weather, the odor in the air, while others shared their most-personal inner thoughts, often about their powerful yearnings for home and loved ones. Some veterans would sit in class week after week, never uttering much but listening, and then, all of a sudden, a story would burst forth, often accompanied by tears of remorse or sadness, frequently laced with survivor's guilt, sometimes full of awe at the miracle of their own survival.

I saw and heard history play out in a compelling and emotional fashion that is simply not attainable from a textbook or film, regardless of how gripping it might be. Yes, there was anguish in the veterans' eyes, but there was humor, as well. This (rather sick, at times) humor was used to show that not all was dark, and for some veterans it provided the only means they had to cope with their harrowing memories. Many young men seemingly aged overnight after experiencing the atrocities that confronted and would forever haunt them. It's been said that there aren't any atheists in foxholes, but as one veteran stated, "There is no God in war."

I heard anger, sorrow, laughter, bitterness, intense patriotism and love of country and fellow man. I saw the desire to restore right and justice. There was acknowledgment of the frequently duplicitous nature of politics during wartime, and on occasion intense political debate would occur. Yet the overwhelming theme of the discussions was the veterans' loyal service, and their pride in their country. They were individually humble and did not look to their own accomplishments. They served willing and eagerly, and when the war was over they returned to their homes and resumed their lives as best they could.

Uppermost in my mind is my deep appreciation for all our veterans and their willingness to fight for our freedom. Our history can be whitewashed in school textbooks, but the experiences related by the veterans in this book provide a permanent historical marker for future generations.

Janice Stevens
March 2007

Author's note: I have tried to strike a balance between leaving each storyteller's words and (sixty-plus-year-old) remembrances as raw and untouched as possible, while correcting major factual errors. Some "lesser" errors (for example, the number of ships in a particular fleet engagement, or the number of casualties suffered during a bombing raid) have been left uncorrected.

THE
PACIFIC
THEATER

PEARL HARBOR ATTACKED

Tension between the United States and Japan had intensified since the beginning of the Japan and China war in 1937. The United States had extended credit to China but placed a "moral embargo" on oil and scrap steel exports to Japan. By 1940, with Japan's occupation of Indochina, the United States ended all shipments of supplies to that nation, froze Japanese assets in America, and prohibited American firms from interacting with Japanese businesses.

In 1941, with negotiations to restore relations between the countries failing to resolve anything, Premier Lt. Gen. Hideki Tojo recommended to the Japanese cabinet that Japan declare war against the United States. Secret plans were put in place for a strategic strike against the United States. Under the leadership of Admiral Isoroku Yamamoto, Commander-in-Chief of the Japanese combined fleet, the intention was to bomb Pearl Harbor in Hawaii, destroying the American Pacific Fleet. Japan could then advance into Thailand, the Malay Peninsula, and the Philippines without fear of U.S. military opposition.

At 7:55 A.M., December 7, 1941, bombs from the Japanese fleet hit Pearl Harbor. The United States was caught unaware. The destruction to military assets at the Naval base and Army aircraft at Hickam Field was massive. By the time the assault ended two hours later the U.S. Pacific Fleet had lost eight battleships, three light cruisers, three destroyers, and four other vessels. The losses included the battleships *Arizona*, *California*, *Oklahoma*, and *West Virginia*, the minelayer *Oglala*, and the target ship *Utah*. All of these ships but the *Arizona*, *Oklahoma* and *Utah* were later restored and returned to service. 170 U.S. aircraft were also destroyed. The Japanese, however, did not destroy the American submarine base, or important fuel storage and repair facilities. More critically, as time would show, they failed to locate and sink any aircraft carriers.

The surprise attack "woke a sleeping giant" and public opinion in the United States immediately turned against Japan. The next day, December 8, 1941, Japan officially declared war against the United States and Great Britain. On that same day President Roosevelt asked Congress for a declaration of war against Japan. His words resonate through history with his reference to December 7, 1941, as "a date which will live in infamy."

REMEMBERING THE ATTACK AT PEARL HARBOR
by Albert Sidebottom

Pearl Harbor, August 1941: I was transferred to the fleet post office. We had a crew of sixteen people, four chiefs and twelve petty officers, and we handled all the fleet's mail. You paid $10.00 for your own bond or you didn't work as a postal clerk. It was a way to stay away from the battleships. I knew people liked them, but I didn't.

After the Christmas of 1940 my wife came out on the 16th of January, 1941, when I made 1st Class Petty Officer. The chief shut down the whole post office for me to change clothes, and they looked in the newspaper for places for us to live.

In February, Admiral Kimmel transferred his fleet from the flagship *Pennsylvania* to the sub base, but the mail clerk at the sub base didn't want to handle his mail. I was the only one of the sixteen men who had a wife on the island, so they sent me over there. Instead of working twenty-hour days at the postal office, I went back to working two hours a day at the flagship to handle their mail. From there, in October of '41, I went back home to Pearl to see my wife and baby. I wanted to go back to sea because at that time you had to have one year at sea or three years on the beach to be qualified to go up for chief. I wanted to go back to sea again and run a division of my own to prove to myself I was qualified to be a chief.

I went home on leave and got back to Pearl on the 4th of December. The ship I was assigned to wasn't in port so I had to go to "receiving" until it came in. It was just a barracks station, and you hang out there and perform duties for them. On the evening of the 6th we had patrol duty at the block arena. There were four first class boatswain mates; two were off-ship to hear the bands play. So they took off upstairs where the bands were playing and left two of us down below.

In those days on payday some sailor would buy a round for the house, and they had cases sitting down inside where the beer was rationed out. We had all these empty cases, and every time they'd buy a round they'd put a beer in your case. By the time we locked the joint up we each had a case of beer. All four of us went on over to the barracks and shoved it underneath our bunks (but on the way over we each drank a can).

For about two years they'd been digging these oil tanks in Red Hill. This is taking a granite mountain and putting these twenty oil tanks inside it—350 feet deep, 100 feet in diameter, suspended in these caves so that the shock doesn't go along with it. Every Sunday they were setting the charges in the mountain blasting the rock out. The island shook from about 6:00 to 9:00 A.M. each Sunday morning.

When the Japanese dropped the bombs on December 7, 1941, the explosions didn't initially bother us. The sound just blended in with the dynamiting in the hills until the planes flew right over our building. We couldn't see the red "meatballs" on them. It sure looked like our planes, but they had torpedoes underneath them. What the hell? We weren't supposed to have drills until tomorrow, Monday morning, not Sunday morning. The second wave came over and we could see the meatballs on the wings. At the same time the gunner's mate on the destroyer that just escorted a submarine in opened up with his .50 Caliber and stitched one plane right down to the torpedo, and he just disintegrated.

Then, the torpedoes blew up along side the *Oklahoma* and the *West Virginia*. We decided it was time to clear out the building. We had no authority except we were boatswain mates. In the old Navy a boatswain mate takes an oath when he makes 3rd Class that he is fully responsible for all government personnel and material within his sight or hearing 24/7 on duty or on liberty. If you take the rate of boatswain mate, you're never off duty.

So we took action, waking everybody up and running them down outside to the main deck, putting them in working parties, sending them around to the officer's housing that was between us and the Navy yard, putting them on fire detail, and anything else. We had an armory on the second deck that had a door with a glass window and inside had fifty rifles and two 45s, but we had no way to get them out. In the room was a first class cook in his bed, and he was still suffering from the night before. We just dumped him and his mattress and springs upside down on the deck. Then we stomped the springs out to bust the window out to get the ammo. Once we could get to the ammo we issued the rifles. We got them all issued and got the guys spread out.

We were out on the front deck looking to see what was going on when Marines came by in a truck. They never stopped but just threw bandoleers of ammunition out to us, to anyone with a rifle. You'd get 200 rounds of ammo right fast like. Those old portable bandoleers would go flying.

We turned around and went out the back door and saw a whole church party on the basketball court in whites. We were in dungarees. In those days you couldn't tell a sailor man from a petty officer. But we had lanyard around our neck and a boatswain collar in our pocket, and that spelled boatswain mate. We were able to walk out into those guys in white and say, "Take 10 men and do this, take 10 men and do that." It took us about five minutes to get the 2,000 men spread out and scattered them so the Japanese couldn't machine gun or drop a bomb on them.

But the Japanese were so well-trained and professional that they were only hitting the targets they were assigned. When they came over us to make their turns to go back and strafe so their high bombers could drop their bombs, the guy in the rear seat was shaking hands with himself—not machine gunning, just all smiles like he was saying, "We won this round," and the pilot would be waving to you.

They only fired at the battleships.

A PEARL HARBOR SURVIVOR
by Joseph A. Ruggles

I do not consider myself a hero. I simply served my country. I was born on December 11, 1911, in Huron, South Dakota. I had three brothers and two sisters. We moved often when I was a child, from South Dakota to Texas to Arkansas to South Dakota again, finally living in Anita, Iowa, from fifth grade to my graduation from high school. I lost my job working for Paramount Publics, a theater chain, and finding another job that would pay a supporting wage was discouraging, so I decided to enlist in the Navy. I left for boot camp in San Diego, and then was sent to Balboa Park for more training as a hospital corpsman. I did well and was fourth in my class of 100.

My first duty was at the U.S. Naval Hospital, Bremerton Naval Yard, Bremerton, Washington. During that time the U.S. Navy was recruiting young men for hospital duty to help give care to WW I veterans. I liked helping and taking care of others, so I decided to stay in the Navy.

From there I was transferred for duty aboard the USS *Saratoga* CV3, a large aircraft carrier with a crew of about five thousand men and officers. Before their removal during WW II, the *Saratoga* had four turrets of two eight-inch guns, two forward, and two aft. The *Saratoga* established a world record for the accuracy of those guns. During WW II the Hawaiian Coast Artillery for defense of the island of Oahu took possession of those guns from the ship.

In 1938 I was transferred to the U.S. Naval Hospital in Washington, D. C., where I met my future wife at an Elks dance. I was twenty-six years old. Soon after marriage I was given the choice of being sent to either Pearl Harbor or the Philippines. It was an easy decision for me. I left for Pearl Harbor.

I arrived at Pearl Harbor in 1941 and in November put in for living quarters for my wife and me. Everything seemed calm there so I made plans for my wife to come out that following January. We weren't prepared for what happened on December 7. Previous to the attack, everyone had been on a two week alert and had just come off of it. To celebrate, there was a battle of the bands that Saturday night. Everyone had a twelve o'clock curfew, which meant they were able to stay up late.

Because I was stationed at the hospital, near the opening of the harbor, I had a good view of what was going on around me, and what I saw remains with me to this day. Four Japanese carriers led the attack. Because the water in Pearl Harbor is so shallow, the Japanese had to develop a special type of shallow-water torpedo. The torpedoes were then dropped into the water by torpedo planes so they ran under the water into the sides of the battleships where they exploded on contact. Dive-bombers dropped 500-pound bombs that could penetrate steel decks and explode inside the hull of a ship. A bomb of this type penetrated the deck of the USS *Arizona* and exploded in the forward magazine (powder and shell storage compartment). That ship sustained the most loss of life—1,117 crew members—out of all the ships in the Navy Yard. There was smoke all around, and burning oil in the water that injured the people who had been blown overboard.

At first I wasn't exactly sure about what was going on, but there wasn't much time to think. Sailors began to pour into the hospital. Some of the soldiers were too badly injured to be saved, but I did my best to help. Morphine was given to the patients to help with pain, but there was chaos and confusion all around. I tried to forget what I saw, but the images are forever in my mind.

During the second wave, soldiers began to fire at the Japanese planes. One aircraft that was shot down crashed into the corner of the animal experimental lab on the hospital grounds. Some of the small animals escaped. A total of about twenty-seven Japanese planes were shot down. When things came to a halt, those who were still alive were left in the middle of total destruction.

The hospital overflowed with the wounded. Later, when the burns and injuries were stabilized, the patients were put on ships with medical personnel and sent back to the States. The hospital ship USS *Solace* was one of the workhorses during this attack and helped to save many lives. They were also able to furnish our hospital with much-needed supplies. I don't remember much about the days after the attack, but I do remember finally being able to wire my wife after three days of worrying to let her know that I was okay.

After Pearl Harbor I went into administration and became a Chief Pharmacist Mate. A few weeks after the attack I was transferred to the USS *Lumberton*, a four-smokestack destroyer converted into a high-speed minesweeper that swept the harbors of islands for mines. After some shore duty at the USN Hospital in Oakland, California, I was transferred to the USS *Chilton*, a troop transport. I was aboard this ship during the battle of Okinawa where I helped to tend the wounded and assign duties to others.

I didn't see my wife until the war ended in 1945. In 1946 she came to Pearl Harbor where I finally had quarters. I spent twenty-four years in the Navy and retired in 1973 from the postal service. In 1993 I became State Chairman for the Pearl Harbor Survivors Association in Florida, before returning to Fresno, where I am active in the local Pearl Harbor Survivors Association. Their motto is "Remember Pearl Harbor, Keep America Alive." Every five years I make the trip to Pearl Harbor in memory of those who were lost.

Briana Pissano contributed to the writing of this story for a Madera High School project.

A STORY OF A U.S. NAVY GUNNERS MATE, FIRST CLASS
by Russell E. Day

I was born in Riverbank, California, on September 25, 1922, to Doyle and Martha Day, and moved many times in California while growing up. I joined the United States Navy in October 1940 at the age of eighteen. After boot camp I was assigned to the battleship USS *West Virginia*. In January 1941 I arrived in Hawaii where I was transferred to the light cruiser USS *Honolulu*. My ship operated out of Pearl Harbor throughout the year doing fleet maneuvers and gun practice. Ralph Engle was my best buddy and we went on liberties together. I still see him twice a year in La Quinta, California. Life was good on the cruiser, and I had no homesickness.

On December 7, 1941, I was washing down the deck when suddenly I heard planes overhead firing on ships in Pearl Harbor. Total confusion reigned. One plane released a bomb that hit only fifteen feet from where I was standing. It hit the edge of the dock and exploded under water making a large hole in our bow. I was sprayed with oily water, and everyone was running in different directions looking for something to shoot at. We were tied to the dock and the USS *Saint Louis* was tied outboard of us. We threw the line loose so she could get underway. Planes were flying over our fantail with torpedoes and our crew was firing shells, which were sometimes landing over in Honolulu. They didn't attack the sub base or the tankers, which probably saved many lives.

During the two weeks following, we stayed in a ready position on board and helped with the wounded and dead as well as cleaning up the many damaged ships. In January 1942 we convoyed troops to Australia, and then sailed on to Alaska and the Aleutian Islands to bombard Japanese bases. The fog was dense and it was bitter cold. We lost two scout planes in the heavy fog. I knew one pilot and one radioman on each plane. I was glad to leave Alaska in September 1942 for the Navy shipyard at Mare Island. There they added new 40mm and 20mm guns to our cruiser, and I had the opportunity to take a short leave.

In November 1942 the USS *Honolulu* arrived in Guadalcanal and engaged in several battles with the Japanese Navy. I was gun pointer in turret one on the *Honolulu*. My first encounter with the Japanese was on November 30, 1942, in the battle of Tassafarongao, Guadalcanal. The Japanese torpedoed the cruisers

Minneapolis, New Orleans, Pensacola, and *North Hampton.* The USS *Honolulu* was the only cruiser to survive the battle even though we lost our entire bow. Other ships in our task force suffered major damage from the Japanese enemy who used Long Lance torpedoes. One observer reported the machine guns were blazing like the Fourth of July off the fo'c'sle deck of the cruiser *Honolulu* during the thirty minute battle against the incoming sweep of Japanese Zeroes.

In July of 1943 our ship was in the battle of Kolondangara where the bow was blown off again. I didn't have time to think during the action. I just reacted to my training on the gun turret, too busy to be scared. Afterwards, while being towed back to Pearl Harbor, I thought I might get a leave for home—but at Pearl we pushed the ship up, replaced the bow, and then set out back to the Solomon Islands to continue operations at Guadalcanal. I earned thirteen Pacific battle stars, one for each engagement.

In 1944 I was assigned to gunnery school in San Diego, California, for four weeks. That gave my wife, Ruth, and me some special time together. I had married Ruth E. Buchanan in Palo Alto, California, on October 13, 1942. We met on New Years Eve 1940 in Long Beach, California, where Ruth had come to see the Rose Bowl parade. She was a beauty operator in Fresno, California, and we corresponded for two years. We were only together five days before I left again for eleven more months of sea duty.

My next assignment was a transfer to the USS *Uvalde* (AKA-88) for moving supplies and landing troops in the south seas of the Pacific, the Dutch East Indies, Philippines, and Okinawa. I was placed as Gun Captain on the 40mm gun turret. During this time we survived several Japanese suicide attacks. On Easter Sunday, D-Day, April 1, 1945, we were at Okinawa. A Japanese plane hit a ship just 100 yards from us as we were firing all our anti-aircraft guns. The landing of our troops was unopposed as the Japanese moved to higher ground in the hills.

In 1946, after the war, I traveled on to China, then to Japan, and back to China to aid the Chinese General in

Russell Day in Navy uniform with his bride Ruth Day, married on October 13, 1942.

their Civil War. I came home in December 1946 and was discharged in February 1947 as a Gunner's Mate First Class.

Since then I established, operated and retired from an agricultural pesticide business, while building two homes for my family. Ruth and I have a son, two daughters and grandchildren. My seven years of service taught me many things. First it provided me with a job and career during the Depression, and secondly, after being in battles and seeing so many lives lost, it is obvious to me that war only leads to more wars. We cannot change the world, and if we could, war is not the way!

DOOLITTLE'S RAID

At the beginning of the war the Japanese, with their ever-expanding empire, were not overly-concerned about a potential Allied attack on their homeland. Their complacency was challenged in early 1942 when a United States carrier task force, in a surprise attack, successfully raided the Japanese-controlled Marshall, Gilbert, and Marcus Islands. However, it was the subsequent legendary Doolittle Raid that forced the Japanese to reevaluate their defensive boundaries.

On April 18, 1942, a fleet of sixteen B-25 Army bombers, led by the famous aviator Lt. Col. James H. Doolittle, took off from the carrier *Hornet*, which was stationed about 650 miles east of Honshu, Japan. Doolittle's risky plan was to drop bombs on Tokyo, Osaka, and other cities. The raid was ultimately successful and none of the planes were lost to enemy fire, although fifteen crash-landed in China when they ran out of fuel. Most of the crew members survived and with the assistance of the Chinese underground (eager to support the Allies' aggression against their mutual enemy) were returned safely to the U.S. The remaining plane landed in Siberia where the crew was detained for some time before eventually managing to escape.

MY BRUSH WITH HISTORY
by Jerry Fisher

The nation was in shock and chafing for revenge after the Japanese sneak attack on Pearl Harbor on December 7, 1941. Morale was at an all-time low as they rampaged through the South Pacific, occupying Bataan, Singapore, Guam, Wake Island, and the Philippines. But Admiral Yamamoto, who led the Pearl Harbor raid, was right when he said, "I fear we have awakened a sleeping giant."

Meanwhile Tokyo Rose taunted us daily while assuring the citizens of Japan they were safe from reprisal. She didn't know Lt. Col. James Doolittle, a hotshot pilot in our air force who went to the President with a daring plan. He proposed stripping B-25 bombers so they could take off the deck of a moving aircraft carrier and bomb Tokyo. The planes would have to fly on to China, so it would be a suicide mission and would require volunteers. Four months after Pearl Harbor, on April 18, 1942, we bombed Tokyo, Osaka, Kobe, Hagaya and Yokohama.

In 1944, a movie was released about this raid based on a book by one of the pilots, Lieutenant Ted Lawson, called *Thirty Seconds over Tokyo*. At this time I worked as a secretary in the public relations office at Hammer Field, the local air base. One of my jobs was to book speakers from the base into the service clubs, like Kiwanis, Lions, etc. One day I was pleasantly surprised when a tall, ruggedly handsome officer limped into my office and introduced himself. "Hi," he said, "I'm Ted Lawson." He was on a speaking tour of the United States and came into my office several times during the next few weeks. I kept asking him about the Doolittle Raid. He told me it was so top secret, they didn't even know where they were going until half-way to Japan.

"All the guys were yelling and screaming, they were so excited, but I went to my quarters and wrote a letter to my wife. I didn't think any of us would make it back. The plan was to get within 400 miles of Japan and take off about dusk on a Sunday evening, but a fishing boat sighted the *Hornet* Saturday morning, so we took off early. This meant we would probably run out of gas before reaching the China coast."

Captain Lawson was in much demand as a speaker. He was fascinating, and each time he came in I peppered him with questions. Once he talked about the actual raid. "We really were only over Tokyo about thirty seconds, but it seemed hours. Nobody shot at us. We took them by surprise. They claimed we didn't do any damage, but we sure did hurt their morale. We were laughing and yelling, feeling pretty good, until we hit a fierce storm. The sky got dark and we ran out of gas. We were about a quarter of a mile off the Chinese coast when we slammed into the water."

I wanted to hear more but he had to leave for a speaking engagement. It was a week later when he came into my office with another officer. "Jerry, meet Captain White. He's the doc that cut off my leg. Saved my life." Captain White was rather short, might be called pleasingly plump, with black hair, what there was of it, and didn't look anything like the tall, handsome Stephen McNally who played him in the movie.

Lawson continued, "I was a mess. Most of my teeth had been knocked out, my face was like raw hamburger, and my left leg was almost severed. The Chinese who drug us out of the water carried us on stretchers for days, evading the Japanese patrols looking for us. We finally reached a small village in the middle of that vast country, but they didn't have any medical facilities or anything for my pain. I figured I was a goner until one night another crew stumbled into the village. The only flight surgeon on the raid was with them."

Captain White chimed in, "Yeah, and lucky for old Ted here, I had managed to grab two vials of morphine when my plane ditched. It helped when we had to amputate his leg."

"He couldn't do anything about my teeth or face," Lawson went on, "but he saved my life. Gangrene had set in."

I asked them what happened to the other crews, and they both broke out laughing. "Well, Doolittle bailed out in a rice paddy," White said. "That wouldn't have been so bad, but they had just fertilized it—with human excrement. He wasn't too happy." Then, seriously, "The Japs captured and executed two crews, and crew one landed intact in Russia and was interned for the duration. It was a miracle that fifteen of the sixteen crews managed to reach China."

When they were flown out of China on June 3, a second amputation was performed on Lawson's leg because of an infection, and he underwent plastic surgery on his face. I thought they did a wonderful job—he didn't have hardly any scars.

The Japanese went after the *Hornet* with a fury, and she went down fighting the following fall. The United States broke the Japanese secret code and one year later to the day, April 18, 1943, we found out where Admiral Yamamoto would be and assassinated him. Captain Lawson died in 1992, and General Doolittle in 1993. As of this date, there are twenty-three of the original eighty on the raid still alive who attend a reunion every year.

TWENTY-TWO MONTHS ABOARD THE USS *ENTERPRISE*
by Albert Fred Blumer

I joined the Navy in July 1941 and trained in San Diego before joining the fleet to sail to Pearl Harbor. I was assigned to the USS *Enterprise* for twenty-two months. We knew the Japanese would be attacking Pearl Harbor and were on our way there but the storms prevented our arriving before the attack. When we got there, we could see the ships burning in the harbor.

The *Dinuba Sentinel* published the following account about me on November 11, 1944:

> On that fateful morning of December 7, 1941, he was on one of the Navy's largest aircraft carriers, the USS *Enterprise*. His ship was due in Pearl Harbor that day but was delayed by storms at sea. This was not only fortunate for Blumer but his country as well because the *Enterprise* was an important factor in turning the tide of no less than ten major sea and air battles. He saw action as a gunner's mate at Midway and fights in the Solomon's. In the Battle of Santa Cruz, 83 Jap planes came over the *Enterprise* and dropped bombs. When bombs hit close the entire ship shook. The ship was hit several times during engagements with the enemy. When there was time, a little patching up would be done, and the ship kept on the job. One of the historic missions of the big flattop was accompanying the aircraft carrier *Hornet* to within a few hundred miles of Tokyo to send Gen. Doolittle and his fliers over Tokyo in a daring raid. He was home for his first leave in 22 months in August 1943.
>
> Participating in nearly every major carrier engagement in the first year of the war, the *Enterprise* and her Air Group, exclusive of her far-flung destruction of hostile shore installations throughout the battle area, did sink or damage, on her own, a total of 35 Japanese vessels and shoot down a total of 185 Japanese aircraft. Her aggressive fighting spirit and superb combat efficiency are fitting tribute to the officers and men who so gallantly established her as a solid bulwark in defense of the American Nation: Gilbert and Marshall Island raid, Feb. 1, 1942; Wake Island raid Feb. 24, 1942; Marcus Island raid, March 4, 1942; Battle of Midway, June

4-6, 1942; Occupation of Guadalcanal, August 7, 8, 1942; Battle of Santa Cruz Islands, October 26, 1942; Battle of Solomon Islands November 14, 15, 1942.

Before coming home on thirty days' leave, Blumer was made a gunner's mate third class. After his leave he was transferred to San Pedro to train on a crash boat for three months. He was then sent to the Hawaiian Islands for several months. From there, he was transferred to the Marshall Islands, where he was stationed as a gunner's mate second class in August 1944. His term of enlistment was up on his twenty-first birthday, August 6, 1944.

The cover of the Dinuba Sentinel *War Album, published November 11, 1944.*

Albert Fred BLUMER

ALBERT FRED BLUMER, son of Mr. and Mrs. Fred Blumer of Dinuba, joined the Navy in July, 1941. He received his training at San Diego and then was assigned to the fleet and went to Pearl Harbor. On that fateful morning of December 7, 1941, he was on one of the Navy's largest aircraft carriers, the U. S. S. Enterprise. His ship was due in Pearl Harbor that day but was delayed by storms at sea. This was not only fortunate for Blumer but his country as well because the Enterprise was an important factor in turning the tide of no less than ten major sea and air battles. He saw action as a gunner's mate at Midway and fights in the Solomons. In the Battle of Santa Cruz 83 Jap planes came over the Enterprise and dropped bombs. When bombs hit close the entire ship shook. The ship was hit several times during . . . the enemy . . . a little p . . . done and . . . job. One o . . . of the big . . . panying th . . . net to with . . . of Tokio t . . . and his fl . . . daring rai . . . his first leave in 22 months in August, 1943. He returned to duty wearing three new ribbons with a bronze star for being pre-Pearl Harbor and two silver stars for action. He has been awarded the Presidential Unit citation "For consistently outstanding performance and distinguished achievement during repeated action against enemy Japanese forces in the Pacific War Area, December 7, 1941, to November 15, 1942. Participating in nearly every major carrier engagement in the first year of the war, the ENTERPRISE and her Air Group, exclusive of her far-flung destruction of hostile shore · installations throughout the battle area, did sink or damage, on her own, a total of 35 Japanese vessels and shoot down a total of 185 Japanese aircraft. Her aggressive fighting spirit and superb combat efficiency are fitting tribute to the officers and men who so gallantly established her as a solid bulwark in defense of the American Nation." Gilbert and Marshall Island raid Feb. 1, 1942. Wake Island raid Feb. 24, 1942. Marcus Island raid, March 4, 1942. Battle of Midway, June 4-6, 1942. Occupation of Guadalcanal, August 7-8, 1942. Battle of Stewart Islands, August 24, 1942. Battle of Santa Cruz Islands, October 26, 1942. Battle of Solomon Islands, November 14, 15, 1942. Before coming home on thirty days leave, Blumer was made a gun-

An article (and accompanying military photo) about Albert Blumer, who served aboard the USS Enterprise, *from the Dinuba Sentinel* War Album.

THE BATTLE FOR THE PACIFIC

The Allies' fight to reclaim the vast Pacific Ocean from imperial Japan began with the Guadalcanal campaign in the Solomon Islands. On August 7, 1942, a force of United States Marines landed on Guadalcanal. The Japanese, having earlier in the year experienced American naval might in the battles of the Coral Sea and Midway, were determined to prevent the Allies from uprooting them from their various South Pacific strongholds, including their major base at Rabaul. The battle was fierce and each side tasted victory and defeat before the Allies' eventual victory.

At Guadalcanal the Allies first encountered the fanatical Japanese code of "Bushido," which inspired Japanese soldiers to fight to the death (and which also inspired that empire's Kamikaze pilots in their suicide bombing runs). It was also during the Solomons campaign that the Allies practiced amphibious warfare and perfected their technique of coordinating air, land, and sea forces. This laid the foundation for their first large-scale victory against the Japanese.

In late 1943 the Japanese controlled and had fortified the Central Pacific's Gilbert, Marshall, Caroline, and Mariana island chains, building airbases which allowed them to project airpower over vast distances. The Allies conceived of a plan to "island hop," capturing target islands that in turn would provide a base for the next assault.

The Allies' first target in the region was the island of Tarawa, heavily-fortified by the Japanese with barricades, underground bunkers and other defenses. Their 3,000 troops and 1,800 civilians (including Korean laborers) were instructed to fight to the death—and did just that. Only 147 Japanese and Koreans were captured; U.S. casualties numbered 3,110.

The United States Navy then launched a fierce attack on the Japanese bases in the Marshall Islands in order to gain the upper hand in the Central Pacific. As a part of the 1,200 ship Central Pacific Command, Rear Admiral Marc Mitscher's Task Force 58, consisting of carriers, battleships, and cruisers, gained control of Kwajalein, in the center of the Marshall Islands, and then Majuron and Eniwetok.

By 1944 the United States had developed the B-29 Superfortress bomber, which was considerably larger than the B-17 Flying Fortress it was designed to replace. The Mariana Islands became a critical next target as Central Pacific islands such as Saipan, Tinian, Rota, and Guam were within Superfortress bombing range of Japan.

On June 15th, 1944, Marines landed on Saipan after a fierce naval bombard-ment, followed by Army infantry the next day. The battle for Saipan resulted in 16,500 American casualties and almost 30,000 Japanese deaths. Premier Hideki Tojo of Japan resigned shortly after Japan's loss under heavy criticism for losing Saipan. A large Japanese naval force struck back in the Battle of the Philippine Sea, but suffered the devastating loss of three aircraft carriers and 395 planes.

The Allies took Tinian by the end of July 1944 and Guam the next month. The Allies immediately constructed bases that would accommodate the B-29 bombers in the Marianas, and Allied forces were now within 1,600 miles of Tokyo and Manila.

Preparations began for the attack on Japan, but first the Philippines had to be secured. With the conquest of Peleliu in the Palau Islands, and Morotai Island in the Netherlands East Indies, the Allies came within 400 miles of the Philippines. In late October 1944, the Battle for Leyte Gulf occurred. It was arguably the largest naval battle in history, with several separate major engagements over a four day period. During this battle the Americans were introduced to the horror of Kamikaze dive-bombing.

The Allies decisively prevailed, as Japan lost three battleships, four carriers, ten cruisers, and nine destroyers. The Allies lost one light and two escort carriers, two destroyers, and a destroyer escort.

In the aftermath of the Battle of Leyte Gulf, the 270,000-man Japanese force on the major Philippine island of Leyte was no match for Lt. General Walter Krueger's invading U.S. Sixth Army. General MacArthur and his staff came ashore at Tacoma five hours after the first landing, thus keeping his promise that he would return to defend the Philippines. The Sixth Army occupied Leyte by the end of the year.

Allied forces proceeded to liberate the remainder of the Philippines by July, 1945, although fierce pockets of Japanese resistance remained until the end of the war.

FORGIVEN TEARS

by Troy Burgess

Troy Burgess in Navy uniform.

I was born in McCurtain County, Oklahoma, in 1924. When my father's cotton farm went bust in 1937 he moved our whole family to California to look for work. My mother passed away that same year. We wandered about the state like so many other Dust Bowl survivors. After December 7, 1941, my life would change forever. Within three weeks I enlisted in the United States Navy. My hard-working father sent me off to war with this statement of sage advice: "Stay tough and never let another man see you cry."

After basic training in Eureka and Monterey, California, my first assignment was to stand sentry duty at night aboard a yacht owned by the Hollywood movie star Joel McCray, whose boat had been taken over for Navy use. I was well-armed for the assignment. I carried a Thompson submachine gun under one arm and packed a 45-caliber pistol in my belt. For some reason, neither weapon had any bullets.

When the opportunity came up, I volunteered for real sea duty. I was a Boatswain 2nd Class in the United States Navy and was assigned to the light cruiser USS *Boise*, where I remained for the duration of World War II. I would see plenty of action aboard the *Boise* in both theaters of war. In the Mediterranean, we took part in the invasion of Italy. The *Boise's* job was to help soften the German line of defense ahead of our advancing troops. As the German and Italian forces pulled farther and farther inland, the *Boise's* guns could no longer reach far enough to be of any effect so we were recalled to the Pacific War.

The *Boise* participated in many pre-invasion attack and logistics operations in the Pacific. We traveled to New Guinea, the Solomon Islands, the Philippines at Leyte Gulf and Sergoya Straights, and Borneo. The battles on the open sea were by far the most harrowing of our experience aboard ship. During the Battle of

Troy Burgess and crew aboard the USS Boise, *May 1945.*

Scrgoya Straight our attack fleet suffered fifty-two air attacks, including bomb-ings, strafing, torpedoes, and even Kamikaze attacks. Twenty-one of our ships were hit that day. The *Boise* escaped harm. I came to believe the claim that there are never any atheists left aboard a ship after an attack at sea.

My most memorable experience of the war, however, was my very first battle at sea. We were involved in the famous battle of Cape Esperance off the Solomon Islands. I was still only seventeen years old at the time. The attack occurred at night—something the Japanese Navy tended to favor. The *Boise* was hit by Japanese shellfire. Although badly damaged and in desperate need of repair that night, she remained seaworthy and was credited with the sinking of three enemy ships and assisted with the sinking of three more.

We were, however, to pay dearly for our successes that night. One hundred and seven of our men were killed in that battle, including a close acquaintance of mine. The following morning a solemn burial at sea ceremony took place for sev-enty of our dead. It was an experience I will never forget. I can vividly recall stand-ing quietly along the ship's rail with my fellow sailors that morning. As I looked into the faces of the men to my right and to my left, I noticed that most of the men who were older than I and a whole lot tougher made no attempt to hold back their tears. As the tears welled up in my own eyes, I recalled my father's sage advice, "Stay tough and never let another man see you cry." I think my father would have forgiven my tears that day.

MY FIRST ZERO

by Leonard Frame

I was born at home on our family ranch in Selma, California, on October 27th, 1917. I was the youngest of three children surviving into adulthood. My mother, Fay Frame, was a housewife and my father, W.W. Frame, was a farmer.

I was working at Sun-Maid Raisin Growers in Fresno, California, in 1940 when the Selective Service Act was passed. At that time enlistees were supposed to serve a one-year enlistment. My draft number wasn't called in the first drawing, so instead of being drafted into the Army I started looking for something I'd like better than walking and carrying a gun. I enjoyed tinkering with ham radios in high school and I had read in the newspaper that the Navy had a communications school. In this program an enlistee went to communications training school for four months and then served eight months active duty. This would take care of the required one-year enlistment.

The Navy Recruiter was located in the basement of the new post office on Tulare Street in Fresno. I went downstairs to inquire about the radio school program. The recruiter asked me how much education I'd had, and I told him, "Three years of college." His reply was, "Oh, go sign up for the Wing Cadets." I said that I thought I'd like radio school better and he said, "Oh, go on, everybody likes to fly." It just happened that there was a Flying Cadet Board in the next

Captain Frame, flight leader of the 70th Fighter Squadron Detachment on Guadalcanal.

room. The Navy Recruiter took me over and said, "Here, sign this guy up," and then he left me there. The Flying Cadet Recruiter told me that if I would come back the next day with a birth certificate and three letters of recommendation, they would give me a physical and, "We'll see where it goes from there."

During my physical it was determined I needed to have my tonsils removed. After my tonsil operation, and some more paperwork, I was accepted into the United States Air Corp. I reported to March Field at Riverside, California, on March 14, 1941. I was off to become a Flying Cadet.

Two years later, in March of 1943, I was a Captain and flight leader on Guadalcanal as a part of the 70th Fighter Squadron Detachment. On April 7th, 1943, the Coast Watchers in the northern Solomon Islands radioed that there

Leonard Frame in his United States Army Air Corp uniform, March 14, 1941.

were a large number of Japanese planes headed toward Guadalcanal. I was sent out leading a flight of four P-39 fighters to protect the Russell Islands off the north end of Guadalcanal. All of the fighters from Guadalcanal were on the same radio frequency, so we heard fighting going on but we didn't see any planes over the Russells.

After the radio chatter quieted down I called fighter control to see if we should stay on station. "Oh, no, you can come home," he said. Our group of four P-39s was flying at 20,000 feet at the time, so I reduced my altitude a little and headed back. As we approached Cape Esperance, at the north end of Guadalcanal, one of my wingmen asked, "How much oxygen do you have?" I looked at my gauge and replied. Then he said, "I'm all out. Incidentally, there is a bogey at nine o'clock."

I saw a Japanese Zero flying the opposite direction. I whipped around and went after him. He made a gentle left turn. I cut him off by diving a little under him. When I came within firing range I lifted the nose of my plane and fired one burst of my guns. His plane immediately flamed and the pilot bailed out. I had my first Zero!

A Japanese pilot was captured in the area soon after. I did not see him after his capture, but it was reported that he didn't see what kind of plane had hit him. I have always thought that he was the pilot that I shot down.

I flew a total of 79 missions and was credited with shooting down one Zero, half a Betty Bomber and another half Zero, but this was the first enemy airplane that I had seen, and that bogey at nine o'clock was my first victory!

After the war ended I returned to Fresno. My wife Cynthia and I bought a ranch in Fresno County where we raised our daughter and son and farmed for fifty years. After sixty-five years I still have an active license to fly. I guess the Navy Recruiter was right after all when he said, "Oh, go on, everybody likes to fly!"

RECEIVING THE BRONZE STAR
by *Thomas McLaughlin*

On December 21, 1944, we invaded the island of Mindoro in the Philippine Islands. As we were going into the beach a flight of about fifteen Japanese planes appeared, and the lead plane decided to use us as his target. He tipped his wing and took a long look at us, and then he just peeled off and down he came directly at us.

My station during an attack was on the bridge, and one of my duties was to give orders to the men at the helm, which I did. I gave the command for a hard left. Unfortunately, LSTs were slow to respond because of their flat bottoms. But it started to turn, and when the plane hit us it didn't crash into the conn where I was standing, but he crashed onto the right (or starboard) side toward the rear of our ship, inflicting heavy damage.

While the plane was coming down on us we were firing and hitting his wings and the body of the plane. That might have also helped to knock him off his course, but at any rate we had to abandon the ship.

All that were able went over the side leaving just the captain, two seamen, and myself. The captain told me to check around below deck, and when I did I went to the starboard side forward from where the plane hit us and saw an Army medic with the wounded. He had placed them on the deck, and he didn't know what to do with them. I went back to the captain and told him we couldn't go because we had wounded men onboard.

One of the seamen said he would go down in the raft, and we would lower the wounded down to him. Unfortunately, the rope we had secured to the raft broke because the water was getting rough.

A destroyer finally came over toward us, so we hailed the skipper and told him we had all these wounded men on board. He told us to put them in the water. I asked him to throw us a line, and we would make it fast on our ship. Then we could pass the wounded over to his ship. He said since we were on fire and had ammunitions on our deck, we could explode at any time, and his ship could explode also. He finally said, "Okay, but if our ship starts to explode, we'll cut you loose." We agreed. It was the only thing we could do. They had a man standing by with an axe to cut us at anytime.

We quickly passed the injured men over to their ship. As soon as the last man was over, our skipper and I jumped over to his ship. At that time, the captain of the destroyer backed his ship away from our ship. It was almost like backing up a car. They put the wounded soldiers in their wardroom, and we worked with their doctor and medics to bandage their wounds.

The Japanese suicide bombers were relentless in pursuing us, but the captain of the destroyer was very skillful in dodging them since the destroyer was very maneuverable. He would wait until the plane was into its dive, then he would make a quick turn and the enemy would splash into the water before they could change course.

When we went ashore to where our crew was we had a very happy reunion. Most of our crew survived, and we went down to Australia on another ship.

Later I received this letter from the Secretary of the Navy:

The President of the United States takes pleasure in presenting the Bronze Star Medal to Lieutenant, Junior Grade, Thomas Francis McLaughlin United States Naval Reserve for service as set forth in the following Citation:

"For heroic achievement while attached to the USS LST 739 in action against the enemy Japanese forces in the vicinity of the Philippine Islands on December 21, 1944. When his ship was attacked and finally sunk by enemy planes, and several of the casualties needed assistance when it became necessary to abandon ship, Lieutenant, Junior Grade (then Ensign) McLaughlin voluntarily remained aboard with the wounded men until he could deliver them to safety. His initiative, and courageous devotion to duty were in keeping with the highest traditions of the United States Naval Service."

Lieutenant, Junior Grade, McLaughlin is authorized to wear the Combat "V".

For the President,
John L. Sullivan
Secretary of the Navy

THE SECRETARY OF THE NAVY
WASHINGTON

        The President of the United States takes pleasure in presenting the BRONZE STAR MEDAL to

      LIEUTENANT, JUNIOR GRADE, THOMAS FRANCIS MC LAUGHLIN
              UNITED STATES NAVAL RESERVE

for service as set forth in the following

    CITATION:

        "For heroic achievement while attached to the U.S.S. LST 739 in action against enemy Japanese forces in the vicinity of the Philippine Islands on December 21, 1944. When his ship was attacked and finally sunk by enemy planes, and several of the casualties needed assistance when it became necessary to abandon ship, Lieutenant, Junior Grade (then Ensign) Mc Laughlin voluntarily remained aboard with the wounded men until he could deliver them to safety. His initiative, and courageous devotion to duty were in keeping with the highest traditions of the United States Naval Service."

Lieutenant, Junior Grade, Mc Laughlin is authorized to wear the Combat "V"

                    For the President,

                    Secretary of the Navy

The document is a Bronze Star citation for, "Heroic achievement while attached to the U.S.S. LST 739 in action against enemy Japanese forces in the vicinity of the Philippine Islands on December 21, 1944."

THE WW II EXPERIENCE OF LT. WILLIAM STELLA
by Wilma Stella

Bill was a senior at the University of Louisiana, Lafayette, when the Japanese attacked Pearl Harbor, Hawaii, on December 7, 1941. Bill thought the wise thing to do was to enlist, and then he would be permitted to remain in school until he graduated. In January 1942 he went to New Orleans and enlisted in the Navy and was granted permission to finish that school year. His orders were to report for duty at Notre Dame University on 20 August, 1942.

At Notre Dame he was given his uniform, the old bell-bottomed sailor suit. He spent four weeks at Notre Dame and six weeks at Northwestern University. Toward the end of his six weeks at Northwestern, when it was evident that the men would graduate, they were sent to the tailor to be measured for their officers' uniforms. These they had to pay for themselves. At graduation he was commissioned an Ensign in the United States Navy.

Bill's first assignment, 2 December, 1942, was to Torpedo School in San Diego, California, where he spent five weeks. He also attended Fireman's School there. Upon completion of his schooling he was assigned to the destroyer USS *Balch* DD-363, which he was to meet in New Caledonia, an island in the South Pacific about 750 miles east of Australia. His transportation out there was on the *President Monroe*, a troop transport ship which had formerly been a passenger liner. He had no duties and had the luxury of being just a passenger. Bill, along with all the others, received a certificate for crossing the equator. The date on the certificate reads "on the military secret day of Janutober 1943."

New Caledonia was a staging area, and Bill was impressed with the great number of ships in the harbor. There were battleships, cruisers, troop ships and many, many destroyers. There were no aircraft carriers because the attack at Pearl Harbor had so depleted the Navy that the carriers were protected from possible attack. Bill's feeling was that at last he was in the war zone.

When he reported aboard the *Balch* his assignment was assistant torpedo officer. The ship soon sailed for Guadalcanal, which had been secured before they arrived. Almost immediately the *Balch* was ordered to the Aleutian Islands near Alaska. This meant going from the tropics almost to the Arctic. The Japanese had invaded the islands of Attu and Kiska. The U.S. Navy was to prevent the Japanese from landing more men and/or supplies. It was so very cold that Bill and most of the men grew beards to protect their faces. The Aleutians were secured and the Japanese-organized resistance there ended 23 May, 1943; the *Balch* was then ordered to San Francisco. Bill was detached and given thirty days leave which he spent at home in Des Plaines, Illinois.

Following this leave he was reassigned to San Diego where he went to the Amphibious Warfare School for instruction in the handling of small boats. Upon completing the five week course he was assigned to the *President Polk* AP103 as "boat officer." This ship had been refitted and commissioned a United States Naval Vessel, having formerly been a passenger liner. The *President Polk* sailed for the island of Tarawa in the Gilbert Islands. The U.S. Marines had invaded the islands 20-23 November, 1943, and because of faulty judgment regarding the tides there were many casualties. The boats were unable to get close in to shore because of the low tide, and Japanese soldiers killed many of the Marines as they waded ashore.

The *President Polk* arrived on D-Day plus five, by which time the island was relatively secure. There was still "mopping up" to do, however, because there were Japanese soldiers loose all over the island. The *Polk* landed the CBs (construction battalion), whose job it was to build air strips, mess halls, living quarters, roads, etc. Bill was in charge of four small boats, LCVPs, with twenty men. They were assigned to the commanding officer of Tarawa (which consisted of several very small islands in addition to Tarawa itself). The job was to transport men and materials as needed among these islands. Bill also had the responsibility of taking tidal readings many times each day.

From Tarawa, Bill and his four boats and crews were assigned to another ship, the *Sands*, and took part in the invasion of Kwajalein in the Marshall Islands. This occurred in early February of 1944. In July and August of 1944 he was involved in the invasions of Ulithi, Saipan, Tinian and Guam in the Mariana Islands. These invasions involved a huge task force and the *Sands*, along with many other destroyers, acted as escorts to the troop ships, which were landing thousands of troops. Bill's small boats were aboard the *Sands* but were not used for minesweeping.

At Saipan there was a report that some Japanese soldiers still remained on one of the small islands in the group. Bill and his boat were sent to investigate. As they sailed around the island their boat became hung-up on the coral reef, and they were unable to break it loose. There was nothing to do but start swimming back toward their ship. An American plane flying over spotted them and, assuming they were Japanese, fired their machine guns at them. Bill and his crew waved their arms showing the "V for Victory" sign, trying to indicate they were friends. Fortunately, the plane crew got the message. The Marines were requested to go out searching for the men in an amphibious vessel; they found the men and returned them to their ship.

When the war ended, Bill separated from the Navy in March 1946, having served four years and two months.

William Stella's wife, Wilma, wrote this story as told to her in tribute of her husband's service.

TWO FAMILIES
by Manuel Toledo

I have had the privilege of having two families. I was born into one on July 13, 1918, and I have served with the other since January 28, 1941. My parents were Catholic Portuguese immigrants from the Azores Islands. We didn't have much, but we didn't suffer during the Depression because we grew and raised most of our food. As the oldest, I had to work the ranch with my dad, so I only went through eighth grade.

In 1934 I was at a wedding and I saw the cutest girl. Six years later I was introduced to that same girl, Lorry Thomas, and we were married on November 21, 1942. I was a wet-behind-the-ears farm boy who had never been very far from home. On January 28, 1941, fifty-three of us local boys were on standby for the draft, and we decided to sign up for one year. At Fort Ord, California, we became part of

Manuel Toledo, National Guard Master Sergeant, 1947.

Company B of the 17th Infantry, 7th Division. We thought we would find a little adventure, but we got more than we had bargained for. By the end of the war, most of us came back wounded, maimed, and scarred for life, but all fifty-three made it home alive.

We only had a few days left to serve when the Japanese bombed Pearl Harbor on December 7, 1941. After combat training in the Mohave Desert under General Patton and amphibious training near San Luis Obispo, in April 1943 we boarded the USS *J. Franklin Bell* and headed for combat. As the ship went under the Golden Gate Bridge I had a sick, empty feeling in the pit of my stomach. Ten miles out at sea we learned that we were going to the Aleutian Islands, not the North African desert. We were young, scared, improperly trained, and wearing clothing unsuitable for the harsh, icy, wet climate and mountainous terrain.

After we landed on Attu on May 11, 1943, we learned to survive. We suffered frostbite. We shot at human beings for the first time. We watched our own men

Manuel and Lorry Toledo were married on November 21, 1942.

die. We lost ten of the forty men in our platoon on the first day. On the second day, our platoon leader was wounded during a banzai attack and I took over command. At the end of that day I had ordered the troops to dig in, but it was hard to dig into frozen ground. After a foggy evening banzai attack we found eighteen more of our platoon slaughtered. Most of them had not dug in and they were bayoneted or shot to death. After all these years the image of the bloody, mutilated bodies of those 15-to-19-year-old boys still haunts me. After the first battles, after watching all those boys die, I didn't want to get close to anyone. It hurt too much. I felt like I was in hell, but we were in hell together. That bond kept us going as it got worse.

On October 20, 1944, during General MacArthur's return to the Philippines, the 17th Infantry was one of the first to hit the beaches of Leyte. The Japanese were ruthless and they were everywhere; we were constantly under machine gun fire. On October 28 our platoon leader was killed, and for the fifth time I took over command.

On October 29, as the 1st Battalion advanced through the swamp, we were hit hard by heavy machine gun fire and lost fifty troops, either wounded or killed. I was one of the lucky ones—I was only wounded. A 25-millimeter mortar shell blasted through a nearby banana tree without exploding. Both the shell and a chunk of the tree ripped through me. It left huge open wounds in my chest and back and knocked me unconscious. I was mistaken for dead and stacked with the dead. As the troops advanced three of my buddies from Tulare—Timmy Lopez, Tommy Fikes, and Manuel Sotelo—happened to glance at the bodies and recognized me. They checked for a pulse and yelled for a medic, who stuffed my wounds with sulfa drugs. The guys risked their lives carrying me through the swamp under machine gun fire to a field hospital.

One of the doctors told the medics to leave me alone and take care of the others because I wasn't going to make it. That doctor may have thought I was almost dead, but I was determined not to die. Eight hours later and after being in and out of consciousness, I still had a pulse, so another doctor cleaned out the wounds and sewed me up. I was critically wounded and my right side was paralyzed. I would later learn that I had two splintered ribs and damage to the upper lobe of my right lung and to my spinal chord.

On November 1, 1944, I was placed on a hospital ship going to New Guinea, and on December 14, 1944, I was on the USS *Monterey*, a damaged aircraft carrier turned hospital ship, en route to San Francisco. On January 1, 1945, I again went under the Golden Gate Bridge, this time headed home, but I was a different man. I had gone from being a strong, healthy 180-pound adventurer to a feeble 115-pound disabled soldier.

Three days after arriving at Letterman Hospital in San Francisco I was on my way to Baxter General Hospital in Spokane, Washington, for experimental surgery. At twenty-six I would either soon die without it, or die on the operating table, or survive it and maybe have a few years to live. In February 1945 I became a guinea pig for numerous surgeries, and was told that I might have two to five years. That was over sixty years ago—I am now eighty-seven years old.

Manuel Toledo with full medals, 1961, is the founder of the Toledo Military Museum in Tulare, CA.

In late June 1945 I was released, returned home for therapy at the Fresno VA Hospital, and became involved with several veterans groups. In 1947 I joined the California National Guard as a First Sergeant and nineteen years later retired as a Captain. In 1948 I met Colonel Ralph Thorpe, a retired WW I and WW II medic. We formed the Tulare AMVETS Post 56 with thirty charter members, of which only two are living—Glen McKinney and myself. The membership has grown to more than 2500, and recently the post was renamed the Captain Manuel Toledo AMVETS Post 56. In March 1987 I was honored to receive the National Silver Helmet "AMVET of the Year" Award. With the dedicated help of Cliff Cates, another WW II veteran, I opened the Toledo Military Museum, which is now housed at the Tulare Historical Museum.

After my discharge on July 13, 1945, I continued rehabilitation and recovered. Then I took advantage of the GI Bill. I was trained as a watch and clock repairman and bought a business in 1947. My wife Lorry and I have owned and operated Toledo's Jewelry in Tulare, California, for fifty-eight years. We have been married sixty-three years and have four children, Yvonne, Michael, Annette, and Michelle, plus twelve grandchildren and twelve great-grandsons.

My life was spared many times during the war, and I owed a debt to all those boys who died and to the ones who came home alive. I'd like to pay tribute to my wife and family, to those who saved my life, to all of those who served, and especially to those who made the ultimate sacrifice for our freedom.

Manuel Toledo's daughter, Yvonne Toledo, wrote this story as told to her in tribute of her father's service.

A TELESCOPIC VIEW OF THE PAST
by Leon Rockwell

About six months ago, while rummaging around one of my closets, I came across a tan case hanging on a hook by a torn strap. Immediately I recognized it as my old WW II Air Force binoculars. There it was in its faded tan case with its pebble-finished leather and a big "USA" with indented print on the front. The case on the exterior did show quite a bit of wear and user scars, as did the torn but useable leather shoulder strap. The G.I. issue binoculars inside the case were of standard size, and as I opened the lid to the case on it was slightly faded but neatly printed, "Major Leon Rockwell—31 Bomb Squadron."

Wow, what memories I recalled as I slowly removed the binoculars from the case. As I examined them, I started to reminisce. I observed that they were black and of metal construction, with black leather on the two adjustable metal cylindrical scopes and black plastic on the adjustable eye pieces and focusing lenses. It was obvious when placed to the eye for sighting that these were originally manufactured for the infantry because imbedded on the lenses were small hair-like lines with tiny calibrated numbers in kilometers.

I wondered why an Air Force bomber pilot would be issued infantry binoculars. As a matter of fact, none of the bomber crews in the Solomon Island/Guadalcanal Theater of Operations in 1942 were ever issued any type of binoculars until one very specific day. On that day, General Nathan Twining, Chief of Staff and Commanding General of the Air Force, was forced to ditch in the ocean in a B-17 from our 23rd Heavy Bomber Squadron.

The general was inspecting the various Air Force bases in the South Pacific and had selected a combat crew from our 23rd Bomb Squadron to fly him around to the Air Force bases in the Solomon Islands. Our Air Force base in the New Hebrides was several hundred miles south of the bases at Guadalcanal in the Solomon Islands. Somewhere in between the B-17 crew ran into a savage tropical storm, became lost, and ran out of fuel. Our weather in the South Pacific was often miserable with tropical storms, heavy winds, and little or no visibility. Usually generals acted as command pilots and did not actually fly the controls in the bombers. During wartime, in the combat zone, radio-navigation is never turned on or doesn't exist since the enemy planes could home in and navigate to a friendly air base to drop their bombs.

Leon Rockwell in his B-17 bomber Aztec's Curse.

The radio operator of the downed bomber was able to send an SOS message that they were setting it down in the ocean, but was unable to give a position report. Immediately a Red Alert was declared throughout both the Navy and Air Force and search patterns were created with all available aircraft. The B-17 bomber crews were ordered to report to the briefing room to plan an organized, methodical search for the general and the downed bomber crew. I never found out where the 13th Bomber Command Headquarters obtained so many field artillery binoculars, but it was that day that I received the now musty, battle-scarred binoculars that had been hidden away in my closet.

There was hope that the general and bomber crew, if found, could have possibly survived the ditching. A B-17 bomber has inflatable life jackets for a crew of about ten men. On either side on top of the fuselage are two large inflatable life rafts, with emergency gear, that pop out when activated for a water landing. Both the Navy and Air Force searched over hundreds of miles of ocean and on the sixth day, when the search was about to be called off, the two yellow life rafts were spotted bobbing up and down among the white cap ocean waves. The entire crew was found well and unhurt except for sunburns, salt sores, dehydration, and hunger.

As I viewed my musty and faded WW II relic, it had quite an impact on bringing back memories of how lucky I was to have survived two years and eighty combat missions flying out of tropical jungles. Of my nine Air Force classmates who were assigned to the Asiatic Pacific Theater of Operations only one other and myself were not forced to make a water landing. Also, of those nine classmates only five of us returned.

I then thought about my tent mate, Andre Temple, handsome, of medium-build, intelligent, and an accomplished graduate of U.C. Berkeley. He was not only a talented artist but a professional photographer. Andre had completed all of his combat missions and tour of duty. He actually had military orders to return to the United States for reassignment after two years of Air Force duty in the South Pacific. Why, I don't know, but Andre volunteered for another tour of duty without any rest leave. He spent his rest leave making a take-off one-day over the harbor at Esperito Santos when the electrical system failed, causing all four propellers to flatten out their pitch, resulting in a sudden loss of power. He immediately spied a U.S. Destroyer in the harbor and proceeded to make a water landing close to it. It was his hope that his crew would be rescued by the Navy personnel aboard the ship. Everyone of his crew got out of the sinking bomber except Andre and his engineer.

It was my sad duty to complete a half-written letter to his girlfriend that was still in his typewriter. I collected all of his personal effects, boxed them up, and along with a very difficult letter to his folks, mailed them to his home.

Captain Rockwell's bomber crew (with Rockwell in the center) of the Air Force's 23rd Heavy Bomber Squadron.

JESS' STORY
by Jess Woodward

It was a warm summer day in California's Central Valley in July 1942. Jess Woodward and his buddy were bored with their summer vacation, so they hitch-hiked to San Francisco to see the merchant marine ships at the docks. When they arrived, they wandered around the docks and checked out the ships. A lady approached them and asked what they were doing. When they told her they did not have a place to stay she offered them food and housing if they would work odd jobs and run errands for her. They later learned that she ran a house of prostitution.

The next day they returned to the docks and met the captain of the merchant marine ship SS *Cedar Breaks*. When he found out where they were staying, he told them that he didn't approve. He told them they could sleep on board his ship that night, and the next day he would send them home. That night he received orders to sail and forgot the boys until it was too late.

Because the country was at war, the captain could not get them back to the mainland. He signed them on as workaways. Because the merchant marine ships were civilian ships, they often had young boys on board. Jess said most of the younger boys were from other countries. Jess celebrated his fifteenth birthday on the high seas of the South Pacific Ocean.

Being on a civilian ship, Jess could sign on for one trip at a time, and at the end of the trip he would be discharged. But when the trip ended, he would more than likely be in another country. He could either sign on that same ship or look for another ship that happened to be in port. Those who were eighteen or older were eligible to be drafted into the armed services if they didn't sign up on a ship.

By the time he was eighteen, he had sailed around the world three times. For the most part he sailed oil tankers, the most dangerous of all ships. They were even more dangerous when they were empty because they floated high in the water and provided an easy target. They also exploded more easily when the tanks were filled only with fumes.

Merchant ships were the enemy's number one targets because they carried troops, tanks, airplanes, ammunition and supplies to every theater of the war. They landed on the beaches right alongside the Marines. They participated in every U.S. Marine Corps landing operation all over the Pacific Ocean.

Jess Woodward in his Merchant Marine uniform in front of his home in the San Joaquin Valley.

There were about 2700 merchant ships involved in the first wave of landing on the Pacific Islands. The SS *Emidio* was the first merchant ship sunk in World War II. A Japanese submarine, eighteen miles off Crescent City, California, sank it on December 20, 1941. Many merchant marine ships were torpedoed. Countless other ships were either damaged or sunk by Kamikaze pilots.

Jess' ships were no exceptions. They fought off numerous planes and evaded many enemy ships and submarines. They used zigzagging actions to evade torpedoes. When attacked by Kamikazes they shot in patterns and prayed that the attacking planes would fly through the patterns. They shot down several planes in this way. One day one of the planes they hit blew apart, and a large piece of the plane landed on board the ship. The sailors salvaged the large red circle of the rising sun on the side of the plane. They cut it up, and each sailor brought home a piece of the rising sun.

It was quite awhile before all of the merchant ships were armed. On November 17, 1941, Congress approved arming merchant ships. They also organized the Naval Armed Guard. But it took many months before guns and crews were put onboard the thousands of merchant ships, and it was a long time before Navy crews were assigned to man the guns on board. The men on all the ships that Jess sailed on had to man their own guns, and many of the guns were of World War I vintage.

One day, near the end of the war, Jess' ship was docked at Guadalcanal when a Japanese submarine snuck into the harbor and torpedoed the ship next to Jess. Painting ships is an ongoing job because the salt air rusts them. Jess was over the side of the ship painting, and the explosion blew him up into the air. When he came down he hit the mooring line and his body wrapped around it. He slid down to the edge of the water and, fortunately, came to a stop at the rat guard. The guard held his head out of the water. He could hear someone yelling, "Save the live ones. We'll pick up the dead ones later." Since he could not speak or move, they passed by him. Finally someone saw him blinking his eyes and they pulled him out of the water. They took him to a hospital in Guadalcanal and then sent him to a hospital in San Francisco.

On June 21, 1945, when he had recovered from his injuries, he signed on again to the SS *Cedar Breaks* in San Pedro and sailed for Saipan. He arrived there on July 15th. It was his birthday. He was just eighteen years old. On August 26, Jess signed on the SS *Maiden's Eye* and sailed from Saipan to Tokyo Bay. They arrived there just before Japan and the Allied leaders, headed by General Douglas MacArthur, signed the surrender documents on the USS *Missouri*, so the mariners watched this historic event from a distance.

Shortly after, their captain gave them permission to go swimming off the side of the ship. After that, Jess' back began hurting again. It was then that he found out he had a fracture of the eighth vertebrae and a dorsal spine fracture. This had previously been missed. He was sent to a Navy hospital. The hospital discharged him as "not able to work." On September 27, 1945, he was put aboard the SS *Benjamin H. Bristow* as a workaway, presumably to get him home. On November 28, 1945, he arrived in Norfolk, Virginia, and was sent to a USPH hospital. It was then that he found he could no longer live the life he loved so much on the merchant ships.

Betty Woodward penned this story, which her husband, Jess, related to her, as a tribute to his service in the Merchant Marines.

Jess Woodward's United States Coast Guard certificate of service.

BELLS

by Louis L. Bestenheider

On December 7, 1941, I was visiting my grandparents and Uncle Ernie in New York City. I was a high school senior in Demarest, New Jersey. Ernie and I were playing touch football when word came that the Japanese had bombed Pearl Harbor.

I went home and told my mom I wanted to join the Marines. Because I was only seventeen I needed her to sign for me, but she said not until I graduated. Immediately following graduation I went to the Marine recruiting office. Things were going fine until I failed the eye test. The recruiting officer told me to eat lots of carrots, avoid reading and watching movies, get plenty of rest, and come back in three months. I really wanted to be a Marine so for three months I stuffed my pockets with carrots to eat during the day and avoided reading newspapers and watching movies. At the end of three months, I still couldn't pass the eye test.

Since the Marines wouldn't take me I joined the Army Air Corp. I envisioned myself as an aerial gunner, shooting down Japanese Zeroes. My training began at Camp Upton, New York. The Air Corp decided my friend Adam Eisenbeil and I would be radio operators, so most of our time was spent learning Morse code.

We were assigned to and boarded the USS *America*, not knowing where we were headed. The *America* was the largest U.S. luxury liner and had been refitted to squeeze in over 10,000 troops. After two weeks at sea, moving back and forth to avoid Japanese submarines, we landed in Sydney Harbor. Adam and I were then transported to Kiriwina Island in Papua New Guinea where we maintained a radar range station twenty-four hours a day. We were not told how long the assignment would last, but others assigned to this duty had lasted just a few months. We lived in a tent with two cots and a hand-crank telephone, which was provided to keep us in contact with the U.S. and Australian Air Force. They would direct us to turn the radar signal on and off. This kept the Japanese from following our planes onto or off the island. We had no vehicle, most of our meals consisted of C-Rations, and the only human contact we had the first year was with a few island natives.

After about a year we were given a Jeep. Adam and I had never driven a car but we learned quickly, and the stress of living on a basically deserted island became slightly more tolerable. We began taking turns leaving our station to find a hot meal in one of the other camps and relax. The stress of our assignment eventually got to Adam. On one of his evenings away he got into some trouble with an officer and he was removed from his tour of duty.

A replacement for Adam was sent, and I remained on the island for another couple of months. After sixteen months on the Island I was sent to Ipswich, Australia, on leave. I met my future wife, Nancy, in Woolworth's, and we fell in love. We were engaged on Christmas Eve, 1944. I was shipped out again but managed to return to get married on May 9, 1945.

I knew we were a very special couple, but I didn't know how special. When we exited the church bells started to ring not only in our church, but also in all the churches in town. I thought, Wow! What a celebration for two young people on their wedding day. Well, I have to admit we were not the reason for all the bells ringing. You see, May 9th in Australia is May 8th in the USA, which happens to be V.E. Day. The war in Europe ended May 8, and that was the reason for the celebration. After sixty years, I still like to think they were ringing for us.

BORNEO BREAK: A WAR STORY
by Robert E. Dyer

From time to time it is the destiny of aging men to recall the past and thereby become the young adventurers they once were. As memories age with those who treasure them, odd variances seem to creep into remembered times and places when shared with friends and loved ones. Such variations are perhaps insignificant, because however expansive the recollection becomes when told and retold, the essence of the story always reflects the spirit of the time the adventure was recorded in our ears and minds. We are thus transformed momentarily by our return to an adventurous hour.

The 2nd Photo Reconnaissance Squadron flew missions over Borneo, New Guinea, and the Southern Philippines from the Puerto Princess Air Base at Palawan, Philippine Islands. My job was radio operator/gunner on a crew of ten men flying B-24 aircraft assigned to the squadron. The aircraft had been modified to carry special cameras on long-range photographic missions. Dozens of photographs collected at the time have been periodically reviewed and have reinforced the clarity of my wartime memories of fellow crewmembers, airplanes, places, and events.

On one most memorable day the sea was a great deep shadow beneath layers of clouds that cut short our photo mission along the west coast of Borneo, near Kuching. The interruption left us with plenty of fuel and time to generate a little mischief before returning to our base. The Japanese had been subdued in this area some months earlier and supply lines were non-existent. A few aircraft were left, but we were confident that the potential for hostile action by the enemy was almost nil. We would later remember this day as one of the last days of World War II.

It was certain that great four-engine airplanes were not all that familiar to the people of Borneo. Someone said the sight and sound of a B-24 at very low altitude could possibly be of some interest to the inhabitants of Kuching. A consensus was reached from much chatter on the intercom, ending in a more serious discussion between the pilot and co-pilot. It became obvious that "buzzing" Kuching at low altitude was the best way to inform the people of Borneo of the superiority of American aircraft and American flyers. Our co-pilot concurred in this idea and the fun began.

The drone of the engines became a roar as I left the flight deck, pushed between the fuel cells, through the camera bay, and to the starboard waist window. The plane banked sharply, the view swiftly changing from clouds to rain forest and back to cloudy horizon. Each of us had braced ourselves so we could avoid being tossed around during evasive action maneuvers. The assurances of two parachutes, emergency vests, Mae West, gloves, and flight jacket seemed amusing but comforting.

The plane descended rapidly, coursing above a river that divided Kuching before reaching the sea. Tree top height at well over cruising speed was exhilarating. In seconds, we were a few feet above the river, rolling slightly, treetops now at eye level left and right. Heavy forestation gave way to intermittent thatched roofs and clearings. The plane seemed to leap, suddenly arching over a wood bridge, a preview of things to come.

Curves in the meandering river tightened, dictating more frequent banking of the plane. Low-rise buildings now lined the river's banks. Larger, solid looking buildings and a riverfront road defined the center of the town. People waved from windows and balconies that were at the same height above the river as the plane. We seemed to have created great excitement as the plane surged upward and over a gray metal bridge, diving nearly to the surface of the river, roaring over small boats and out over the harbor.

We rose two or three hundred feet above the open sea turning gracefully back toward land. The plane descended swiftly again to tree top height, parallel with the shore, sweeping past the water's edge, docks, boats, and people crowding the embarcadero. Up again and over the town, skimming over the neighborhoods and jungle paths, finally rolling into two or three tight turns around a radio antennae mast we believed to be about a hundred feet high. Gaining altitude, we flew over the town and out to sea.

We did not try to contain our excitement as we shouted accolades over the intercom. The co-pilot had flown the B-24 beautifully and I believe each of us felt deeply satisfied with the episode. We climbed slowly to the northeast on a heading that would take us across the South China Sea. The navigator confirmed my sighting of a distant waterspout in an approaching storm front to the northwest. We outdistanced the storm narrowly and reached the air base five uneventful hours later.

Flying over Borneo.

MYSTERY IN NEW GUINEA
by Edward Roddy

I was flying a P47-Thunderbolt for the 342nd Fighter Squadron in World War II when my wing pilot, Wilfred J. "Bill" Desilets, Jr. disappeared during a mission over a dense rain forest in New Guinea. It was on August 18, 1943. Fifteen members of the squadron and I had been flying a mission escorting C-47 cargo planes from Dobodura, New Guinea, to the Wau-Bulolo area.

The squadron commander had briefed us, saying, "We don't want any nonsense, no more radio chatter, keep quiet, don't say anything." Well, the squadron commander had the first eight P-47s, and I had the second eight. We kind of scissored back and forth because the C-47s going as fast as they could were about as slow as we could go without falling out of the sky.

We were at about 10,000 to 12,000 feet with a speed of 185 to 200 miles per hour. We passed through a dense cloud, and the C-47s went under some clouds. The squadron commander circled back under the clouds descending to a level below the clouds trying to follow a C-47 as it rose above a canyon. The rest of us went up a valley and circled a little grass landing strip. Of course, I was following where we were on my map, and I knew this was the strip called Garaina.

We then headed up a valley, which soon became very narrow, too narrow to do a 16-ship formation 180-degree turn. Soon the floor of the valley came up, and we were forced to pull up into the clouds or crash into the hillside. All of a sudden the walls of the canyon were too close. We were at the end of the valley, and it's nothing but rocks. We weren't prepared for that. We had been cruising at fuel-saving power settings, since we had much more speed than the C-47s. We pulled up into the overcast, adding power, and I think each pilot realized that on the heading we had been on there was nothing but trouble.

We went full throttle, full mixture. We had no external tanks yet because they hadn't figured out how to do it. We went into the clouds at about 6,000 feet. When I spiraled out on top, some twelve to fifteen thousand feet above sea level, I was shocked to see no one else. Gradually P-47s were popping up out of the clouds, and I gathered about five or six of them and led them back to Dobodura. When the fighters landed, two were missing. Desilets had been flying on my wing that day when he vanished.

When I landed back at Dobodura there was a big discussion with Colonel Kerby, the group commander, as to what happened, and exactly where we were at the time. When I pointed out where I felt we had been the squadron commander came in. He heard me and said, "We're nowhere near that!" In other words, I was a big liar. I just kept my mouth shut, and when he was finished shooting off, I went to the group commander and said, "Obviously, he and I don't see eye to eye. I need a transfer out of this outfit."

When the weather broke, and I got back to flying, I knew where the crash was and went up looking for any evidence of our two missing pilots, Desilets and Andrews. Although I never actually saw Andrews down below, he knew that was me up there, flying around looking for his crashed plane. The foliage was so thick from the trees that signal bearers wouldn't do anything. We didn't have a signal radio or anything like that at that time. I got a copy of his report and felt that it verified my position, so I went to the group commander and asked that I be transferred out of the 342nd. He asked me if I knew that this would not bring Desilets back. I said that I understood, but that I just had lost all respect for the squadron commander and wanted out.

The report is as follows:

On 1 September 1943, a statement to Intelligence Officer, He, 348th Fighter Group, A.P.O. 929 wau/Bulolo area was given by Lt. C. O. Andrews on Mission of August 18, 1943. Andrews said, "After plunging into an overcast at 6,000 feet as No. 2 in the leading flight, my plane went out of control, and I bailed out when approximately 1600 feet from the ground. In descending, my parachute became entangled in the tree tops and left me dangling about 100 feet from the ground, suffered a fracture of the right leg between the hip and the knee. Unable to move any appreciable distance, I lay on my rubber boat using parachute cloth for covering. Plenty of fresh water was available from a nearby stream which I was able to reach with my left hand. My only food was a "D" ration bar from my jungle kit.

I lay in the same place for three days and two nights and was about to attempt an escape by crawling on the ground when some friendly natives spotted me. They placed a splint on my leg and carried me by stretcher to a village where they kept me until ANGUA troops recovered me. I was then carried to Garaina strip and returned by an AAF Rescue Squadron plane to Fort Moresby where I was hospitalized.

The exact spot where I descended was on the side of Mt. Batchelor about 20 miles SW of Garaina. I never once gave up hope and felt confident right along that rescue attempts were being made. On the second day, I spotted a P-47 presumably flown by Captain Roddy, searching the area. I believe that with a mirror or tracer ammunition I might have been able to attract his attention.

I saw no trace of my plane after bailing out, but heard it explode nearby shortly after I reached the ground. (Pieces of the wreckage have since been recovered.) I saw nothing of P/O Desilets or of his plane.

I have acquired a healthy respect for the jungle and advise all pilots to do the same."

Everyone in the squadron knew the facts. After Col. Kerby died, they found the airplane right where I said it was reported.

I didn't get a transfer for another five or six months. It was April 1944 before the group commander could accommodate my request, but I did get out, and later became a group commander at the tender age of twenty-five years with three American squadrons of 25 P-47s each.

We had lost two pilots, two airplanes. Andrews was found, injured but survived, and Desilets' remains and the wreckage of his plane were found in 1996. His sister said that finally knowing what had happened to their brother was both painful and comforting. The comfort came from knowing he died quickly, and would finally be laid to rest.

There are only three of us left in that sixteen that went off on that flight.

A CLOSE CALL
by Jack Knight

I was born at the Burnett Sanitarium on March 20, 1925, to Hugh Felix Knight and Floy Ellen Ledbetter Knight. Growing up in Fresno, California, in the 1930s and early 1940s was good. Times could be hard because of the Great Depression and bad things could happen, but people pulled together and that made all the difference.

After graduating from Roosevelt High School I joined the Army Air Corp and spent the next year training in California and Montana to serve my country. Following training as a nose gunner in a B-24, I was assigned to the 7th Army Air Force operating from the Hawaiian Islands chain. This area was designated the Central Pacific Theater. The 7th Army Air Force was supported by multiple wings, one of which was the 30th Bombardment Group. The 30th Group was based at Wheeler Field on the Island of Oahu with Pearl Harbor only minutes away. Within the Group functioned the 38th Squadron, a unit of a dozen aircraft and hundreds of "fly boys" and support personnel. I had recently been assigned to this squadron, and they would become my extended family.

The job I had trained to perform was to operate a tandem 50-caliber machine gun mounted in the nose turret of a B-24M Liberator long range bomber. On the morning of 26 June, 1945, our plane #44-42223 took off from Wheeler field with two other planes at about 07:50 for an air-to-air gunnery mission. After take-off all the planes flew directly to the designated ranges. Firing started at 08:00 and continued until 09:00 when we had finished our mission. Our pilot received permission from the flight leader of 392nd Bombardment squadron to leave formation and return to base. The pilot left the mission area, then took a course to the Oahu coast, and from there headed down the valley toward Wheeler Field. We were about three miles from Wheeler flying at 3,500 feet altitude when the pilot called the tower and received permission to enter the traffic pattern.

I had cleaned and blocked the nose turret guns, and had gone back to the waist to take some photos and wait for the landing. As we neared Upper Post (Schofield), I was standing at the left waist window watching the ground. Suddenly, there was a fairly loud explosion. The accompanying concussion thrust the sixty thousand pound bomber forward like a leaf and downward. I thought the left waist gun had "cooked off." Upon closer examination, I could see that both the rudder and elevator control surfaces of the left side had been shot away. The pilot no longer had radio contact with the Wheeler Tower and the airplane would not respond to the controls for a right turn.

Finally the pilot was able to contact "lizard" control, and through them obtained permission to make a left-hand approach and emergency landing at Wheeler. There was no room for turbulence or sudden corrections. As the Liberator flew slowly toward its destination each crewman aboard contemplated the time and distance between them, the base, the valley floor below and the encircling mountains. These were the same mountains that had recently devoured another bomber and crew returning from Guam, a flight I had just missed because my seat was taken by another gunner.

I knew, as did all aboard, if the remaining stabilizer should suddenly go, landing would have been impossible and at such a low altitude all parachutes would be rendered useless. Seconds became minutes and minutes seemed to become hours with the phrase "sweating it out" taking on an entirely new dimension. This day, however, the Liberator and its crew would not fail, and this moment would not be the last for our eight crewmembers. Everyone was prepared to bail out if necessary, but the pilot decided to land the plane. We were told to brace for a rough landing, but with pilot skill and some luck the pilot brought the wounded plane in just fine and we landed safely.

Jack Knight's damaged B-24M Liberator shot en route to Wheeler Field, June, 1945.

Upon the landing approach the astonished ground crews stood with their arms limp at their sides as they gazed in amazement that we had engaged the enemy so close to Wheeler Field; moreover, they were amazed that we were able to make it back at all, considering the amount of damage visible from the

Jack Knight with his crew in the 7th Army Air Force, 38th Squadron.

ground. During inspection of the damage to the bomber, it was discovered that only about twelve inches aft of the left fuselage window was a fist-sized hole. This was the window where I had been standing and photographing when we were hit by the errant round. Following the blast, all endeavors had concentrated on securing the bomber and its crew. The gash in the thick aluminum skin where a piece of shrapnel had ripped into and through both sides of the fuselage had gone unnoticed. This shrapnel had missed me by a mere foot. Photographs of the grounded and damaged plane revealed the degree of destruction and how close we came to not making it. Unknown to us at the time, our Liberator had been hit by an errant 81mm mortar round from the Schofield training range some 3,500 feet below. This near disaster was caused by "friendly fire."

It is said that life moved at a slower pace 60 or 70 years ago, but to me things were moving pretty fast. I graduated from high school, joined the Army Air Corp and became a nose gunner. I found out that at the age of nineteen I was going to become a brother for the first time. After I returned home at the end if the war I went to work for Dutch Boy Paint Co., returned to school, married and started my own family. This all happened relatively fast.

Almost getting shot down in our B-24 was probably the most dangerous event in my life, but it was all worth it to be able to have the life we have enjoyed in the "good Old USA." My wife Lorraine and I have raised two boys, Craig and Gary, whom we are very proud of, and we have two great daughters-in-law and four wonderful grandchildren. I guess the world has sped up, but my life has slowed down some. I guess all things work out the way they are meant to.

IN THE DRINK
by Lowell Ivan Horton

I was born at home on December 17, 1917, in northern Independence County, Arkansas, and was there to greet the doctor when he arrived to deliver me. There were six boys and one girl in our family. Times were very lean with patched clothing, one pair of shoes per year, and eating whatever we could grow or catch. My mother died in June of 1934 when I was sixteen years old, and the following year I joined the CCC Camps, which was a program of President Franklin D. Roosevelt's "New Deal" program. I was married on January 5, 1941, while war clouds were gathering. I worked for a couple of months in the wheat harvest in Kansas, then my new bride and I joined some friends and headed west to California with $16.00 in our pockets.

After doing farm work for a while, I enlisted in the Navy Sea Bees in October of 1943. I had five younger brothers and all six of us served in some branch of the service during WW II, and we all returned home without a scratch.

I had boat training in Camp Perry, Virginia, and later moved to Port Hueneme, CA. I left for Pearl Harbor and was promoted to 1st Class Petty Officer. I was one of the first in the Navy to receive the refrigeration rating of MMR1C.

The most frightening event of the trip was when I almost fell overboard. On January 6, 1945, we left Hawaii for Iwo Jima on a cargo ship, which carried 3,700 barrels of aviation gasoline and aerial torpedoes. We were six weeks at sea. One hot humid evening, we were sailing along on a glassy sea near the equator, and all except the crew was asleep on the deck. I climbed on top of one of the walk-in refrigerators. Later in the night the ship began to roll with the sea. I woke up just as my legs bent over the side of the refrigerator. The top of the metal refrigerator was slick, and I found nothing to grasp onto. I looked down and saw the frothing sea below, just as the ship fortunately rolled the other way. I found a safer place to spend the rest of the night!

My job on Iwo Jima was to distill ocean salt water into drinking water. We had two crews that worked around the clock to perform this huge task. It was on Iwo Jima that I discovered war was larger than myself. I asked the Lord to watch over me and give me the courage to do the tasks at hand. We assisted at an emergency evacuation tent, and the doctors on duty were very appreciative of the fresh water after long hours of dealing with the sick and dying. Heroes were all around—most were unaware that they were heroes, but they did what came naturally and whatever needed to be done without thinking of the consequences that might harm them.

My most memorable moment of WW II was when the flag was raised by the six Marines on Iwo Jima, and I was there to see it. The flag was raised and after a few minutes that flag went down. I later learned a picture was taken of the first flag, and it was removed and sent to the archives of the Smithsonian Institute in Washington, DC. Another flag was then raised and remained there. That moment defined patriotism for me, and whenever Old Glory is flown I stand proud to have been able to serve her and my country.

After the war I returned to California to my wife, Ethel, and two children, Gail and Linda. I worked my entire life mostly in the refrigeration and engineering business and enjoy recreational activities such as golf. Ethel and I had two more children, Gary and Susan. I have lived a full life with family and friends close at hand. I have been active in the Visalia First Baptist Church and have many close friends whom I still enjoy. There have been sad times, too. I have lost three of my four children, but I have five grandchildren and two great-grandchildren. My eyes are growing dim, but my memories of WW II are still sharp, and I can say that I am honored to have been able to serve my county.

OPERATION BARNEY

by Robert Owens

I joined the crew of the submarine USS *Tinosa* at Majuro Atoll on 3 June 1944, my birthday, as an Electrician 3rd Class. We left Majuro for the East China Sea where we sank two merchant ships and numerous fishing boats. On completion of this patrol we were sent to the shipyard in San Francisco for a major overhaul. It was here we received a new sonar that would detect mines.

For some time it was a known fact that Japan was bringing raw materials from the mainland to their home islands by the way of the Sea of Japan. In *Hellcats of the Sea*, by Charles A. Lockwood and Hans Christian Adamson, Lockwood said, "The principal object of the Hellcat invasion was not only to disrupt life lines and sink as many Japanese ships, large and small, as possible, but also, in fact, chiefly, to destroy Japanese confidence in the ability of its military leaders to maintain those supply lines against American or other Allied attacks. It was no secret to the rank and file of Japanese that the uninterrupted operation of the trans-Sea-of-Japan shipping lines meant the difference between food and no food; between survival and starvation, victory and defeat."

Several of our submarines attempted to get into the sea but failed. We lost the *Wahoo* at the north end of La Perouse Strait, for instance. The planners developed a plan to enter the south end of the Sea of Japan through the minefields protecting this entrance. Nine submarines with the new sonar were tasked to make the attempt. This group was known as the Hell Cats. The nine submarines were divided into three groups of three boats each. The *Tinosa* was in the third group known as the "Bobcats."

While en route we were notified of a downed B-29. The estimated position was about 200 miles north of our position. We went full on four engines at about twenty knots. We arrived at the estimated position about midnight in a heavy fog. Visibility was about 100 yards. At about nine o'clock, the next morning, the search airplanes had located the lifeboat of the crew. We still didn't see or hear them and steamed in circles blowing our foghorn a few miles off the shore of Japan. We finally recovered ten men. Only one didn't make it, and that was the chief engineer whose chute failed to open. We later transferred them to another submarine that was returning from patrol. We then continued on to the Sea of Japan.

We arrived at our entrance point and proceeded to enter the Sea of Japan, the first group of U.S. submarines to do so. As we proceeded at 120 feet and at 21/2 knots speed on course north, we picked up our first mine on the port (left side) bow fairly close. The ship was maneuvered to the right, and there was the second mine on the starboard (right) bow very close. The *Tinosa* turned slowly to the left at 21/2 knots. It seemed to take forever. As we came closer, the signal on the sonar faded away and showed "all clear." Right about then, we came into contact with the mine anchor chain.

My duty station at this time was in the ring room which is the next to last compartment on the boat. We could hear the chain scraping down the side of the boat for a long period of time. It seemed like an eternity. Fortunately, the chain cleared our stern planes. We were now in the Sea of Japan headed for our assigned area.

Our area was the east cost of Korea known as Bokuko KO. We all had to wait until sunset on 9 June to start shooting. However, at about 2:30 P.M. a freighter was sighted headed into the port. The Captain couldn't wait and shot three torpedoes at about 2200 yards. We fired a normal spread of one ahead, one middle of target (MOT), and one astern. Because the target was slowing to enter the port, the torpedo aimed to for the stern hit the freighter and down she went—2,300 tons.

On 10 June at about 3:30 P.M. we had a target on the radar at 60,000 yards. We proceeded on the surface of the water for four hours plotting all the time until we had the target course and speed cold. The Captain decided to fire the torpedoes from the stern room and placed the boat to do so. At a generated range of 1,200 yards, we fired three torpedoes. The soundman reported, "Hot, straight and normal."

All of a sudden, he shouted that the torpedo from tube eight was changing course and was making a circular run. This meant the torpedo was coming back to the ship. The Captain

The submarine USS Tinosa *(SS283).*

Robert Owens at sea.

called, "Ahead flank, go deep, flood negative." Down we went.

The skipper had ordered us to go deep 700 feet, although our test depth was only 350 feet. Shortly the diving officer reported 250 feet and asked again what depth the Captain wanted. By now some calm had returned, and he ordered 300 feet. The high-pitched whine of the returning torpedo was heart stopping as it passed by. We had already lost two submarines from circular running torpedoes. Since we missed the target ship with a dud torpedo and also missed with two other torpedoes, the target then attacked us and dropped depth charges. Fortunately, no damage resulted.

On 12 June we spotted a 1500-ton motor ship. As we made our approach a heavy fog set in, so the Captain surfaced. There was the motor ship about 6,000 yards away. The Captain decided to sink him with our 5-inch deck gun. The plan was to approach closer in the fog and then shoot. However, the fog lifted, and there we were three miles off the coast fully exposed. The target had a deck gun of her own, and it was manned and ready. When the range closed to 4,000 yards we opened fire. What luck! Our first shot hit the bow gun on the target. We then hit the waterline in the area of their engine room. The crew took off in their lifeboat as we shot up the freighter until it sank. All of this took place within a mile off the Korean coast.

The next target was a 4600-ton freighter. We shot him with three torpedoes at about 750 yards. At sundown this same day, smoke was sighted at 2600 yards. We tracked the target until 7:30 P.M. and fired four torpedoes at 1200 yards. Two hit. The first hit the stern of the freighter and caused a spectacular ball of fire. It must have been from aviation gas. This was our last shot in the Sea of Japan. We had steamed 3000 miles in the Sea and sunk over 12,000 tons of shipping. We happily joined the other submarines and departed the area leaving behind the USS *Bonefish* and her crew.

Fleet Admiral Chester W. Nimitz, USN, recalled in the foreword to *Hellcats of the Sea* in 1955:

"Operation Barney was a break-through into the well-defended Sea of Japan, hitherto considered so safe and impregnable that Japanese shipping and navigational aids followed peacetime procedure. Here nine American submarines spent fifteen days of destruction and general hell raising before eight of them escaped to the Pacific Ocean and safety, leaving behind on the bottom one American submarine, the *Bonefish*, and her crew, and some twenty-eight assorted Japanese ships, including one large Japanese submarine, for a total tonnage of 70,000 tons."

"Operation Barney took place between the dates of June 9 through June 24, 1945, and was successfully completed at least six weeks before the first atom bomb was dropped on Hiroshima.

"The success of Operation Barney can be attributed primarily to the unlimited faith Admiral Lockwood had in his submariners, and in his never-ending drive and zeal for the production of some device which would permit his submarine navigators to locate underwater minefields in time to pass by or through safely."

USS Tinosa *crewmembers enjoying a respite from life at sea (1944).*

THE BATAAN DEATH MARCH

With confidence levels high after their success at Pearl Harbor, Japan continued its offensive in the Pacific by capturing American bases at Guam and Wake Island, as well as many other islands throughout the South Pacific. In early 1942 Japan captured the Philippines, entering the capital of Manila on January 2. The previous month General Douglas MacArthur, commander of U.S. Army Forces in the Far East, declared Manila an open city and withdrew his troops to the Bataan Peninsula. The American and Philippine troops fought valiantly against the Japanese aggressors, but as the enemy continued to encroach President Roosevelt was forced to withdraw MacArthur to Australia, prompting the general's famous proclamation, "I shall return."

Lt. Gen. Jonathan M. Wainwright took control of Bataan. Unfortunately, shortages of food and supplies compelled the Allied force to surrender Bataan on April 9, 1942, while the 11,000-man garrison on Corregidor, a rocky fortress in Manila Bay, held out until May 6. The Japanese forced some 60,000 prisoners to march seventy miles to prison camps. About 10,000 of them died en route from starvation and maltreatment.

WILD BILL'S WAR STORY
by Bill Begley

I was born on September 21, 1921, in Hyden, Kentucky, and was raised primarily by an aunt. She encouraged me to graduate from high school, which I did in 1940. I attempted coal mining but gave up that idea when a mine I was working in collapsed and I narrowly escaped. It was about that time when someone said to me, "Go West, young man." I ended up in San Francisco working at a gas station until the owner suggested that I join the Army. He explained that it would give me some direction, and at the same time pay for an education.

I began basic training on February 7, 1941, at Monterey in the Army Cavalry. After basic training—eighteen days before the war started—I received orders to go to the Philippines. Once there, we were positioned in what had been a sugarcane patch. Although we had been trained with P-40 aircraft, all the aircraft available to us were some P-35s that had been abandoned by the Philippine Air Force. They were an unsightly mess with parts missing and grass growing up through their cavities. Amazingly, however, we were able to salvage about twenty planes from the thirty-five we had found.

About that time we heard on the short-wave radio that Pearl Harbor had been attacked. General MacArthur then grounded all planes, but our commander decided he could not sit idly waiting for something to happen. We agreed with our commander, and we went into battle with the Japanese. The enemy outnumbered us two-to-one, but we were still able to shoot down three of their planes which were seen badly smoking while trying to fly back

Bill Begley (right) as an Army recruiter.

to their carrier at sea. Our ground crews shot down another two. No credit was ever given for this battle, nor was it ever mentioned, but most of the men involved did go on to become Ace pilots.

We were then sent into combat against the Special Japanese Marine Landing Forces without any additional training, and with equipment that had been left over from World War I. Our only orders were, "Do not fire until you see the whites of their eyes." Under those circumstances, the outcome was destined to be bad. What followed was the fall of Bataan, our capture by the Japanese, and subsequently the "Death March of Bataan."

When the Japanese took over Bataan they decided to brutally march the American and Filipino prisoners to POW camps many miles away. Approximately 10,000 died on the march. Many were already malnourished because rations had been cut severely. During this hellish journey, sick and starving prisoners were beaten randomly and denied any water. Any prisoner who asked for water was executed on the spot. When the Japanese guards needed a rest, they forced us to sit in the hot sun without any head covering. Any prisoner who fell behind or collapsed was executed on the spot unless his comrades could carry him. During the week-long march prisoners were denied food apart from a few handfuls of contaminated rice. We were expected to walk over any of our fellow comrades who had been shot or bayoneted. I also witnessed comrades who were forced to dig their own graves, and than have a rifle put to the back of their heads. They were shot in this way so that they would fall easily into the grave.

I vividly recall a small girl about five years old giving the "V" for victory sign. She was immediately bayoneted. Her mother tired to shield her from further harm and was also bayoneted. I, along with several other soldiers, reacted to this horrific sight and we, too, were bayoneted, while others were shot. I cried at the brutality of it. Others sobbed or cried as the little girl cried out. The situation was so awful it was beyond comprehension.

Bill Begley in a photo from the Fresno Bee *is shown at a tribute to POWs.*

Once we finally reached our destination things grew even worse. I was bayoneted multiple times and was even scheduled to face a firing squad. But the bomb was dropped on Hiroshima. I recall thinking that the bomb saved my life. Of the huge numbers of us taken as POWs in our unit, only about forty were still alive at the end of three-and-a-half years in the POW camp. Those that didn't die of starvation or diseases such as malaria had been tortured to death.

After the war ended and we were liberated, I remained in the service as a radio operator. There are only two of us remaining from the 34th Pursuit Fighter Interceptor Squadron.

Bill Begley is the leader in this veterans group photo.

A POW FROM THE BATAAN DEATH MARCH
by Jay Rye

As the Japanese advanced their invasion of the Philippines, the province of Bataan fell on April 9th, 1942. The Bataan Death March of American war prisoners, of which I was a part, moved into the valley of Luzon. We passed artesian wells shooting water three and four feet high. If someone got thirsty and tried to get to water the guards would use a rifle or Samurai sword to kill that person. We learned that if you could take a hard pebble and roll it around in your mouth, it would ease the thirst. It was more than seventy miles to the town of Tarlac, where we were packed in metal boxcars, jammed so tight there was only room to stand. A lot of the soldiers died that way, standing up. We were moved into Camp O'Donnell on Luzon. So many men died along the way that they had to be buried, but the water level was so high that they could not dig any deeper than five feet. Some bodies would float up, and people would take their clothes.

We were eventually moved to Sendai, Japan, and spent 350 days working twenty-four hours a day, three shifts. Another POW camp was on the other side of the mountain from ours. On one particular day in this Japanese village they supplied a meal for eighty or ninety in the first shift. They then took us in drives to the Venture house where we were going to eat lunch, and then back to camp at 9:00 P.M. After all these months of captivity we wondered what was going on, but remained silent. Everything went smoothly, and at 10:00 P.M. they didn't wake us up for the next shift. The Japanese commander, who was of small stature, got upon a stool and spoke before the 100 British and 200 American soldiers. In a powerful voice he announced, "The war is finished."

The British Major made no attempt to gain any demands. The P-51 American Fighter pilots demanded a bull be butchered and brought in for our meals, plus rice and vegetables. Unbeknownst to us, a few got together earlier, acquiring paint and materials, taking nice white sheets from the Japanese officers' beds, and painting the Union Jack and Old Glory on them. They then went down to the river behind the camp felling two tall trees, dragging them up to the base of buildings, digging and burying the posts to fly the flags. The British wanted to fly their flag to the right, but the Americans thought they should fly their flag to the right. When those flags came out the next morning and the bugler sounded we were still in our own dirty clothes, but our shoulders were squared at attention. You cannot know what that flag meant to me!

On the second or third day a Navy fighter craft came over, rocked his wings, and dropped a parachute with cigarettes, candy, etc., and a promise that more would be coming the next day. It did come over the high mountain, a big Air Cargo C54 plane that began throwing stuff out during two runs. A message also came down telling us to remain where we wcre, until a train was sent for us.

You never stop appreciating the flag of the United States of America and what it represents.

This story was written by Aileen Bos based on an oral presentation by Jay Rye.

THE CHINA-BURMA-INDIA THEATER

After freeing the Philippines, the Allies' next priority became securing southeast Asia and the Chinese mainland. Earlier in the war Japan had seized control of the Burma Road, which connected the Burmese capital of Rangoon with China, thereby cutting off the Chinese from all supply routes and isolating their country. Air transport became the only means to supply the Chinese, and the legendary American Volunteer Group known as the Flying Tigers, operating under Maj. Gen. Claire L. Chennault operating out of an airbase in China, was a vital part of the effort to control the skies.

In 1943, the Allies were determined to build a new route called the Ledo Road in the same region, connecting the railway system in northern India to China and thereby reopening supply lines. Rough jungle terrain, steep mountains, and fierce Japanese resistance slowed the Allies' efforts, but various Allied forces such as Merrill's Marauders, Wingate's Raiders, and General Joseph Stilwell's Chinese troops cleared the path for construction. In February 1945 the first Allied convoy drove into China on the Ledo Road (later renamed the Stilwell Road).

LONGBURST: THE STORY OF FIGHTING WITH THE FLYING TIGERS

by Jim Dumas, Jr.

The road to any goal is long, hard and circuitous. My road to becoming a U.S. Army Air Corps pilot began when I awakened under an olive tree, homesick and lonely, on a hot July afternoon just outside the small town of Chowchilla, California.

I was born on February 25, 1917, on a red clay Arkansas hillside farm, the eighth of ten children. As far back as I can remember I dreamed of flying. From the first time I saw an airplane fly over my family farm I knew I had been born to become a military fighter pilot. I graduated from high school on April 12, 1934, in the depths of the Great Depression. My parents could not afford to send me to college, so I went to California in July to earn enough money for the two years of college the U.S. Army Air Corps required of each aviation cadet.

I worked at various jobs, picking peaches for thirty-two cents an hour, picking cotton for seventy-five cents per hundredweight, and driving tractors for farmers—anything to earn a buck I could save so I could go to college. When I had saved $800 I returned to Arkansas to attend college. I enrolled in a government Civilian Pilot Training Program and earned my private pilot's license while attending school.

On the last day of school in January 1941 I took my physical in Little Rock and joined the Army Air Corps as an aviation cadet. I reported to March Field in Riverside, California, for induction on April 23, 1941. I was assigned to Cal-Aero Academy in Ontario, California, for primary and basic training, followed by advanced flight training at Stockton Air

Jim Dumas standing next to his P-40.

Jim Dumas flying over Lake Kunming in his P-40, spring 1942.

Base. I graduated and received my pilot's wings on December 12, 1941, five days after the attack on Pearl Harbor.

After advanced training I was sent to China in April 1942 as one of the first four Army Air Corps replacement pilots for some of General Claire Lee Chennault's "Flying Tigers," the American volunteer group. I flew, trained and fought with the Second Squadron of the Flying Tigers until they were deactivated in July 1942.

I remember well my first mission. That spring morning in 1942, three days after I had been assigned to join them, our flight of seven P-40s were stacked in echelon to the right of our flight leader, David "Tex" Hill, commander of the Second Squadron. We were circling at 21,000 feet over the Flying Tiger base at Kweilin, China, waiting for a flight of Japanese planes from the Canton area the warning net had told us was headed our direction.

We spotted fifteen twin-engine Japanese Mitsubishi 97 type bombers below us escorted by the same number of single-engine Zeros. I was flying right wingman for our flight leader, one of the best, if not the best, of the Flying Tiger pilots.

When Tex radioed, "Let's go get 'em. Follow me." I was second to attack behind the tall Texan. I attacked the last bomber in the flight, the most vulnerable because it lacks the supporting firepower from other planes in the formation. We called a plane in that position "Tail-end Charlie." After shooting at him, I dove below the formation to make sure no Zeros were on my tail. As I pulled out of my dive, I was surprised to see a Zero in front of and below me that had followed Tex down after he attacked the bombers.

He rolled out on top of his half-loop headed directly toward me almost at my altitude. My greatest fear at that time was that we would collide. I wasn't going to be "chicken" and break first to have him think me a coward and make myself more vulnerable. We were closing at over six hundred miles an hour, both with guns blazing away. I could see the red blast from each of his guns as he shot at me. That dirty bastard is trying to kill me, I thought, as we flew directly toward each other. We continued toward each other until we had to break to avoid a head-on collision that would have killed both of us in a fiery crash.

At the last possible second we each broke to our right and passed belly to belly not more than fifty feet apart. Wow, I thought, that was a close one. My heart was pounding in my earphones. I tried to straighten up and come around in time to make another pass at him, but he was gone.

I ended the dogfight with a battle with another Zero above our base, and it was seen smoking as it disappeared out of sight headed toward Canton. I thought maybe I had put a bullet through it as I fired at him from above. It that was true, the pilot didn't get back to his home air base before he ran out of oil or caught fire and had to bail out. However I never got credit for shooting it down, not even credit for a probable. The Flying Tiger pilots ended the day after having shot down seven of the Japanese planes, three bombers and four Zeros, and all the planes in our flight returned home safely. What an exciting first combat mission.

Pilots from the 76th Fighter Squadron.

To even be associated with the Flying Tigers was an honor for me, and to think about flying and fighting with such an elite group was almost unbelievable. When I first met them I thought these guys were supermen. That day's combat convinced me it was true.

After I had been in China less than a week, the day dawned bright and sunny. Little did I dream that before it ended I would have earned a nickname that would gain me notoriety throughout the Army Air Corps and remained with me for as long as I was on active duty.

I was flying wing for Flying Tiger ace Tex Hill again when we were alerted about approaching Japanese planes. I was at 20,000 feet circling our base when I heard over my radio a warning of a Japanese Zero climbing up underneath my plane. The message probably saved my life. I rolled over immediately until I was upside down and did a split-S. From my inverted position I pulled the nose of my plane toward the line of his. As it approached his nose I started firing. His plane didn't explode as I had expected, so I fired again and again, and kept wondering why he didn't go down. I fired as long as I could before I pulled through him. I was not leading him enough. Being a hunter from the hills of Arkansas, I should have realized why I wasn't hitting him with my machine gun fire.

During the critique after the fight General Chennault asked, "Who was the pilot who made that long burst right over the field?" I very sheepishly admitted I was the pilot. The name "Longburst" stuck, and I have never lived it down.

I flew sixty-two combat missions with the Flying Tigers and with the 76th Fighter Squadron, 23rd Fighter Group, 14th Air Force, which replaced the American Volunteer Group in the skies over China in July 1942.

MY MILITARY CAREER
by George Delbert Middleton

I am a third generation native Californian. I was the oldest of three children born to John George and Letha Chamberlain Middleton. Following old English customs, my father had always been known as George, so I went by my middle name until I went into the Army Air Corps in 1942. At that time it was easier to use my first name and I have continued to do so professionally although I am still "Del" to my family.

My great-grandfather was born in Lumly, England, where he was reared and educated. In 1855 he and his family made their way from England to the Isthmus of Panama, walked across, and caught a boat to California. Anthony Cooper Middleton, my grandfather, was born in Kingston, which was in the Laton area of the San Joaquin Valley. It was the site of a ferry over the Kings River.

I grew up in the Selma-Kingsburg district. My family farmed and had a dairy. I spent many long hours on horseback riding herd on my uncle's cattle in the high meadows of the Sierra Nevada Mountains. I was fascinated by aircraft from an early age and was flying off a cow pasture before I even had a driver's license. I graduated from Kingsburg High School and was taking CPT (College Pilot's Training) at Reedley College when World War II began.

In October of 1942 I reported to the Army Air Corp Induction Center at Santa Ana, California. From there I was sent to Arizona State at Tempe for preflight training. Actual Primary Flight Training began at Rankin Field in Tulare, California, with the class of 44-D where we were checked out in Stearmans, P.T.17. I enjoyed being close to home and the girlfriend I had met at Reedley College.

George Middleton in flight gear, 1944.

From Rankin I went on to Basic Training at Gardiner Field in Taft, California. There we flew B.T.13s. Advanced Training was at Ft. Sumner in New Mexico where we were introduced to A.T.17s and B-25s. I graduated, was commissioned as a Second Lieutenant, and pinned on my wings on April 16, 1944.

In a blinding rainstorm, April 19, 1944, Pauline Opal Martin and I were married in the Methodist Church in Reedley, California. Pauline was born in Sanger, California, and grew up in Reedley, where her father was the principal of the Riverview School. Our first home was in Austin, Texas. I was flying C-47s at Bergstrom Field, a Troop Carrier Base. Instead of being sent to Europe I was assigned to Malden, Missouri, where we instructed crews in C-47s and C-46s. When that base was closed I was returned to Bergstrom for Combat Crew Training for China.

Three crews for each C-46 left Dover, Delaware, for India and China by way of Scotland and Iran. Our mission was to ferry supplies and personnel across the Himalayas. We became known as "Hump" pilots. My crew and another got off the C-46 in Chabua, India. One hour out of Chabua the other plane blew up in the air.

George Middleton preparing for flight. Middleton, known as a "hump pilot," ferried supplies and personnel across the Himalayas.

I was assigned to the 332 TC Sq. 513 Grp. in Luliang, China, and remember weather as the major enemy in flying supplies back and forth to China. At the end of hostilities, I was moved to Shanghai where I flew the Chinese officials to Taipei to accept the surrender of Formosa (Taiwan) from the Japanese. Theirs was the first U.S. plane to land on the island after the war. I flew support for General Marshall's peace effort until July of 1946, and was decorated in person by Chiang Kai Shek and presented with Chinese wings.

Upon returning to civilian life, I finished at Reedley College and went on to graduate from Cal Poly at San Luis Obispo, California, in 1949. I taught Ag at Clovis High School in the Central Valley until recalled to the Air Force in May 1952. I was assigned to the 86th Wing in Germany and spent three years in the NATO Aircraft Control Center out of Landstuhl. The next two years were spent at Tyndall AFB, Panama City, Florida, as an instructor.

I returned to Clovis High in 1957 as an agriculture teacher. After several years I became part of the administration as a counselor. I joined the Air National Guard in '57 where I flew a progression of fighter jets: T-33, F 86-F, F 86-D, F86-L, F102 and F106. I continued my dual professions simultaneously fourteen years and was the commanding officer for the 133rd Fighter Interceptor Group in

Fresno when I was retired as a Brigadier General in 1971. I retired from Clovis High School in 1983.

During my years with the Air Guard I had several interesting assignments. The "Grizzly" VC117 (DC-3) was the plane used by California governors. When its pilots were returned to active duty during the Vietnam Conflict, I helped fill in and enjoyed flying Governor Pat Brown for several years. My most dramatic experience was Hurricane Camille in 1969. As commanding officer, I had six hundred men on a training mission in Gulfport, Mississippi. The wind tower blew over at 220 knots and the death toll and damage in Gulfport was staggering. I ordered my troops to clear the airport runways allowing relief supplies to land and 200 to 300 bodies to be flown out. I ordered my doctors and corpsmen to scatter throughout the town giving aid to the injured. Due to decisions I made to protect my men they returned to Fresno without a scratch. Thirty years later when I see some of those same men they greet me with, "Here's the one who saved all our lives!" I received a letter of commendation from President Nixon for my professional handling of a serious situation.

Pauline and I have been active members of the Clovis Memorial United Methodist Church for over fifty years. We have volunteered many hours and summers for "Y's Men's" projects at the YMCA camps. I served on the Central Valley YMCA Board of Directors for over twenty years. In June of 2000 we were honored by induction into the Clovis Hall of Fame.

We have two children. John Mark Middleton is a graduate of the California Maritime Academy. He has an engineering company and is the resident engineer for two hydroelectric plants in the Trinity Alps above Eureka. Marsha Sue Robinson graduated from Cal Poly and teaches at Cuesta College in San Luis Obispo in California.

OKINAWA

The Battle of Okinawa was fought from March through June 1945, and was the largest, and last, of the Pacific Theater's major battles. The fighting was excruciatingly intense, amplified by the wet, muddy conditions on the island. The Japanese suffered more than 60,000 military personnel killed in action, as well as horrific civilian losses. The Allied toll was over 70,000 casualties.

Allied military planners considered the capture of Okinawa, part of the Ryukyu island chain south of Japan's main islands, to be a strategic necessity as it would provide a critical forward base for land, air and naval operations should an invasion of Japan's homeland become necessary. The daunting prospect of such an invasion was averted when the Japanese surrendered after the atomic bombing of the cities of Hiroshima and Nagasaki in August, 1945.

I LOVE MY FLAG
by Victor Smith

I love my flag. It represents what my country means to me. I have a flagpole in my yard and every morning, without fail, I raise my flag in honor of the greatest country on earth.

I arrived at Ford Island, Hawaii, on Thanksgiving Day 1944 after completing boot camp with my buddies from Fresno, California. We all five had pre-enlisted and were on a troop train to Farragut Island, Idaho, the morning after our high school graduation. I loved the marksmanship competitions, and our company won the Bennion Battleship Award.

At Pearl Harbor the American Flag was flying over the battleship *Arizona* and gave this 18-year-old boy his first glimpse of the reality of war and the price paid to protect the country you love. All those men were killed by Japanese bombers while they lay in their bunks. I remember hearing about the attack on Pearl Harbor as I drove home from church with my family on December 7th, 1941. Seeing the flag flying there was a real eye opener.

My closest buddy, Joe Opazda, and I were assigned duty to Commodore Wallace M. Dillon's plane staff and awaited the gathering of ships and personnel for a flotilla to attack Okinawa. I remember standing on deck, and all I could see was ships of every size and purpose from me to the horizon.

Knowing Joe became a real learning experience as we read scriptures from our Bibles, and then prayed before attempting to sleep. It is important to point out that Joe was a devout Catholic and I about as Protestant as you could get; but I found that we prayed to the same God. Every night, Joe prayed for my safety and the safety of his brother serving in battle in the European arena, but he never prayed for his own safety. He always put others ahead of himself; that's the kind of man he was.

The fleet hit the beach on Okinawa at 8:00 A.M. on Easter Sunday, April 1st, 1945. Joe and I were a part of the operations unit onshore to set up a tower to track enemy aircraft. It seemed we were always under fire by heavy artillery, bombing or strafing.

The night of April 27, 1945, we took shelter in the cover we had built for that purpose. Joe said to me, "Smitty, we are going to have to get the fellows out of

Sailor Victor Smith arrived at Ford Island, Hawaii, on Thanksgiving Day, 1944, after completing boot camp in Fresno, CA.

their sacks, or we might have a lot of our people killed or wounded." I think he must have remembered the pre-dawn attack at Pearl Harbor and could see the same thing might happen here.

I stood by the entrance to our shelter and watched for impending danger so I could warn Joe as he moved from tent to tent and woke the men. After Joe returned to our shelter, searchlights found a plane at about one o'clock in the night sky. With gusto Joe shouted, "Get that sucker!" Then we heard another plane closing in. Joe yelled at me to "Hit for cover!" Those three words were the last Joe would say to me or anyone else. The concussion blew me through the entrance and into our shelter. I hit something with my head and someone hollered, "Smitty lost his hand!" I felt for my hand; it was cut up from shrapnel but still attached.

I screamed, "Joe is still out there!" At the same time, I pushed the debris and sand bags off of me so I could get to him. I took a couple of steps and nearly stepped on Joe as I heard him coughing his last. He was lying face down in his bloody navy dungarees. That vision is imprinted in my mind, and I feel overwhelming survivor's guilt to this day. Why did Joe die, and I lived?

We buried Joe the next morning in the 1st Marine Division Cemetery on Okinawa on the 28th day of April, 1945. Joseph John Opazda AMMIC made the supreme sacrifice. Had Joe not realized the seriousness of the moment and reacted to wake the men, they would have been casualties as well. The beds where they lay sleeping were all destroyed.

What is my definition of courage? Joe had courage. What is my definition of hero? Joe Opazda. Every night I lower the flag at my home in Central California and think about Joe. I know I've lived the life I've had with my wife, Lorraine, and my sons and daughter because Joe saved my life that morning so long ago. The older I get, the more I think about Joe. I know he is with his Maker, and I know he would not have changed anything he did that fateful morning. He willingly gave his life so others and I could live. He did not die in vain. I've lived my life with honor for both of us, and I hope I've done him proud. I'm grateful to have been a friend of Joe Opazda. I'm proud to be an American, and I love my flag.

Rachel Frauenholz contributed to the writing of this story for the Stories of Service on DVD project.

FIRST AND LAST
by Charles H. Jones

I was born April 16, 1919, in Egan, South Dakota, in the same house my mother had been born in. She worked as a telephone operator before becoming a home-maker. I was the third child in a family of nine. Driving in a 1913 Model T, my father moved the family to Escondido, California, in 1924. He was a plastering contractor, and in 1935 he purchased a ten-acre land parcel for $600.00. During the Depression we were very poor, and times were very hard.

I was drafted March 11, 1941, when I was twenty-one years old. My draft number was sixty-eight. I understand number sixty-eight was the first draft num-ber drawn by President Franklin D. Roosevelt. That makes me the first soldier to be drafted from Escondido, California.

I entered the Army at Fort MacArthur, California. When the war broke out, my unit was sent to guard the railroad tunnels outside of Los Angeles. I then went to the 7th Division, 48th Field Artillery and got my first Dear John letter. Next, I was sent to Camp Adair, Oregon, on a cadre that was to become the 96th Infantry Division. The 96th Division's nickname was the "deadeyes," and you had to be a marksman to belong.

In 1944, after amphibious training at San Diego, I was sent overseas. We invaded two islands: Leyte and Samara. We landed in Leyte on October 29, 1944. While on Leyte I slept in foxholes filled with rainwater for days on end. I became covered with ringworms, from my waist to my knees. I had to paint iodine on myself to get rid of them. I think I was the first to be told I could die from iodine poisoning in WW II.

I left Leyte on March 25, 1945, and headed for Okinawa. I made the invasion of Okinawa on April 1, 1945. This battle was one of the bloodiest of World War II. Our unit was in battle for eighty-two days. Thousands of the enemy and thou-sands of our own soldiers were killed or wounded. The only thing that kept me going was the music I played on my harmonica. The first thing the guys asked for when the shelling slowed down was for me to play for them to lighten the mood. Many times the last thing they heard at night was the sound of my harmonica.

The most important job I had while serving my country was being a gunner on a 105mm Howitzer. The twelve guns in the 921st Field Artillery fired 93,000 rounds of ammunition on Okinawa. As the guns were firing, my ears rang, having no ear protection at that time. My ears still ring today. When I am asked how I lost my hearing, I tell people I didn't lose my hearing, I gave my hearing to my country for freedom.

I was given the privilege to have fired the last artillery round in the last battle of Okinawa. I knew the battle was almost over and started saving the casings. As each round was fired, I would throw that casing away and wait for the next one to be fired. I wanted a souvenir to take home and didn't realize that a very important part of history was to be mine. I still have the last casing fired, and I had a plaque made up listing all the soldiers who were assigned to that gun.

I was discharged from the service on December 22, 1945, and got my good conduct medal. After being home a few days I went to a dance with one of my younger brothers. He introduced me to the most beautiful girl in the world. After three months, we were married. We have three children, eight grandchildren, and sixteen great-grandchildren.

I entered the service because my draft number was the first number to be drawn by the President of the United States, and I fired the last shell in the Battle of Okinawa. America has always been first in my heart, and I will defend her to my last dying breath.

Donna Pearce contributed to the writing of this story.

OKINAWA: WORLD WAR II, 1945-1946
by Betty Jane Lynch (excerpts from my diary)

I am a 22-year-old U.S. Army nurse during WW II. I arrive on Okinawa during the heavy bombing of Naha, Sugar Loaf Hill, and Half Moon Hill.

May 21, 1945: The day passes swiftly, and when night falls, the bombing begins. It doesn't take long before we hear the siren go off—Red Alert. All of us nurses in the tent must rush to get out of the tent, and we crash up against one another trying to reach the opening. I head for the ravine wall. I refuse to get into a foxhole, as they have a most dangerous snake on this island, the Habu. After we hear the all-clear signal, we return to our respective tents.

May 22: We are finally ready to take in the wounded soldiers. I am assigned to the "shock tent." This is where the wounded will be brought in, right from the battlefield where they fell. There are medics in the field of battle with the infantry and Marines. When they hear the cry "Medic" they rush to the side of the fallen soldier. The medic applies first-aid, such as pressure dressing to stop bleeding, bandaging wounds, and administering a shot of morphine, which they carry with the needle attached. Then a litter bearer carries the wounded either on his own back or, with the help from others, the wounded soldier is put on a litter and carried to an ambulance or any vehicle—tank, Jeep or truck—to a field hospital where surgery and post-operative care can be given.

It is a difficult task to get the wounded to our hospital because the roads are terrible. As we are on the China Sea side of the island, and our hospital is near the beach, some of the wounded are put on small boats, LCVPs (Landing Craft, Vehicle, Personnel), and brought up the China Sea coast to us. As night falls, the wounded start to arrive. There is nothing to prepare one for the sight of so many wounded soldiers. As each wounded soldier comes in he is placed on a stretcher that is on two sawhorses. The doctors immediately start triage.

This is heartbreaking to watch. Immediately I start to get vital signs and to suction out throats so the soldiers can breathe. I also cut off their blood-soaked uniforms. Each soldier has a tag on a button on his jacket. The tag tells me if the medic has given the soldier morphine, what his blood type is, his religion, and what service he is in, Army or Marines. The priest, rabbi, and protestant minister are in the shock tent to give comfort and last rites.

I look into the eyes of these young soldiers, their eyes glazed over in shock, not knowing where they are. I glance over to one side of the tent and see many stretchers with young brave men who have given the supreme sacrifice, their lives. An arm has dropped off one of the stretchers and I see a wedding ring. My heart aches.

The only way I am able to function is by instinct and the acquired talents of being a nurse, so I just keep going. The wounded men never cry out. They are so brave. All the doctors, nurses, and medical corpsmen carry on into the night. We can hear the firing going on outside the tent, and the planes flying overhead, and sirens going off with the Red Alert. No one leaves the shock tent. As the doctors remove bullets and shrapnel from arms, legs, abdomens, faces, heads and backs, one hears the sound of the extracted metal hitting the pans below the operating tables.

Dawn finally comes, and no more wounded come in. My duty is not over, nor is it over for the other medical personnel. The wounded soldiers who have survived surgery that night are taken to surgical tent wards. I go to my assigned surgical tent and continue starting plasma. While turning one soldier, I see where the doctor missed another wound in the soldier's buttocks. Back to surgery he goes. Our shifts are twelve hours long, but many times it is not uncommon to work fourteen hours. We are very short of nurses. When I am relieved of duty, I don't go to eat. I go to my cot to lie down, and fall fast asleep.

May 23: Going to church: if it is not raining, the sides of the tent are rolled up; however, it is raining today. The pulpit is a wooden box. There is a small compact organ, and one of the talented GIs plays hymns on it. The patients who can walk come in wearing their blue pajamas. We all sit down on sandbags. We hope to get some chairs or benches some day. We sing "Be Still My Heart." The tune sounds to me like "Finlandia," very beautiful. For an hour the roar of the planes and the sounds of the big guns on the battleships in the harbor are silent. As we pray and meditate in the simplicity and humbleness of this setting, time stands still.

The same flood of wounded arrive. When night falls, I speak gently to each one as I check the tourniquets on their arms or legs. I tell them they are safe, that they are in a hospital. I feel if they see a nurse smile they will think maybe they are out of harm's way. At least I am silently praying they will feel safe.

Tonight there is a full moon, so I know the enemy can see the big red cross painted on the large white square of canvas on the top of the tent. So far we have been lucky. Oh, the sirens go off screaming Red Alert, but we all keep working. My courage comes from all these brave, young men. I am amazed that not a sound of screaming in pain is heard. When we get the wounded men stabilized, bring up their blood pressure and their pulse, they become aware of where they are. They usually ask about their buddies.

Most of the soldiers are seventeen or eighteen. They come into the armed services and are toughened up in boot camp. Their youth and their strength give them a fighting chance to make it through surgery, plus their faith in God and wanting, desperately, to make it home to loved ones.

A GOOD FRIEND LOST

by Herbert Spencer

My Navy military service began at age seventeen, the day I boarded the Santa Fe train at the Depot in Fresno, California, waving adios to my parents and grand-parents as they stood there waving with shining wet cheeks. I was whisked away to the north and all of the unimaginable events that were immediately beginning to unfold before me.

I boarded at the rear of the train and proceeded forward through the empty car to the next one forward until I spotted a fellow my age, the only person in that car at the time. I asked him, "Where you headed?" He said "Farragut-Navy." We exchanged names, his being Ed from Bakersfield. In Stockton Bob came aboard.

We three had enough in common to keep us occupied the rest of the trip, which turned very uncomfortable from Sacramento to Spokane and on to Farragut, Idaho. The train cars were antique and drafty, and there was no water, other than the toilet, no food, and no GI escort. We arrived at Spokane, were loaded on buses to the base, stripped, inspected, inoculated, issued GI gear, and assigned a company barracks and a leader, who was a chief assigned to each new company formed for boot training.

I was cold upon arriving at Farragut, which was covered with a foot of snow. My warm San Joaquin weather clothing hadn't been any help from the Oregon border all the way to Farragut. My new clothing issue plus some boiler duty seemed to acclimatize me, at least enough to continue throughout basic, and I realized that all these great peo-ple I was with were as anxious to protect the "Good ole USA" as I was.

Herbert Spencer enlisted in the Navy at seventeen years of age and was assigned to the West Virginia.

A memorable time for me happened on a clear, calm day in early January 1945. We were in the Philippines on a smooth sea, no clouds, and sun up at about 70 degrees. I was serving on the battleship USS *West Virginia*—the *Weevee*—and I was on watch in the 02 deck 20mm group. I was looking off the port side at about 300 degrees or about 60 degrees left of our course heading. The carrier *Ommaney Bay* was on the same heading running parallel with the *Weevee* about a half-mile off of our port beam, and her birds were returning from patrol, circling and landing one at a time. I don't know how many had been on patrol, so I don't have an idea what number might be returning or from what direction to expect them.

I was scanning the sky in every direction, which is pretty customary anyway. During this search of the heavens and the usual thorough scan of and around the sun, I detected a speck moving out from the sun, and as I continued to attempt to distinguish its shape, figuring it was probably an F6F from the *Ommaney Bay*, it didn't take long to see the twin engines. I reported to the bridge, "Bogie!"

All I could do was pray that the returning birds would see what I saw and pursue, attack, and down, but no such luck. The twin engine nick slipped right in behind a F6F that was about to land and ahead of the next one banking in to approach his landing. The nick was then in where he wanted to be and flew right into the hangar deck where the next flight was all fueled and ready to elevate for the next go. The next instant there was a flash—a monstrous flame—and the entire forward half of the carrier was a mass of fire. I could make out personnel jumping into the sea. Destroyer escorts moved in to pick up survivors and all hands would immediately abandon ship. The destroyers delivered all needing medical attention to the USS *West Virginia* plus some others. As personnel recovery was done and darkness was setting in a destroyer sent the remainder of the burnt-out hulk to the ocean floor where it would no longer present a navigational hazard to the ocean's highways.

I shall at this point jump directly to the South Pacific to relate two specific battle engagements that did damage to our ship and at the same time to my friend Truj, four others, and myself. The first was during a Kamikaze attack during which two planes came in at main deck height toward the starboard bow. Both were shot, hit, and crashed into the sea close enough to shower the bow with airplane parts. One was a Judy (dive-bomber) and the other was a Zeke (a Zero), and the Judy's wing came flying right at Truj like a boomerang. He was in the starboard forecastle AA group, and I saw him dive for the gun shield. Then the wing smacked into the main turret just beyond him. Well, he must have hit the deck just in time. A chunk of metal from one of the planes hit me in the knee and I got one of my gun crew to assist me down to sickbay after we were secured from air defense. That piece of metal is in use today as one of my belt buckles.

The second event was D-Day plus one, Okinawa, when we received word from our landing force nearing the middle of the island where we had been firing the big guns on call. The report was "enemy planes heading your way." I was on watch in 02 Deck Group and dashed to my group on the bow. I slipped on the head set, scanning the sky and telling the bridge, "They are over the beach at Bearing 020, maybe a half dozen, they fanned out, two crossing a distance beyond our bow, and the others turn-

A depiction of the West Virginia *under attack.*

ing away. One is roll curving toward our stack." The Zeke crashed outside the stack and his 500-pound bomb went down to the 2nd deck below, not detonating, but the nose cone came off, and incendiary fluid covered the deck.

We lost four wonderful friends, exceptionally fine men in that gun group, and right after the Kamikaze hit my friend Truj came running to my gun group in severe shock saying, "Hos, I've been hit." He was covered with blood so I asked another friend to take Truj down to sickbay, which he did. After the all-clear, I went to sickbay to see how Truj was, and the medic said he didn't have a scratch on him but was in severe shock. I didn't see Truj after that and was never able to make contact again, so perhaps the lingering wonderment of it all is an unshakable thing.

AN EXCERPT FROM ACE, A MARINE NIGHT-FIGHTER PILOT

by R. Bruce Porter

My flying career began on a rainy southern California Saturday morning in December, 1939. I was nineteen years old and a member of the University of Southern California Class of 1942. I had only a vague idea of what I wanted to do with my life; perhaps I would become an engineer, like my father, or a lawyer. The world was wide open to me and the future seemed bright, for all its haziness. Whenever I had a spare moment to myself the thought of flying came up. Roy, a friend of mine, after hearing two ensigns recruit officer candidates for the Naval Aviation Cadet Program, was impressed with the uniform and, more than anything, with the level of excellence represented by those gleaming Wings of Gold.

As Roy and I stepped out of the recruiting office I happened to see another sign which read, "Join Marine Aviation." Just then a dashing Marine captain, dressed in a blue tunic crossed by a leather Sam Browne belt and shod in high leather boots, tucked his head through the doorway and said, "Hey, boys, come in. I want to talk to you." He then explained that the Marine Corp program was identical to and interchangeable with the Navy's except that all Marine aviators received advanced training as fighter pilots and would eventually have to qualify for aircraft carriers. By the time I left that cramped office I felt like a Marine.

Okinawa: Yontan Airfield

June 15, 1945, was not a particularly noteworthy day. Early in the day my flight officer, Captain George Gelsten, told me that I was slated to fly nightcap from 20:00 hours until midnight. This pleased me because half the squadron's kills had been scored during this active period. As I suited up for my patrol I had an all around good feeling, but I could not decide why. My fiancée Pat Leimert's letter, I supposed.

The night was completely dark; there was no moonlight whatsoever and an extremely thick cloud cover. I checked my airplane in the darkness, just as I always did before a mission, but that was more customary than practical. I could not see very much. My plane captain, Technical Sergeant G. M. Stanley, helped me on with my harness and told me that my radar and radios were in top working order.

He gave me a thumbs up and yelled in my ear "Good luck, Major!" just before jumping off the wing.

I ran up the engine to check the magnetos. Everything there was fine so I released the brakes and taxied slowly to the pitch-black runway. I told the tower that I was ready to go, and I was given immediate clearance to take off. I pushed the throttle lever forward and took my feet off the brakes. Within seconds I was rapidly gaining speed. My feet worked the rudder pedals to keep me on an even keel and I slowly pulled back on the joystick. I became airborne with plenty of room to spare. As I cleared the abyss at the seaward end of the east-west runway I retracted *Black Death's* landing gear and prepared to climb.

As I headed out over the empty sea I listened intently to the sound of *Black Death's* engine and felt for unusual vibrations through the seat of my pants. Everything sounded and felt fine. Then I fiddled with the instrument lights to set them where they would be most comfortable for my vision in this night's total darkness. I tested each of my radios, primary and spare. All okay there. My radar was perfect, too. I armed my four .50-cals and two 20mm cannons and test-fired them, first the machine guns with one trigger, then the cannon with the other trigger; just a squirt from each to reassure me that they would fire when I needed them. My fuel supply was normal. I reported my position to my GCI officer on Ie Shima.

I was already in a climb and passing through 6,000 feet when the order arrived. I turned to the new course and continued to climb to my patrol altitude. Suddenly my GCI officer called excitedly, "Hello, Topaz One from Handyman. I have an unidentified bogey for you. Target range 30 miles at 10 o'clock. Angel 13. He's indicated 170 knots. Handyman out."

Well, that started my adrenaline flowing. The intruder had 3,000 feet on me and was quickly closing. I dropped my belly tank and threw the throttle all the way forward, which added considerable power by engaging the water-injection system. This was good for an extra 15-knot burst of speed in emergencies. I also increased the engine RPM and nosed up into a steep climb. I made sure my guns were armed.

The GCI officer reeled off the distances. Fifteen miles, ten miles, six miles. "Hello, Topaz One from Handyman. Target range three miles at 11 o'clock. Bearing one-one-one (110 degrees). Target crossing your screen. Go!" I changed course and muttered aloud, "Steady, Bruce. This is it." If Handyman had vectored me correctly I would be turning right onto the bogey's tail. If not, I was going to be flying up nothing but empty sky.

I flipped on my finder as I came out of the turn. (The radar was on but we kept the screen off to preserve night vision until we knew a target was out there.) My eyes became riveted to the orange scope on my instrument panel. Nothing there yet. I was glad to note how cool I was. This was just like a textbook practice mission, of which I had flown hundreds. I was on full instruments and radar. All I needed to do was remain steady and do what my instruments and Handyman told me to do. If I trusted in the system I would be coaxed into a perfect firing position. If the Hellcat could have flown itself there would have been no need for me.

I did precisely what I was told, totally without ego. Bingo! My scope indicated a tiny orange blip at the very top. I was dead on target. The bogey was straight ahead. It had been a letter-perfect vector. "Handyman from Topaz One. Contact!" I watched as the blip got larger and closer to the center of the radarscope, which represented my position. The bogey remained dead ahead, flying straight and level, as I crept up on its tail. My ghost blip, which indicated the bogey's altitude relative to me, rapidly clarified itself. If appeared that the bogey was just a little higher than *Black Death*.

I flicked my eyes up to see if the target was as yet in sight. I thought I saw something so, after one more check of the scope, I peered at a slight ripple of movement dead ahead and slightly above my direct line of sight. A second or two later I knew I was staring at the bogey's exhaust flame. My long training with similar practice approaches gave me ample reason to believe that the bogey was only about 350 feet ahead of me—within *Black Death's* boresighted firing cone. I flew in a little closer in order to positively identify him as an enemy warplane and to learn precisely what I was facing. I was certain that he was a K145 Nick twin-engine night fighter. Thus, there was an outside chance that he would be able to find me before I could open fire.

I climbed slightly to get right over him and then marginally increased my speed to close up. If he did not detect me and did not change course this was going to be a sure kill. As I nosed down slightly to bring all my guns to bear I decided to fire everything in my armory. When I was in the best possible position, and only 300 feet from the target, I gently squeezed both triggers. My .50 calibers roared and the 20mm cannon blew off rounds in a surprisingly slow, steady manner.

My initial target was the right engine and right side of the fuselage, where some fuel was bound to be stored. *Black Death's* outpouring of lead had a literal buzz saw effect upon the enemy airplane. I eased off the 20mm because of a limited supply of ammunition, but I kept putting .50 caliber armor-piercing and incendiary rounds into the fuselage. I wanted him to burn so I would know beyond a doubt that I had scored a kill. Licks of flame showed up on the leading edge of the wing. Then a fiery orange tongue swept back over the fuselage. Suddenly the twin-engine Kawasaki stalled and lurched heavily to the right. My rounds poured into her vitals. I saw tracers strike the canopy. I doubt if the pilot ever knew what hit him. It was over in about two seconds. When the Nick nosed over and fell away toward the sea he was wrapped in flames from nose to tail. Okay! My fourth confirmed kill.

I heard from Handyman again almost exactly an hour after he had called out the first bogey. "Hello, Topaz One from Handyman. I've got another bogey for you." Wow! A double night contact! As far as I knew, this was only the fourth such the squadron had encountered since deploying on Okinawa in mid-April. Two of the double contacts had resulted in dead night stalkers. "Topaz One from Handyman. Bogey at Angels 14. Indicated 180 knots. Vector 145 at Angels 13." I pushed the throttle downward to get the water injection going and then I hauled back on the stick to rush to the required altitude. Even with luck I was facing a stern chase. I had the speed advantage but it would take time to close on him because I had to use most of my power to climb.

I reached 13,000 feet and leveled off for my approach. Ahead I could see fingers of light reaching into the black sky—searchlights. Farther on was Okinawa's west coast. As with all tail chases it seemed to take an eternity to note any relative progress. Handyman kept reading off the closing distances and I kept monitoring the rapidly approaching pillars of light from the anchorage ahead.

I flipped on my finder for the second time that night. The scope flared orange. The bogey was right at the top of the scope and just a little way down toward the one o'clock position. My closure rate was too fast. If I kept it up, I would overshoot before being able to line up my gunsight. I eased back on the throttle but the blip remained too large. Then I saw flames from the exhaust stacks. He was definitely a twin-engine airplane, but it was still too early to identify the type. The real danger was that he was a bomber with a vigilant rear machine gunner. If there was a stinger, I stood a good chance of being shot out of the sky. I dropped down a little so the bogey would be silhouetted against the dark canopy overhead. As dark as the sky was, the solid airplane would stand out against it.

My quarry was definitely a Betty medium bomber, a fast, maneuverable thoroughbred. It had a stinger, all right! Something at the corner of my attention noted that the Betty was carrying an external load on its belly. I thought it might be a so-called Baka bomb, a manned rocket-propelled suicide missile typically hauled to the target by a mother plane, the Betty, and dropped.

I drifted upward a bit to get a good belly shot. By the time I reached a comfortable height I had closed to within 250 feet. I put the illuminated gunsight pipper right between the body of the aircraft, right beneath the flight deck and the right engine. Then I slowly squeezed both triggers. For the second time that night *Black Death's* .50 calibers roared and the 20mm cannon slowly spit its flaming popcorn-ball rounds. The tracer and the popcorn balls fell right into the target area. After only a second or two the wing fuel tanks ignited in a garish explosion and the sky in front of my windscreen was filled with an expanding ball of flaming fuel. I instinctively ducked as pieces of the Betty scraped along *Black Death's* wings and fuselage. Then I dived away as the first fingers of friendly tracer reached up around me from the darkened fleet beneath *Black Death's* wings. I caught a momentary flash as the Betty's cargo, the Baka bomb, blew up.

"Handyman from Topaz One. Did you get the picture on your scope?"

"Topaz One from Handyman. Roger that. Congratulations. The time is 22:26 on confirmation. It's a kill, Topaz One. Resume patrol."

Before I got to sleep that night I heard from the squadron armorers that I had fired a total of 500 rounds of .50 cal and 200 rounds of 20mm for both kills. Since the squadron average was 785 rounds per kill I was thus the squadron champ for kills per rounds fired, less than half the average. I chalked that up to having the 20mm cannon on board.

What a night! Handyman and I had scored a rare double night kill and I had fulfilled my fondest ambition as a fighter pilot. I was an Ace!

This excerpt was taken from Colonel Porter's story as told to and recorded by Eric Hammel.

LETTERS HOME:
JULY 23, 1945, TO AUGUST 28, 1945

by Richard Y. Johnson

July 23, 1945, Okinawa Shima

Dear Folks:

Just a line to let you now that I am still well and in the best of spirits. Things have finally come to a victorious end as far as front line fighting is concerned, but we still have to patrol every day or so, and you would be surprised how many of the rats we find. While the fighting is going on the tension is quite heavy. Everyone is always on the alert, and everyone is a little nervous. Our day doesn't actually start with the rising of the sun because all through the night we keep constant guard. Every night is just like the preceding night. Darkness there at home doesn't mean much, but over here it's hell. The Japanese are pretty good at sneaking around at night, but they have found out that it is death to get too close to our lines at night, but they still come.

I was on guard one night and I heard something to my right front. After watching for awhile I noticed three dark objects against the side of a rock possibly thirty yards away. After awhile these objects moved and something else moved with them—me. Well, next morning there were three dead Nips out there and two of them were officers. I got a beautiful saber off one of them and am sending it home.

Richard Johnson served in the Army and was on Okinawa when Japan surrendered.

As soon as it gets light enough to see next morning, a fellow has to watch out for snipers who might be close to our front, and make sure he doesn't show himself too much. The Jap sniper is very hard to locate—it is almost impossible to see where he is firing from. Then we start out for our objective which has been made for that day and which we generally get by the time night comes. The frontline troops have it pretty tough, but someone has to be the nose of the whole thing, and the infantry man is it.

At dusk everyone knows what has happened in his area, but not what has happened in other areas. News travels pretty fast around here, but most of it's uninteresting to a certain point. Then a fellow looks around to see how many of his buddies weren't so lucky this day, buddies who but just a few hours ago were talking and laughing—joking about what might happen, and what did. It's rough, but it's passed off casually as just in a day's work. Then we settle down for another night in our foxholes. This is just an average day for the U.S. infantry man who is trying to do a job.

Well, maybe I have written about enough and anyway it's time for chow. I have a squad of men under me now, so maybe I will get a raise in salary soon and rank, too. Well, I send my love to all, and Boy! I wish I had a nice big glass of cold milk about now.

Love, Richard

July 25, 1945, Okinawa Shima

Dear Mother,

While the battle was going on we didn't receive mail every day, but when it did come up to the front the expressions on everybody's face would change, and then with the sound of battle everywhere you could see each man in his hole reading his mail from home. His mind wouldn't be on the things around him, but on the things that he had left behind. Things that someday he would get to go back to.

Many times I have thought of the same things and with that thought and God I got through this great battle of life or death without a scratch. I have received a couple citations, but they were given to me because someone thought that I had done more than my part in a couple of incidents, but I figure differently. I don't believe I can ever do too much for my fellow man or for my country. I have always tried and shall continue until the enemy is beaten or I am, and I know it won't be me.

Well, Mother, it is growing dark so I will bring this note to a close. I will be looking forward to the next letter, and I hope this finds you all there in good health. I am having a life of Riley at the present am really enjoying it.

Give my love to all and God bless you.

Your son, Richard

August 28, 1945. Okinawa Shima

Dear Mother,

It's All Over!

When the first news of Japan's surrender reached us here on Okinawa, it was raining cats and dogs. It was at bedtime, and I was knocking off some good sleep on my innerspring Army cot which any GI knows hasn't any springs in them, and all at once, I was awakened by what sounded like all the guns on Okinawa opening up. I figured it was an air raid so out of bed I came. I didn't have time to get into my clothes, so outside I ran with nothing but my steel helmet and my shorts on. When I got outside tracer bullets could be seen flying in all directions. Search lights were on and going back and forth across the sky. It was a sight that can't be put into words. I thought and imagined everything from paratroopers to Kamikaze planes coming. Then all at once, I heard someone yell that the war was over. Soon everyone was yelling and laughing as loud as they could.

Upon recovering my senses after hearing the news I also joined in with the yelling and I, shorts and steel helmet soaked from the rain, really cut some capers in the mud. After things calmed down, I found out that the report was not confirmed by the President, so then just a little doubt came into my mind. Days went by and still no confirmed report came through. Then finally it was confirmed by President Truman. This time no celebrating was heard. Not in our outfit anyway. I guess all the fellows thought the same as I did. I believe there was a prayer in each man's heart not only for himself, but mostly for you folks at home and for those who have suffered so under the rule of the Axis powers. I did my very small part, but I don't believe I did enough. There is still much to do to make this world a Christian world, and not one of us should slacken our strides until this goal is reached.

Well, Mother, I shall sign off for now. I, like my buddies, hope to be home in the very near future. It is growing dark on this island in the Pacific, so I shall say good night and may God protect you.

Your son, Richard

SANGER, CALIFORNIA, FEBRUARY 18, 1949

Richard V. Johnson Awarded Oak Leaf For War Dead Work

Richard V. Johnson, now a master sergeant at the Oakland Army base and a former Sanger resident, has been presented with the Commendation Ribbon Oak Leaf Cluster for his work in the return of World War II dead.

Sgt. Johnson's wife, Mrs. Jane Johnson, informed the Herald of the commendation awards in a letter this week. Mrs. Johnson is a former employee of the Herald.

Maj. Gen. Walter M. Robertson, deputy comander of the Sixth Army, Presidio, of San Francisco, made the presentation.

The cluster was given for ". . . meritorious and superior performance of duty as chief non-commissioned officer of the escort finance section of the Sixth Army, escort Detachment.

"Master Sgt. Johnson," the commendation continued, "displayed exceptional ability in originating, perfecting, instituting, and executing the technique governing the preparation of travel and reimbursement vouchers for escort personnel in connection with the program for the repatriation of World War II deceased.

"By initiating improved forms and techniques for supplement and implementation to standard Army finance procedures, Sgt. Johnson's ingenuity facilitated the ultimate production of efficiency in the overall financial phase of the escort services.

"The enlisted man most capably established and maintained procedures without a precedent to serve as a guide and together with his outstanding qualities of leadership has developed the finance section into a highly efficient and superior organization.

"Through outstanding skill, technique, ability, and untiring efforts, Sgt. Johnson performed a distinct service and contribution in organizing an efficient operation of the finance section."

The former Sanger resident earlier last month had received a Bronze Star Medal (First Oak Leaf Cluster) for ground operations against the enemy on April 15, 1945, on Okinawa.

A Sanger Herald newspaper article and photo depicting Richard Johnson's receipt of the Oak Leaf Cluster commendation ribbon.

UNCLE SMOKE'S STORY

by Hubert B. "Doc" Harmon

I was born Hubert B. Harmon on August 31, 1922, in Branch County, Michigan. I was the middle son of three boys and one girl. My parents, Henry and Pearl, sent me to St. Charles School in Coldwater. During the height of the Great Depression I left home to ease the stress on my family of feeding four kids. I was sixteen years old as I hopped freight trains south through Missouri, to Texas, and eventually on to California.

The family called me "Smokey" because I started smoking when I was eight years old and didn't stop until I got cancer in my 70s. A hobo friend of mine called me "Down the Road Doc" and the moniker stuck for the rest of my life. I spent two years working as a "hoe boy," a term later shortened to "hobo," to feed myself on my journey west. One of my "hoe boy" jobs paid three dollars a week. Come Friday, the farmer tried to cheat me out of my money and told me to hit the road. I hid in the woods and waited until his family left for town on Saturday morning.

Hubert "Doc" Harmon served in a Navy amphibious unit in the Pacific theater.

I stole three chickens out of the hen house and sold them on the road to recoup the three dollars the farmer owed me.

I traveled on to Texas where I arrived starving, my clothes in rags and my shoe soles flapping and tied to my feet with string. I went to the undertaker and got outfitted with new duds. I left town in a new suit, shoes, and bowler hat and looking like a million bucks. I was still starving, but I looked good.

I eventually arrived in California and worked for North American Aviation in Southern California. When the Japanese bombed Pearl Harbor I tried to enlist, but my employer had classified my position as essential to the war effort and would not release me to go to war. So I showed up to work every day dressed in a suit and tie and sat on a stool and refused to work. After two weeks they agreed to release me if I'd train two other men to do my job before I left. My second day at boot camp I questioned my sanity for making such a choice. I enlisted in the United States Navy and served in an amphibious unit in the Pacific Theater. I served honorably and with courage in the battles of Guadalcanal and Okinawa.

Hubert "Doc" Harmon (middle) and friends on Okinawa.

My most memorable war experience was when I tried to pull a dead man out of his grave in the middle of a dark night on Guadalcanal. I was pulling guard duty on a night dark as coal, and I was just a scared kid. You couldn't see your hand in front of your face. As I walked back and forth on the perimeter, I tripped each time I passed a certain place. I knew I couldn't be tripping all night because it was distracting me from listening for any approaching enemy. So finally I put down my rifle and tried to pull whatever I was tripping on out of the ground so I could move it out of the way. It was too dark to see what I was doing. I finally struck a match and saw that I was pulling on a man's foot. His unit had buried him in such a hurry as they retreated they'd left his feet sticking out of the ground. I'm not pulling your leg either. I was pulling his leg though.

After fighting in the battle of Guadalcanal, my unit moved on to the invasion of Okinawa on Easter Sunday, 1945. After fighting in the bloodiest battle of the Pacific and after the Japanese surrendered, my buddy and I cleared tunnels and caves where the Japanese enemy hid from the G.I.s. It was dangerous duty. Along with enemy forces, we found Japanese-Americans who had been stranded on Okinawa while visiting relatives when the war broke out. They couldn't get back to the U.S. when the war started and hid in the caves for protection from the occupying Japanese forces. In one cave, my Navy partner and I found a young Japanese-American woman. My buddy fell in love with her. She had destroyed her passport to hide her American identity, and it took two years to eventually get her back to Los Angeles where I was best man at their wedding.

As owner of Doc Manhattan Bar and Grill, I met and married a beautiful young stewardess, Joyce, and had twin boys, Michael and Paul. Later we had another son, Tim. I owned Clingan's Junction Restaurant in Squaw Valley and retired to the foothills of Kings Canyon.

When I was seventy-five years old I put a credit card in my shoe and jumped a freight train out of the Fresno rail yard. I took one last trip to Britt, Iowa, the home of the National Hobo Convention. When a brakeman found me in a boxcar, he took me to the engine and I rode up front with him and the engineer the rest of the way. It was the first time in all my train trips I saw the scenery from the front instead of from the side.

I was honored to be able to attend the dedication of the WW II Memorial in Washington, DC, during the summer of 2004 with my niece, Deborah, her husband and my grandniece. During the summer of 2005 illness intruded. I could no longer hit the road so they came to me. Their visit rallied my spirit and I told jokes through labored breath and with that old twinkle in my eye. I was suffering from congestive heart failure.

My M1 Garrand rifle, the one I carried during the war, stood in the corner of my living room as I relived many stories with friends and family those last days. My poetry was inspired by my "hobo" days, my military service and my satirical view of life. Mixing wit and humor, I became a masterful poet and enjoyed regaling friends and family. I was published in several magazines and newspapers. They especially liked to print my poems that pointed out the absurdity of political figures.

I have no doubt the next generation will tell my jokes and stories. I am the family legend, and legends don't die. They're passed down by word of mouth and tradition. By any name, "Doc," "H.B.," "Unkie," or "Uncle Smoke," my legend lives in those who loved me.

Life is like a poker game
You play it like a man.
You play the hand that you were dealt
An' do the best you can.
My life is slowly winding down,
I'll soon cash in my chips.
With nothing left but memories
Of all life's wandering trips.
I've been most every place a man can go,
Seen most everything a man can see.
I've riddin' every railroad line
From the B&O to the Santa Fe.
The day of reckoning is drawing near,
T'will be no more riding the rails,
Or sittin' around a jungle fire
Or sleeping in small town jails.
But after all, what is life
As we live it day by day?
It's made up of deeds you do
An' those you meet along the way.
Life is made up of memories,
Think about that my friend.
That's the only thing you'll take with you
When your life comes to an end.

H.B. "Doc" Harmon died on August 26, 2005, just a few days short of his 83rd birthday. This story was revised and written in the first person by Rachel B. Frauenholz, caretaker of Doc Harmon during his last few months of life.

THE
EUROPEAN
THEATER

NORTH AFRICA AND THE MEDITERRANEAN

Prior to the United States entering the war, the British, led by General Bernard L. Montgomery, fought a desert campaign in North Africa against the Germans, commanded by Field Marshall Erwin Rommel, and their Italian allies. The British scored a major success in late 1942 at the Battle of El Alamein.

Led by Lt. General Dwight D. Eisenhower, the United States invaded the coasts of Algeria and Morocco on Nov. 8, 1942, as part of Operation Torch. In the following months the combined British and American forces attacked the Axis on multiple North African fronts, eventually causing their surrender in May of 1943.

With the success of the North African campaign the Allies ended the Axis threat to British oil resources in the Middle East, and could commence their next major objective in the European Theater—the capture of Italy.

FORGOTTEN HEROES
by Harold Coon

I believe that all the women and men who have served and died for their country are heroes, but there is one group that has been forgotten by most Americans. These are the men who lost their lives because of the sinking of the HMT *Rohna* on the day after Thanksgiving, November 26, 1943. The ship was sunk in the Mediterranean by a German radio-controlled guided missile. Out of 2,000 troops, five officers and a crew of 195, a total of 1,150 lives were lost, of which 1,015 were American soldiers. This was the largest number of lives lost at sea during World War II, second only to the USS *Arizona*, which was in port. Everyone has heard of Pearl Harbor, but how many people have heard of "The Rohna?" It seems that the attack was kept secret for security reasons as well as the fact that the British were ashamed that the ship wasn't fit for troop transport. The lifeboats didn't work, and it had an Indian crew.

My husband, Harold Coon, was on this ship and was one of the survivors. He was in an infantry unit and left Newport News, Virginia, on the *Betty Zane* for

Oran, Algeria, in North Africa, along with some of his buddies. They boarded the *Rohna*, which was part of a convoy, on Thanksgiving Day, November 25, 1943. His unit was on the way to India and then to Burma and China to tour with the Chinese Army for combat. The next day he and his buddy, Dean Glancy, were on gun duty on the top deck and had just been relieved by two men, one of whom was from Fresno. Harold and his friend saw the torpedo coming. He said it had wings and a red nose. They were lucky to have been on the top

Harold Coon was an Army infantry man traveling to Oran, North Africa, when his ship, HMT Rohna, *was sunk in the Mediterranean by a German radio-controlled guided missile.*

deck because many of the men were trapped below on the lower decks. He and Dean were knocked down by the blast. They were unable to get the lifeboats to work, so they took off their shoes and jumped overboard. They kept afloat with the help of their life belts. When they saw a man who couldn't swim, they told him to hold onto them and to keep kicking his feet.

The three of them were picked up approximately seven hours later by what they presumed was a fishing boat. It was full, so they had to hang onto the side. They were taken to Bezerte, Tunisia, and several weeks later they boarded another ship which took them to India. From there they flew to Burma. Harold served there and in China until the end of the war.

In 1993, after fifty years, the surviving members of Convoy-KMF had their first reunion, along with their rescuers, mostly from the USS *Pioneer*.

As a tribute to his military service, Harold's wife, Nina, wrote this story as he related it to her.

WAR STORIES
by Thomas Gilpin

Darkness held us in its arms like a protector. The only sound you could hear was the tramp of boots. Me and Zot were marching toward the beach in North Africa, near Tunis, each wrapped in our own thoughts, wondering what fate held in store for us.

The 809th Aviation Engineers, my outfit, were in Oran, North Africa, building an airport.

We had been training for six weeks and the scuttlebutt was that we were going to invade some place, but nobody knew where. We were the 809th Aviation Engineers, builders, not fighters, and we were apprehensive about having to fight our way in somewhere.

We reached the beach and saw a lot of big barges with their loading ramps down. What looked like the outline of small ships lay about half a mile offshore. We correctly assumed we were going to be loaded on them. By daybreak we were aboard the ships, called LCIs (short for Landing Craft Infantry), and the commander finally told us we were going to Sicily. We were to take over an airport, hold it until our equipment arrived, then rebuild it. Our forces had been bombing the airport for several days, and the commander thought it would just be a matter of walking in and taking over, since the Germans had supposedly left. We hoped he was right.

A couple of days later we landed in Sicily. The LCIs rammed into shore and grounded themselves—doing just what they were made to do. The loading ramps were dropped so we began unloading. There was not a sign of life anywhere.

As soon as we got on shore we formed in squads and began marching inland—very cautiously at first, because we did not know if any enemy might still be in the area. We felt a little more at ease after marching a mile or so. It must have been about five miles to the airport. When we got there, we split up into groups of six to search the buildings and surrounding area. Still no sign of life.

Our commanding officer ordered us to split the force in two. One-half would bivouac on the south side of the airport, the other half on the north side. Me and Zot went to the south side.

Thomas Gilpin served in the 809th Aviation Engineers in Oran, North Africa.

I don't recall what month it was, but it was hot as hell. Each G.I. was given half a tent, so me and Zot put our shelter halves together to form a shade. The spot we picked to setup was about fifteen feet from a small shack. Next to it, the Germans had dug a pit to bury their garbage. Dirt had been pushed in to cover it, but it left a hole about three feet deep. You could see pieces of broken glass, tin can, lids, and stuff like that. One thing about the Germans, even their garbage dump was neat.

It had been a long, hard day. Bed consisted of laying one blanket on the ground, strip to your waist, remove your boots and socks, pile it all beside you and try to get some sleep. It wasn't easy. Hard clods of dirt gouged you in every place that touched the ground. Being so tired, I went to sleep pretty quick and slept soundly until the droning of a plane awakened me. By the sound of it I knew it was not one of ours, so I yelled to my buddies. We heard a whistling noise. No one had to tell us what that was, so we grabbed our helmets and headed for the garbage pit. The bomb exploded about the same moment we slid to the bottom of the hole on our stomachs. Dirt and debris rained down on us, but no one was hurt that we could see. Me and Zot sat there at the bottom of the pit until the plane was so far away we could no longer hear it. We thought it strange the plane dropped only one bomb but didn't worry about it. Soon we were fast asleep again.

At first light Zot was up stirring around, trying to heat water in his canteen cup for some hot instant coffee. We were on field rations and did not have a kitchen setup. Also, there were no latrine facilities to answer the call of nature so we had to walk a ways from the camp area with our foxhole digging shovels. Corporal Stone was on such a mission when he came on something lying in his path. It looked very similar to a thermos bottle. He rolled it around with his foot a bit, then there was a god-awful explosion.

Me and Zot heard his screams of pain and went running to him, calling for the medics. When we saw how badly he was hurt, I think we went into shock. Both of his legs had been blown off. He begged us to shoot him or give him a rifle so he could do it.

The medics arrived and began injecting him with morphine and putting tourniquets on what was left of his legs. After a while, the morphine began to take effect, so he quieted down. A radio operator put out a distress call for help, but since we had just landed on Sicily, it was a long time coming.

Corporal Stone called for his best buddy, Sergeant Bitters, who knelt beside him. "I'm here, Buddy. What can I do for you?"

Stone said, "I'm not going to make it, Sarge. Will you write to my wife for me? Tell her I love her. Tell her I'll love her forever. Will you do that for me, Sarge?"

"Sure I will," the Sergeant answered. "But you're going to be ok, Buddy."

Stone was getting weaker. He grasped his buddy's hand and in a hoarse whisper pleaded, "Promise me, Sarge. Promise me you will write to Nora."

"I promise you, Stone," the Sergeant said with tears glistening in his eyes.

Finally, a G.I. ambulance pulled up, loaded him on it, and took off, but Corporal Stone passed away before they reached a hospital. Scuttlebutt was, Sgt. Bitters fulfilled the promise he made to his buddy.

RECOLLECTIONS OF WORLD WAR II
by Hugh E. Johnston

It was December 7, 1941, when the air attack at Pearl Harbor by the Japanese occurred. The United States was at war. The enlistment draft started, and I didn't like the thought of going into the infantry—all that marching and crawling in the mud. I enlisted in the Air Corp, but they were only taking twenty people a month. Before I could be called up by the Air Corp I was caught up in the draft. In April of 1942 I reported to the induction center for my physical. At first I didn't think I was going to pass because it took three doctors to find my pulse.

I was sent to The Presidio of Monterey, California, where I was kept busy marching, doing K.P. (kitchen) duty, and painting buildings. After a month of misery at Monterey I bid the place adieu and left for greener pastures at Sheppard Field, Texas. You might be asking what I did in Texas. Well, every day in the boiling hot sun I marched and marched. Forward march, to the rear march, to the left flank march, to the right flank march. I didn't know my left flank from my right flank.

The next think I knew I was leaving Texas and headed for Camp Williams in Wisconsin. I could never figure out why I was stationed here. I did pull M.P. duty on the main gate, we marched a little, and I repaired faucets in the latrine, which was essential to the war effort.

The next assignment was Sadalia Army Air Field, Missouri, then Scott Field, Illinois, and then Seymour Johnson Field, North Carolina. It must have been while I was stationed at Billie Mitchell Field, in Milwaukee, Wisconsin, that the Army decided to make a radio operator out of me.

I was assigned to the Trans-World Airlines School in Kansas City, Missouri. There I put in 384 hours of intensive training, learning to operate aircraft radios and other related equipment. When I answered "yes" to all the questions like "do you get motion sickness, do you get sick on a boat or swing," I thought I'd be assigned to a control tower. But NO, I was radio operator material. After graduation I was assigned to the 20th Ferrying Group of the Air Transport Command, Nashville, Tennessee, as a flight operator.

My first training as a radio operator was on a B-24 Bomber. I wondered what I did wrong when I was selected to be the radio operator on a C-47, loaded with aircraft parts and equipment that we would fly to London, England. I was issued all the flight equipment, and I especially wondered why I was issued a 45 pistol and holster.

We took off from Miami, Florida, and landed in Brazil. The next day as we taxied down the runway for liftoff the pilot discovered we had no brakes. It was the same thing the next day. The third time was the charm as the mechanics finally got it right. The next stop was the Ascension Islands out in the middle of the Atlantic Ocean. It is an eight hour flight from Brazil and there was just enough fuel to go this distance. The navigator told the pilot exactly the right time to make a descent, and as we came down out of the clouds there were the Ascension Islands—a beautiful sight to see. We took on fuel and headed for the Gold Coast of Africa and landed at Acera, Liberia, then up the coast past France. France was occupied by the Germans at that time, and we were glad when we didn't see any German planes. Now I know why I was issued a pistol. I could shoot down a German plane.

As we neared the coast of England we were picked up on radar by an English base. We had to identify ourselves or British planes would be sent up to shoot us down. For all they know we could be an American plane captured by the Germans. I was trying to make contact with the ground station. The co-pilot was standing right behind me and kept saying, "Did you get them yet?" He was scared, and so was I. There were fifteen or twenty planes all trying to contact the ground station at the same time. Trying to pick out our call sign out of all the others was very nerve racking, but I finally was able to do it—the crew all relaxed and we had a safe landing in London.

Our crew was picked to take a beat-up B-17 back to the United States. Extra fuel tanks were installed in the bomb bay so we could make such a long trip. We had an extra passenger—a fighter pilot who was being reassigned after serving his time in Europe. We were high over the Atlantic Ocean and I was just ready to radio our position to the ground station when we went into a vertical dive. Talk about being scared. We dropped several thousand feet before the plane pulled out of the dive and leveled off. We found out the pilot let the fighter pilot fly the plane and I think he forgot to tell him, "You don't fly a bomber like a fighter plane."

I was stationed in Memphis, Tennessee, with the 4th Ferrying Group Air Transport Command when I got my overseas orders. Our first stop was Casablanca, where I was stationed for about a month. Then I went on to Tripoli where I spent the duration of the war. I was radio operator on C47 cargo planes and occasionally on a B-24 and B-25. I never got enough sleep because the cargo planes were flying constantly. I landed an office job in the Navigation and Radio Briefing Office. I remained there until the war was over.

Do I have some stories to tell.

THE STORY OF A U.S. NAVY GUNNER MATE
by Fred Nicholson

Fred Nicholson after Navy boot camp in 1943.

I joined the Navy in December 1942 to serve my country during its wartime need. I was a gunner's mate third class aboard the Naval Destroyer 168, the USS *Amick*, and completed my service in February of 1946. I was just a skinny kid from Columbus, Ohio, weighing only 110 pounds when I enlisted in the Navy. My sisters and I had happy childhoods growing up in Columbus where I was born on New Year's Day, 1925. My father worked in optics manufacturing, and I had a stay-at-home mom.

I first heard about Pearl Harbor at the Palace Theater when I was seventeen years old. I don't remember what movies were playing, but I will never forget the day Hawaii was bombed. My sister Marty's fiancé, Bob, whom I'd worshiped as a boy, had already enlisted, and I signed up for the Navy. I couldn't wait to start my basic training at Great Lakes, Illinois. It turned out to be harder than I thought, both physically and emotionally, but after Boot Camp I weighed 140 pounds. My training was putting weight on me and turning me into a man.

After Gunner School, I went to Williamsburg, Virginia, for Ammunition School. I was beginning to see the world as the Navy recruiting poster promised, first in America, then across the Atlantic Ocean. I was deployed overseas November 3, 1943, into the North Atlantic where German U-boats patrolled. The nine convoys I accompanied from America to Europe helped turn the tide of war with none of our ships lost. We were six naval destroyers constantly circling the outer perimeter of 350 to 500 ships, providing protection to Allied ships that gathered and deployed into different arenas of the war as we traveled across the ocean.

We ended up in the Mediterranean—I remember seeing the Rock of Gibraltar and was in awe of the battle-mounts projecting out of caves. What an amazing fortress it was. I saw Casablanca, Morocco, where Franklin D. Roosevelt and Winston Churchill demanded unconditional surrender earlier in the war. I was at Oran, Algeria, and saw the devastation of the German sinking of many Allied ships in the harbor as Rommel's defeated forces left the area. Palermo, Sicily, and its people are among my favorite memories. I was seeing the world after all.

Everybody on our ship wanted action. We were idealistic young warriors with patriotism in our hearts. When action arrived, it wasn't fun and games any more. I lost my right eye and almost lost my hands in action. We were firing a 40mm gun, and my hands caught in the breech of the weapon as I dropped shells into it. I couldn't jerk them out, and each time Carl Neff fired the cannon, it sucked my fingers deeper into the mechanism. Carl finally stopped firing, and the medics drilled holes into my fingernails to relieve the pressure from the crushing injury.

Fred Nicholson was a gunner's mate third class aboard the Naval Destroyer 168, the U.S.S. Amick, and completed his service in February of 1946.

My ship helped sink the last German U-boat, the *U83*, off the Boston Harbor, where it could be seen from the New England shore on May 6, 1945. The *Amick* and *Atherton* dropped depth charges on the German submarine and brought its reign of destruction to an end. The *U83* had sunk an American ship, the USS *Black Pointe*, outside of Boston harbor the night before our battle. Most Americans don't realize just how close to American soil the Germans brought the war.

After the war was over we returned to the states. Everyone was so happy, and some went wild. We kissed and hugged whoever we could find. I returned home and worked in my dad's optical business for a while before moving to California and working with McDonald-Douglas building moon rockets. That's where I met my wife, Mary. Mary worked at McDonald-Douglas also, and wrapped bandages on the home front during the war. We moved to Squaw Valley, California, in 1978. I have a picture of my ship, the USS *Amick*, on the wall to remind me of my service, and I enjoy building airplane models from that time.

I was twenty in 1945 and I was scared most of the time. It was so cold, but I'd do it again tomorrow if my country needed me, and I were able. Now in 2005 I'm eighty, sixty years after the end of WW II. Patriotism to me is to obey your country's laws and defend it against all enemies. The war taught me courage is the ability to enter just about any situation without fear, and that war is the last resort.

UNSUNG HEROES
by Robert Brummer

The families of my parents made the decision to immigrate to the United States of America to be a part of the promise of freedom offered here. My mother's French-Canadian family settled in Kansas, and my father's family came from Germany to Illinois. My parents met, married, and on December 20, 1923, I was born in Litchfield, Illinois. I was the first born of four children, and at the age of eleven my father died. He was a WW I veteran. Mother returned to Kansas to raise the four of us with the help of her parents, as it was a very difficult period of time in our nation, especially for a widow with four young children.

In June 1941, at the ripe age of seventeen, after just completing my junior year of high school, it seemed logical to join the Navy and lighten the burden at home. What a shock I had when I did not pass the physical exam. I spent the summer in the Civilian Conservation Corps on a survey crew instead of seeing the world in the U.S. Navy as I planned. But earning $30 a month was a big help to the family.

Before starting my senior year in high school, my attempt to enlist in the Navy failed again. I was rejected because of high blood pressure, even though I had been eating garlic as was suggested. A few months later, December 7, 1941, Pearl

Harbor was attacked, and many of the young men who got in the Navy when I first tried to enlist were killed in that horrendous slaughter. Apparently, there was a reason I was not supposed to be there.

After high school, I went to work for the Boeing Company in Wichita, Kansas. Upon completion of training, I was assigned to building the gliders that would be used in the invasion of Europe. After several months on the job, and being deferred from the draft for being in an essential war industry, I still felt

Robert Brummer, serving as a Merchant Marine, delivered fuel, tanks, planes and troops around the world.

the need to serve my country in another capacity. A school friend came home on leave from the Merchant Marine and talked me into joining them. I went to Omaha, Nebraska, and was able to pass their physical exam. I immediately was sworn into the U.S. Naval Reserve and found myself on board a train to the U.S. Maritime training Station in Sheepshead Bay, New York.

After three months of training off I went to Norfolk, VA, to be assigned a ship. My first voyage was on a tanker in a forty-ship convoy taking supplies to Casablanca, Morocco, which had just been secured from the Germans. When we arrived the Vichy-French fleet of ships had been sunk in the harbor. What a sight to see! While in Casablanca some of our entertainment was to dive from the deck of our ship, swim to a partially sunken battleship, and walk up to the side of it. I had the experience of participating in the dangerous refueling of a destroyer. During rough seas and because of the close proximity of the two ships, there was a very real possibility of collision and explosion.

Robert Brummer posing with his mother, a widow, who raised her four children after her husband died.

After returning to N.Y. for supplies and refitting we again rejoined a convoy to Curacao, Venezuela, to refill with crude oil. One of my jobs was to look out for the dreaded sight of a wake from an approaching torpedo. Fortunately I never saw one, but on this journey a ship behind us received a direct hit and sank in a short length of time. It was dark at night when the ship exploded, caught fire, and a huge fireball lit up the sky as we continued on and sailed away. We didn't stop as we had a job to do. It leaves a sinking feeling in your heart and soul. While never having a direct attack, I saw the results of enemy action and never knew when we would be in their crosshairs. In fact, over 1554 merchant ships were sunk during the war with a high loss of life. The Merchant Marines had the highest percentage of casualties, losing 1 of every 26 men.

This was only the beginning of many ports of call on a variety of ships going to South Pacific Islands, Australia, Philippines, Persian Gulf, India, Africa, South America as well as the east and west coasts of the United States and Hawaii. We delivered planes, tanks, fuel, troops and all kinds of supplies. Later, President

Harry Truman stated: "During the black years of War the men of the Merchant Marine did their job with boldness and daring."

After the war I came to Visalia as my mother and siblings had relocated to be near her sister and were able to purchase a small home. In October 1946, while viewing Visalia's Harvest Festival Parade, I couldn't help but notice the festival's Queen riding on a float and thought I would like to meet her. By a stroke of good luck, a year-and-a-half later, my brother and her sister arranged a blind date, and as they say, "The rest is history."

We were married in 1949 and moved to Tulare in 1955 where we raised five children. Those were busy, joyous years and many summer vacations were spent camping and fishing. I retired after thirty-seven years with Southern California Edison Company and have remained active in many veteran, church and service organizations, in addition to family times with grown children and grandchildren.

Having visited many places on this earth with a wide variety of people and cultures, there is nothing like the United States of America, and it is worth defending from all enemies. I think of the fact my grandparents provided for my future by coming to this great nation, even though it must have been a sacrifice for them. God Bless Them and God Bless America.

Robert Brummer aboard one of the ships he served on.

THE INVASION OF NORMANDY

In December 1941, Roosevelt and Churchill met to discuss war plans with the intention to "Defeat Germany First" (in large part to assist the beleaguered Russians). General George C. Marshall, Chief of Staff of the U.S. Army, insisted that the main drive should be in northern France. He asserted that a successful invasion there would likely bring a decisive victory.

In August 1942 the Allies launched a raid on the port of Dieppe in Northern France. The assault was unsuccessful and costly, especially in casualties to Canadian troops, but proved invaluable in terms of gaining an improved understanding of amphibious tactics.

In 1943 plans began for the invasion of Normandy under British General Frederick E. Morgan, who was Chief of Staff to the Supreme Allied Commander. The invasion was code-named "Operation Overlord." General Dwight D. Eisenhower was selected by Britain and the United States as the supreme commander of the Allied Expeditionary Force.

The Allies—Canadians, British, and Americans—assembled more than three million men and stockpiled some sixteen million tons of supplies in Britain in preparation for the invasion. They possessed a combined force of 5,000 large ships, 4,000 smaller landing craft, and more than 11,000 aircraft. Prior to the invasion, Allied bombers and warships attacked the Normandy coast to degrade German defenses.

Although the invasion was scheduled for June 5th, Eisenhower postponed it by one day because of severe weather. In the early morning of June 6th, paratroopers and gliders landed behind the frontline German defenses to destroy railroads and bridges, and to accomplish other preliminary objectives before the main landings.

Historians note that Eisenhower said to his troops, "You are about to embark upon a great crusade," and indeed they were. The invasion of Normandy, although costly in terms of loss of human life, was highly successful due to the foresight of its planners. D-Day, June 6, 1944, became symbolic of the tide turning in World War II, despite the bitter fighting that lay ahead.

I'M NOT OKAY, YOU'RE NOT OKAY, THAT'S OKAY, GOD HEALS
by Stan Lindquist

World War II played a significant part in my life. Drafted, assigned to the medical corps as an aid man and sent to Europe, we landed in Normandy on D-Day plus 5. After crossing France, Belgium, Holland and into Germany, a life-changing event occurred.

I was standing on a little hill gazing across a large meadow bordered by beautiful woods. Cattle were grazing knee-deep in rich green grass. Birds were singing. Squirrels were chasing. Flowers were budding. Bees were buzzing in search for nectar. Everything whispered peace.

Could this be war?

Yes. And I was a medical aid man with emergency medical supplies in a khaki bag slung over one shoulder contemplating my incomprehensibly threatening future. This peaceful meadow was a minefield at a strategic point to deny military access through a crucial break in the woods. U.S. Army trucks were scattered about waiting. Long Tom 155mm cannons were in place at the edge of the forest ready to fire life-destroying projectiles ten miles away.

The crucial points for me as an aid man were two wounded soldiers in the middle of the minefield crying for help. Squads of men were looking and listening, wondering what to do in this impossible situation, expecting a medic to somehow help. Two recruits were jabbing bayonets in the ground at the edge of the minefield searching for hidden mines.

As I stood there, strange thoughts blew through my mind. Was this scene to depict my destiny—fail to rescue the two men—and end my life in a futile gesture...shattered by a mine?

Nagging doubts and fears tore at me. Indecision tormented my deeper being. What should I do? What was my responsibility? Why did I have to be here at this place and time? Then a fragment of the words from Jesus came to mind, "He who lays down his life for another is a friend indeed." Apostle Paul's assurance flashed, "I can do all things through Christ who strengthens me."

In this mind-fog I called to my buddy, McGraw. "Let's go this way. We can see where the mines are by the dug-up grass." We strode into the minefield past amazed soldiers and the probing neophytes whose procedure was by the book and might be safer, but the injured men would die by the time a path was cleared that way. We safely threaded our way a hundred yards into the minefield. Stymied we stood together searching for the next faith-step. McGraw later said he moved his left foot a fraction of an inch, and we were both propelled skyward by an appallingly destructive blast.

It was this deed which changed the direction of my life. I had been an elementary school teacher, a car salesman, a government food inspector. Now I was capitulated into a new life as a permanently disabled soldier. Barely alive, I was hospitalized for nine months recovering from that one-second blast. Larger mines designed to stop the behemoth tanks were booby trapped with smaller anti-personnel mines to keep out the mine sappers. These shaped my destiny.

As I lay in various hospital beds for those nine months, I had the leisure to review my decision. Why had I volunteered to try to save the wounded? What possessed me to take this risk? No doubt, the words of Jesus, which had become part of my life—do unto others as you would have them do to you—played an unconscious part in my decision. The many times previously when I had risked my life and lived gave me false confidence.

At the time I felt as if I were in a trance. It didn't seem like a courageous act. There was a job to do. We had been trained to do it. With vigilance we had strode out to meet the crisis. With our bodies we made a path on which our rescuers could walk safely in our footsteps to save the other wounded men and us.

I entered the University of Chicago on crutches to learn skills to help the emotionally wounded, instead of physically shattered, soldiers…became a psychotherapeutic counselor…a listener…a different kind of helper…a professor. I majored in Psychology and taught at our Free Church school, later called Trinity International University. I became a Research Associate at the University of Chicago and taught at Herzl College, where many future rabbis took my course because they discovered a professor open to a religious interpretation of the subject.

Our family's next move was to Fresno to teach for thirty-six years in what is now known as California State University Fresno. Off campus, I simultaneously had a part-time practice as a psychotherapist. In 1965, I, with my wife Ingrid, and two brothers-in-law as board members, incorporated the Link Care Foundation, established to counsel concerned missionaries and ministers from the world as well as others in the community. Link Care Center is now a campus of eight acres, with 104 apartments, motel rooms, and offices, and staffed by 14 to 17 counselors, and 17 support personnel. 5,000 missionaries and ministers with families have lived on campus recently, their lives being renewed by the combination of faith which uses psychological tools.

FOLLOWING YOUR INTUITION MAY SAVE YOUR LIFE
by Jose Sanchez Salazar, Sr.

Jose Salazar in his Army Air Corp uniform, 1943.

I'm a World War II Veteran who served this country in a time of economic despair. It was a challenge to live in that generation when hardships were a way of life.

I was born in San Pedro, California, in 1924. I was the youngest of four, with two sisters and one brother. I attended Barton Hill Elementary School until 1933. I experienced the economic depression of our society. I thought of the things we lost as a family but we made adjustments. My father was laid off from his job in a foundry. I remember going to bakeries and grocery stores looking for day-old bread or discarded food. I brought it home and my mother made us soup from the scraps.

We eventually moved to Woodlake in the San Joaquin Valley. I picked grapes at one cent a tray and averaged 150 trays a day, which was pretty good at that time, considering milk was ten cents a quart and gasoline was twelve cents a gallon.

I went back to school and graduated from the eighth grade. Since times were hard, I eventually dropped out of school and helped my family's income by picking oranges and other fruits and vegetables.

Our lives were pretty simple then, until I heard of the 1941 bombing by the Japanese of Pearl Harbor, Hawaii. I remembered one of those ships that was sunk. It was the *Arizona*. I remembered the sailors who gathered as many kids as they could when they docked at the Los Angeles Harbor near our old home in San Pedro and fed us a Thanksgiving meal onboard the ship. I was heartstricken to know that some of the sailors I knew died in that bombing.

I was inducted into the Army Air Corps in April of 1943, then attended basic training at Jefferson Barracks, Missouri. From there I transferred to Mt. Home, Idaho, and was assigned to the 453rd Bomb Group as a waist gunner on a B-24. Jimmy Stewart, the famous Hollywood actor, was also assigned to the 453rd Bomb Group.

I really enjoyed this training, but I guess fate stepped in and changed my assignment when they found I had perforated eardrums. I was permanently grounded and reassigned to the Motor Pool. I was eventually shipped out to Europe aboard a British ship called the *Queen Elizabeth*. Near Attleborough, England, I drove aircrews to the mess hall, briefing rooms, or the hardstands when their aircraft were ready to go. It was hard to be close to anyone because you had to deal with their loss if they never returned.

I volunteered and was picked for an unknown mission. I was assigned to the 1st Engineer Special Brigade. During this advanced training I learned to make bridges for water crossings, scale high cliffs, and other types of maneuvers and tactics for our upcoming operation.

Then on one awful morning I found myself in the middle of "Operation Overlord." I remember it was cold and stormy that day, and the soldiers were scared and sick from traveling in the landing craft prior to hitting the beach (later I learned it was called Utah Beach).

This experience is forever embedded in my mind. It was June 6, 1944. I was assigned to hit the beach in the second wave. I remember seeing the ramp go down and I saw dead soldiers floating on the water as we jumped in. Some of these soldiers were missing body parts. I remember jumping into chest high water, and I started to release the non-essential gear I was carrying in order to make the shore before being shot.

After reaching the beach I heard rifle and machine gun fire with an occasional mortar being launched, and heavy artillery firing in the distance. I followed the other soldiers to an embankment barrier wall. We went over the wall and moved further inland. It was scary and very confusing. I was so frightened I didn't feel anything, not even numbness. I could hear soldiers crying and yelling for help, but we keep moving and digging in. I also remember there were airplanes flying low. I believe they were strafing areas to support the ground troops.

We started to push ahead farther inland meeting resistance from the Germans. We were ordered to head toward St. Lo where I and five of my squad buddies started searching buildings. All at once we were pinned down by a sniper. Out of nowhere a small white dog came to me. I tried to push this dog away, but it was very insistent. It tried to pull me by my pant leg, but it couldn't. I followed my intuition and followed the dog staying low. It led me to a place where there was an open field.

Shortly thereafter I heard a big blast and ran to see if my buddies were okay. I found them all dead. I went looking for the dog, but he was nowhere to be found. I felt bad for my buddies and even worse because I was alive, and they weren't. By following my intuition, this experience forever changed my life.

We then proceeded toward Paris, and the war ended ten months after the invasion of France. When I first learned the war had ended I was in a village talking to other G.I.s. The local villagers came out and greeted us with cheers and hugs and threw flowers at us. Afterwards, we stayed at a Chateau and marched in Paris, France, through the Arc de Triomphe.

I boarded the aircraft carrier USS *Enterprise* in South Hampton, England, and headed across the Atlantic Ocean to New York Harbor. I was never so happy to see the Statue of Liberty. It made me feel proud that I served my country. The war was over but not for me. I have lived with its horrific thoughts and memories in my mind for more than sixty years.

Jose Salazar, Jr. contributed to the writing of this story.

IN HONOR OF MY BROTHER, HAROLD
by Stanford S. Lee

I was born on April 5, 1930, in Hanford, California. My mother delivered eleven of us siblings in our parents' bedroom at home. Nine of us survived.

My brothers Gilbert, Harold and Ray served in the military during WW II. Gilbert entered the Army at the age of twenty-two on 15 December 1942 and was discharged on 9 January 1946 by the reason of "Convenience of the Government" (demobilization). He was a chiropractor and served in the medics in China. Harold graduated with honors from Hanford High at the age of seventeen in 1943 and was drafted into the Army in November of 1943 after turning eighteen. Ray, also an honor student, enlisted into the Navy at the age of seventeen right out of high school because of Harold having been killed in Normandy. Ray was a signalman on the island of Oahu during the bombing and was on three different points of the island. He thought that he would not have returned home alive due to the bombing in 1944 and 1945.

Harold was my favorite brother, although my other brothers and sisters were very encouraging to me in my youth. Harold spent time teaching me how to ride a bicycle, shoot basketball, and play softball. He was given a party at the Chinese Pagoda before he went to basic training and sprained his ankle. He ended up going into basic using a cane. He returned home once and that was the last time we saw him alive. Upon his arrival in England, he sent a "V" letter home to our uncle and aunt in Visalia, which read:

Dr. and Mrs. Wm. F. Lee
311 E. Mineral King
Visalia, California
From: Somewhere in England

Dear Uncle and Auntie:

Just dropping a line to let you know that I said good-bye to you. Am doing okay over here. Everything is almost perfect. Beautiful country, but give me the good old USA.

How's everything getting along back home? By this time you must be well settled in your new house. Certainly feels funny to be riding in a vehicle driving on the left side of the road. Every time we meet a car going the opposite direction, it makes me feel we're going to run into it. The beer taste very different. I can hardly wait to get some good stuff of the States! Cousin Henry still in North Carolina? Haven't heard from him since I was home.

Well, so long for now. Write soon.

Love,
Harold

I had forgotten this for many years, but I remember that when the messenger delivered the telegram notifying my parents of the death of Harold, I answered the door. It was on the second Tuesday morning of July of 1944. He asked for Mom, whom I got from the kitchen. She must have sensed it was bad news for she opened it right away at the front door and read the devastating news to my sister Dorothy and me who were in the living room. Live military personnel were not sent to homes in those days. On July 20, 1944, the *Hanford Sentinel* wrote on the front page about the death of Harold and said he was the first of his high school's class who was killed in war. It also said that he was hospitalized before he died of wounds. In 1997, however, I received a copy of Harold's medical record from the National Personnel Records Center in St. Louis, Missouri. Harold's death was prior to being in a medical facility. That tells me that he died on the battlefield of Normandy.

In 1990 I was encouraged to write my family's history. I donated copies of the research to the three museums in Hanford. A former classmate of Harold's, Doris Roberson Polley, read the article and wrote an article for the *Hanford Sentinel*. I then created an Army display of Harold and his service. From that display, I gave a copy of the picture of it to our late family friend, retired Army Colonel Won Loy Chan, formerly of Visalia. He met a military historian film producer, Montgomery Hom, who put Harold's picture in the film "We Served With Pride," about Chinese Americans who served in WW II. It was premiered in Washington, DC, October 26, 1999, at the Smithsonian Museum Theater. I was asked to represent Harold, and although I did not plan to go, the organization of Chinese Americans felt that my presence was important enough that they paid all my expenses.

The day before we left Fresno, they left a message for me to be ready Monday (the day after the ceremony at the Smithsonian) at 3:00 PM to be picked up at the Red Roof Inn in Chinatown to be taken to the White House. Without any schedule, I thought we were to be given a tour; instead we were taken into the Cabinet room after going through security with identity tags that had been given to us. Laura Effurd, who worked for the President, told us that usually no one is allowed into the Cabinet room unless the President is there, too. Thirty minutes later we were escorted into the Oval Office where the president of the United States of America, William Jefferson Clinton, was expecting us. It happened so fast that I was thinking, "How did I get here, and what am I doing here?" Only the Lord could have allowed it to happen.

I believe the example shown to me by my brothers, and the direction of the Lord, led me to also serve my country. I did not want to be drafted into the Army, having just received my draft notice during the Korean War. I attempted to join the Navy at the Fresno Recruiting office because of Ray being in the Navy but was rejected due to my flat feet. I enlisted into the Air Force in Bakersfield on 6 September 1950.

I served in Korea from 1953 to 1954. Major John Cummings awarded me airman of the month and somehow the Air Force gave me three battle stars for serving in three campaign areas in Korea. Because I worked on confidential information in Korea and Japan, I did not have to be in hand-to-hand combat of which I am grateful, for I cannot forget my brother, Harold.

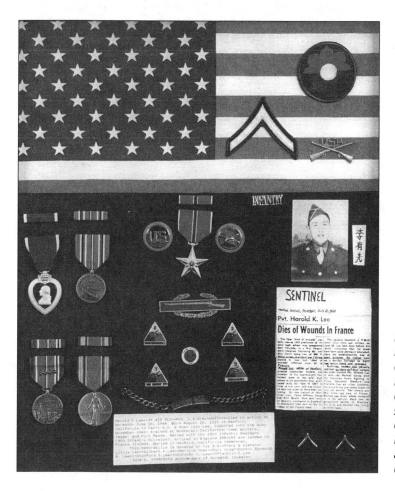

In tribute to his brother, Stanford Lee contributed Harold Lee's photo, an article describing Harold's service, and a display of the medals and r ibbons Harold was awarded for the ultimate sacrifice.

THE BATTLE OF THE BULGE

The Battle of the Bulge, which lasted from December 16, 1944, to January 28, 1945, was the largest land battle of World War II involving U.S. forces. It was also America's bloodiest. The German assault, codenamed "Watch on the Rhine," began under cover of fog. On December 16, 1945, thirty-eight Nazi divisions struck along a fifty-mile front in the Ardennes Forest. Mechanized units overran several U.S. First Army positions.

In the days that followed German forces were successful in driving the Allies almost to the Meuse River, in the process surrounding American units in the Belgian town of Bastogne. When offered a surrender ultimatum, Brigadier General Anthony C. McAuliffe of the 101st Airborne Division at Bastogne offered a single-word reply: "Nuts!" General Patton's Third Army was soon able to break through the German lines to come to the aid of the garrison at Bastogne.

Although the Germans were temporarily able to create a "bulge" in the American lines, they suffered massive losses with 100,000 casualties and another 110,000 troops captured. The Allies also paid a steep price: American casualties were more than 81,000, including 23,554 captured.

A SOLDIER WITH A THOUSAND LIVES
by Juan Cedillo

I served as a technician fifth grade during WW II and ended up serving in the Rhineland Campaign in the 23rd Armored Infantry Division at the Battle of the Bulge. I was born in Texas in 1925. My father moved there from Mexico to make a better life for his family. I worked as a farm laborer making only two dollars and fifty cents, working from sunrise to sunset. At the age of sixteen I left school to help support the family.

In 1943 I was drafted into the United States Army. WW II had begun and Uncle Sam decided he wanted me. I was afraid of heights so I didn't join the air corps. I was afraid of sharks so I didn't join the Navy. I chose the Army as a rifleman and became a sharpshooter.

After six weeks of training in San Antonio, Texas, I boarded the *Queen Mary* for England. Upon arriving I remember hearing all the people shouting, "Here come the Yankees." I thought that was funny. I had never been called a Yankee before. When my unit arrived at our first duty station in Luxembourg, in November 1943, the battlefield was littered with guns and fallen soldiers. The sergeant told us to pick up any gun we wanted, oil it, and test it in the woods. I received special training launching hand grenades from my Browning automatic rifle. My job was to find the enemy and flush them out. My team searched foxholes, basements, and anywhere else we thought German soldiers might be hiding.

Juan Cedillo in his Army uniform, 1943.

Juan Cedillo served in the 23rd Armored Infantry Division. He is kneeling in front of a farmhouse during the Rhineland Campaign.

I remember when I went in to my first battle. I was scared. My buddy to the left of me was killed. Then my buddy to the right of me was killed. I wasn't scared no more. I was mad! Mad was better.

In the Battle of the Bulge we traveled from Luxembourg to Belgium. It was an exhausting experience. I remember crossing the Rhine River, and I remember living in the snow for months. We fought in the snow. We even slept in the snow. A lot of men lost fingers, toes and feet from frostbite. Some even died. It was terrible time.

One time I recall they sent an armored battalion through a narrow canyon. There was a German pillbox ahead of us. They could easily have killed us and destroyed every tank in the battalion unless we did something. My team of six men was ordered to take them out, and we did. We got up close behind the pillbox; we waited a long time for the right moment. The moment came, and the bazooka man fired the bun and destroyed the Germans, and our convoy was allowed to continue. We saved our tank that was pinned down.

We traveled more than eighty miles through the snow and chased the German soldiers ahead of us. They were running so fast we couldn't catch up to them. We arrived at a German airbase, which they had deserted. My job was to destroy all the parachutes, and my buddy did something to all the engines so the planes couldn't take off.

We were on our way to Antwerp and came across a concentration camp the Germans had deserted. There were no guards. They left the POWs locked inside. We cut the chains on the gate and let the prisoners out. There were thousands of them; they were all starving. They were so hungry that as soon as they passed through the gate they fell down and started eating the weeds and grass. We gave them what food we had with us, and they went into the houses in the town looking for food and clothes.

We got medical help for the really sick ones. The prisoners of war were nothing but skin and bones. A Polish man kneeled down in front of me and said, "The Lord has sent me an angel." I never forgot that day. It was the most horrible thing I ever saw. I want people to know what happened to those poor souls—and never forget it.

We did what we could in a short time; then my division kept moving forward and we met with the Russian forces in Berlin. I was part of the German occupational forces for a while before I went back home to Texas and began working in construction. I met a beautiful young lady, but when I asked for a date she told me, "No! I don't date." So I said, "OK, will you marry me?" She said, "Yes," and we were married in 1951 in Atchington, Texas.

We moved to California and raised three sons and two daughters. We have over seventeen grandchildren and great-grandchildren. My wife and I have celebrated a fiftieth wedding anniversary, and we felt truly blessed to have such a wonderful family. We really come together and support each other. I am very proud of them.

I have tried to live my life in such a way that they will see me as a hero. They are the reason I want to tell this story. I want my grandkids to know what we did over there, and to remember, "No matter how bad things can be, the Lord can carry us through."

THE BATTLE OF THE BULGE
by Art Hill

I was born in 1915 and grew up in the coastal city of Coos Bay, Oregon, with my six brothers and one sister. As a young man in the Depression years it was hard for me to decide what I wanted to do with my life, but by December of 1941 it was clear.

At twenty-seven years old I enlisted in the Army with a good friend after listening to the radio broadcast of President Roosevelt's "This Day Shall Live in Infamy" speech. My basic training was at Camp Swift, Texas, and after Officer's Candidate School I was assigned to the 146th Engineer BN as HQ-Company Commander and Battalion Motor Officer. Later, I was involved in five European campaigns: Normandy, Northern France, Ardennes/Alsace, Rhineland, and Central Europe.

In December 1944 we were on reconnaissance near Malmedy, Belgium, when we saw a big sign on a house with a picture of a t-bone steak on it. We thought, well, that's for us, and stopped for dinner. While waiting to be served, the owner suggested that we move our Jeep around to the rear. It turned out that German SS troops were in the restaurant the night before and the owner was afraid they would see our Jeep and shoot up his establishment. We polished off our steaks in a hurry and hightailed it back to report the incident to our Battalion HG at Eupen. We had occupied the territory for months, and these were the first German troops sighted in the area. Little did we know that the Battle of the Bulge was about to begin.

German divisions attacked and made deep penetrations, or "bulges," in our American frontlines. It was bitterly cold at the Bulge, and I'll never forget hearing the eerie sound of crunching, frozen snow becoming louder and louder with every footstep of either friend or foe. I also remember the artillery shells bursting on the trees above us, and the branches and treetops falling all around us. After the shelling the German paratroopers would land in our immediate area and attempt to secure the key road junctions that we were guarding. They would follow the sound of each other's cricket clickers and birdcalls.

Later on, we learned of the capture of approximately ninety or so American soldiers near the same place in Malmedy where we had ordered our steaks. The

Germans lined up these American soldiers in a field and machine-gunned them. When their snow-mantled bodies were found this became known as the Malmedy Massacre, the worst atrocity committed against our troops in the European Theater.

After the Battle of the Bulge, and the eventual liberation of Europe, the U.S. Army Engineers stayed on to help these newly-liberated countries rebuild. In Pilsen we helped clear the demolished streets and buildings of rubble and rebuilt all of Pilsen's utilities. I was named director of a school in Czechoslovakia teaching the Czech civil engineers the proper use and capabilities of our road-building equipment. They later went on to build a highway between Pilsen and Prague with their newly-acquired U.S. Army equipment.

I'll never forget returning home from the war. As our ship entered New York Harbor I looked up to see what seemed like a thousand flags waving from every warehouse rooftop lining the harbor. The entire harbor was filled with ships of every description, all waving their flags and blasting their horns. When I saw the Statue of Liberty my eyes filled with tears of joy for being home, mixed with tears of sadness for those we left behind.

Looking back at the war, I am happy to have served my country and help rid the world of Hitler's tyranny. We went to Europe to help these countries regain their freedom and then rebuild from the scars of war. Many young men died fighting for this freedom, and since I returned from the war I tried to figure out a way to make sure they were not forgotten. I now volunteer as Director of the Legion of Valor Veterans' Museum in Fresno, California, where we remind the public of the sacrifices made by veterans of every war. Let us never forget those who have made the ultimate sacrifice for our freedom, and the freedom of other people throughout the world.

REMEMBERING THE BATTLE OF THE BULGE
by LeRoy Jenks

I grew up on a farm south of Mitchell, South Dakota, the home of the world's only corn palace. You get out of school at noon during corn palace week so you can go down and spend your pennies. And you didn't have much more than that during the Depression days. I went to high school one year and figured I knew everything there was to know—what the heck? Why spend that time? I was out for two years and finally went back. I didn't graduate until I was twenty-one. But I worked for a year and I still have the bankbook at home: $125.00. I was able to save that in one year at $2.00 a day. The job I was working in was agriculture, where we had to measure farms. Doing that I met the people who decided I'm going to go to college. Once there I found out everyone was in the United States Army ROTC, so I participated in that, too.

After Pearl Harbor things changed in a hurry. Kids were getting drafted. I was a little bit different in that I didn't have as many credits, or I guess I had a few more credits. It was finally decided to let these people who were in college stay until they completed school. I got my degree in 1943. I came home for a month and then I was called to Fort Benning for Officer's Candidate School for three months. Then I came home again and got married. 1943 was a good year for me: I graduated from college, got my commission, and got married. The only good thing is I'm still married: fifty-seven years.

I was a Lieutenant Commander, Company Commander in the infantry. I served in France and Germany. My Company took Frankfurt. We destroyed that place, nothing left of that when we got done. I got wounded on patrol in France. I remember waking up laying on the floor on a cot and some general up there handed me a Purple Heart. Now I'd have been interested in most anything but that. They put me on a plane, and I tell people that I crossed the English Channel without any clothes on. They just wrapped a blanket around us and by not taking any equipment with us, shoes or anything, they were able to get two or three more patients into the plane. Then I was in Army hospitals.

I recovered from that and even though you want to go back to your company, you don't want to volunteer until you're stateside. But what happened? The Battle of the Bulge. Out of the hospital, back to our units. I went to the same Company I'd been with and from there on it was the Battle of the Bulge.

We'd take a town, and then we'd wait for another unit to come through. They'd take their town. We were never in a place more than three days until finally we were at a small village in Germany, I think it was April or May, in the spring. Three days went by, four days, five days, six days. We couldn't figure out what was happening. That's when the governments were signing the papers, I guess.

I returned that summer and was in two or three different Army hospitals, finally ending up in San Antonio. My wife was able to get a job there, and after I got out of the hospital I looked around to see if I could do something. I got a job teaching veterans the farm trade. My wife always talked about Uncle Oscar sending oranges from California, so we decided to go to California and see what's there. I bought a Jeep, a station wagon type that was one of the first automobiles made after the war. We threw our things in the car and took off to visit a sister in Los Angeles. Once we got out here we didn't want to go back. I checked around and had to go to Cal Poly for six months to get the units I needed for a good job. The first job I had was in a place forty miles west of Chico. I was there until I came down to Fresno in 1955. I've been here ever since. I taught at Clovis High School for twenty years, built my home here, raised two girls, and have a grandson.

The Battle of the Bulge was the biggest battle in the history of the American Army. I meet with a Battle of the Bulge group four times a year, especially on the 16th of December, the anniversary of the day the Bulge started. I'm grateful to have survived.

Soldiers in the 3rd Platoon, Co. F, 2nd Battalion, 5th Division, Siegfried Line. (Image from the Clovis Independent.*)*

Soldiers in the 3rd Platoon, Co. F, 2nd Batallion, 5th Division lined up for a hot meal at an outpost near the Siegfried Line in Germany on February 18, 1945. The photo, taken by a U.S. Army Signal Corps photographer, was submitted by local veteran LeRoy Jenks. He is featured in a story included in the Welcome Home America special section in today's Independent.

A PRISONER OF WAR REMEMBERS
THE BATTLE OF THE BULGE

by Judge Frank J. Creede, Jr.

My time in combat was fairly abbreviated before I became a guest of the German government. Lest any think I raised my hands the first time I saw a German, I had lots of company, 7,000 men, two regiments. I served in the Selective Service two years before participating in the Battle of the Bulge with the 106th Division, 423rd Infantry Regiment, 2nd Battalion, H Company, Heavy Weapons Company and Machine Gun Squad. I was just nineteen years old, just turned nineteen two weeks before the Battle of the Bulge broke out. I was a dumb kid, only had a year of college.

The 106th Division landed in the Schnee Eifel (snow) Mountains off the Ardennes forest on December 11, 1944, just over the border between Belgium and Germany into the Siegfried line. Of course our American Intelligence was up to its usual excellence because we were assured this would a good place to break into combat. The Third Army was on the offensive. There hadn't been any engagements so no heavy offensive was anticipated even though the Germans were prepared to go on December 16, 1944. We were also told not to shoot when the Germans came in. "Break your weapons if you are going to be captured," we were ordered. My job was to get ammunition from the jeep to the guns without getting shot.

While we were talking, the Germans had 250,000 troops, 1,000 tanks, and 2,000 artillery pieces ready to go at 5:30 in the morning. We were spread out over twenty miles with many gaps and no armor when the Germans approached us from the rear on December 16, 1944. In two days we were surrounded, and two days after that our colonels surrendered 7,000 men to the Germans. The colonels who surrendered us to the Germans really saved our lives. The F1 rifles were destroyed when the Germans took over. I broke mine by striking it against a tree. I was captured, and then we were marched off to a POW camp.

Anyone who engaged in radio or telephone communication on the German side would be shot. The only way they communicated was by courier and hand-to-hand messages. I would find out later they would have an armored division at Cologne, and it would gradually move on, but the normal radio transmit would come from an armored division saying they needed more tanks, equipment and supplies as if the armored division was still at Cologne; however it had already moved up to the Ardennes forest.

We ended up marching for several days until we got to a rail yard garrison that had boxcars down for repairs and maintenance. We arrived at Stalag IX B which was 37 miles northeast of Frankfurt on the Rhine. Fortunately, and I don't know the reason, but probably because the Third Army came through so fast, they didn't have a chance to move us out. We were liberated on April 2nd, 1945, which was a month before the war was ended. I was back in San Francisco by V.E. Day. I was very fortunate indeed that in any event they didn't march us halfway across Germany. That probably was because we were so close to the front line they didn't have the railroad cars to put us in. We heard stories of other POWs that got terrible cases of frozen feet and trench foot when they were marched halfway across Germany to Poland in the winter.

I remember the day, April 2nd, 1945, that we were liberated. There was a white flag flying from the flagpole in front of the gates of Stalag IX B. At 9:00 A.M. the American troopers came right through those gates. The front line troops had no food for us, because they just had enough for themselves. They lined up in the kitchen, and it was the day we had mush. One of the troopers said, "Let me taste that stuff." I handed him my wooden spoon, and he took a bite, then spit it out. I said, "Don't spit that out! It's the best food we've had in months." We could tell how the war was progressing because we could hear the heavy artillery to the west, and to the left we could hear our heavy artillery. To the south and to the east, we heard more fire fighting activity. The Americans couldn't tell our POW camp from a German camp, so our camp was strafed, but we were still lucky to be in West Germany.

I was in the POW camps in Germany for three-and-a-half months. I lost over thirty-five pounds. The Germans threw away our gas masks, but, I would find out later from liberated German soldiers, "The original plan was to kill all of you in the POW camps, but now that we know that you treated our people so well, we will let you live." The Americans who captured the Germans carried the Germans up the front lines.

One incident vivid in my mind happened on January 28, 1945. The Germans didn't open the barracks as usual at 7:00 A.M. but waited until 9:00 A.M. Our shoes were taken, and we had to stand three deep in snow and formation for two hours with an entire squad of men wearing helmets, with machine guns trained on us. Two Americans had gone into the kitchen and were caught by the German guard. They hit the guard on the head with a cleaver. The American men were from the 106th Division, 424th Regiment, serving in the Battle of Bastogne. Protestant and Catholic chaplains went through the barracks trying to find out whoever did this. They were two men looking for bread to feed themselves, not doing it for the rest of the soldiers. The chaplains found several with blood on their overcoats and transferred them to another camp. The Germans eventually restored their privileges, not really wanting them to starve. The German guards said, "If you don't cause us trouble, we won't cause you trouble." I don't know how we managed to save our feet from frostbite that day.

The captives from the 106th eventually added up to more than 7,000. It was touch and go at times, and in the fray, I was injured. I was awarded the Purple Heart, but I'm grateful to have survived the war. Over 2500 POWs were held in Stalag IX: British, American, some Italians and the Russians. The Germans treated the Russians pretty harshly.

After repatriation, I had done my duty and had risen to the high rank of PFC. I was most anxious to get back to college, and I was very happy to see that discharge paper. In the prison camp I wore the same uniform and was allowed an ice cold shower for three minutes once every month, and I have worn the same black uniform my whole [professional] life.

THE AIR WAR IN EUROPE

Although Germany's air force, the Luftwaffe, was quite formidable in collaboration with Nazi ground forces in blitzkrieg campaigns, it had difficulty countering the Allies' devastating advantage in long-range strategic bombing. By 1942 thousands of Allied bombers were partaking in highly-successful daily sorties over Axis-held Europe.

The Royal Air Force Bomber Command preferred "saturation bombing" (dropping waves of bombs in a location) with the assumption that at least some of them would hit the target; however, the United States 8th Air Force perfected a style known as "pinpoint bombing," strategically dropping bombs on a selected target from a high altitude during daylight. Eighth Air Force pilots flew the Flying Fortress and Liberator heavy bombers, and the Thunderbolt, Lightning, and Mustang fighters.

Allied air forces scored a critical success during five days of clear weather in February, 1944—known as the "Big Week"—when they conducted a massive continuous bombing assault targeting German's military-industrial infrastructure. Historians note General Henry H. "Hap" Arnold as stating, "Those five days changed the history of the air war." The Allies degraded aircraft plants, assembly factories, and railroads in Germany, and the Allies' reach extended into Romania, stopping oil production, destroying or damaging dams in the Ruhr Valley, hindering power sources, and targeting machinery, aircraft and tank factories.

During the course of the war the Allies destroyed more than 56,000 German aircraft and dropped about 2,700,000 short tons of bombs in Europe. American pilots flew over 750,000 bomber sorties and nearly a million fighter sorties. The British flew nearly 700,000 bomber sorties and almost 1,700,000 fighter sorties.

FLYING THE PT19s
by Robert Francis Dunbar

I was working in the Mare Island shipyards when Pearl Harbor was hit. A school friend, Buddy, and I, the same age, born on the same day, decided to go Castle Field in California to sign up for the cadet flying program. At the time I had a brand new 1941 Chevy Coupe when I passed the test. It was months after I passed the test before they called me up for training. Buddy didn't pass the physical which I was pretty sorry about. I decided to go back to Mare Island to finish paying off my new car while I waited for my orders.

I ended up being sent to Texas for training and then to the University of Wichita, Kansas. On leave one night, I was attending a show when I eyed an attractive usherette, sending her a handwritten note asking for a date on the back of his popcorn box. It worked. After I graduated we were married, the weekend before I left for overseas. Her family never forgave me for having her visit me when they wanted her presence with them at a family reunion in Iowa.

I served in WW II in the Army Air Corp from 1942 through 1945 as a fighter pilot, flying PT19s in Italy. The first flight I was able to do myself, I thought I'd go up and do a loop. I went through the proper height and everything and started to do this loop, but not being accustomed to doing it, I stalled out and killed the engine. The crank is on the outside of the PT10 to start the engine, so

I just pointed the plane to the ground and hoped to heck it would start. Sure enough it did. I went back up again—if something happens you can't let that hold you back, so I went back up again, and did it properly.

Morris Field in the Rio Grande Valley near McAllen, Texas, was my next assignment. I trained on P47 Thunderbolts there. I was then transferred to Pocatello, Idaho, for further training in P47 Thunderbolts. The weather was terrible. And finally, they ended up closing the whole base.

Robert Dunbar served in the Army Air Corp from 1942-1945 as a fighter pilot, flying PT19s in Italy.

The war in Europe ended two weeks after I arrived in Italy. I was a Second Lieutenant and flew thirteen missions as a fighter pilot, near Pisa and Naples. When we heard the news the war had ended we had a meeting in the Officers' Club. Two days before we had gotten there, the atom bomb was dropped in Hiroshima. We were in a meeting in the Officers' Club for a briefing on the situation in Okinawa. At 9:00, they stopped it all and announced the war was over. We knew we would be going home. The next day they started to delay departure time, but they let us go off the base where we hadn't been allowed to before. We went into town and celebrated while the MPs and Shore Patrol turned their heads. One fellow didn't make the ship for home, and the next morning as we were going through the last lock he jumped aboard. When we got across the isthmus he was thrown in the brig.

Out of the 1,000 men we had onboard ship, he was the only one who didn't make it back on time. It was quite a special event when we got back to the States. We were served fresh food by German prisoners of war.

The emblem of the 347th Fighter Squad Robert Dunbar served with.

Dunbar also trained on the P-47 fighter-bomber shown in the photo.

WARTIME MEMORIES OF ONE AIR FORCE MAN
by Eugene Enderson

I'm with the 452nd Bomb Group and we're stationed in Norwich, England. Our base is called Deopham Green. We're here to bomb and annihilate Hitler and Germany. The weather here in England is cold, damp, and foggy, almost every day. These are some of the missions our crew lived through.

Mission #1: January 15, 1945
Target: Augsburg, Germany

It was a jet fighter plane. Heavy flak and this being my first mission, it was overwhelming, exciting but also very scary, not knowing what's going to happen! My top turret guns were loaded and ready. That is after I checked them on the ground before take-off. Our squadron of twelve bombers was being cleared for take-off. Our meeting for this mission was previewed with all the crew and all the planes who would partake in it. Maps were described and the destination was briefed, and the 8th Air Force brass chose the target. Chaplain said a few words and wished us the best.

We flew over the Swiss Alps and headed for our target. We had a lot of flak and quite a few holes in our plane. None of us were injured. It took us nine hours. Oxygen masks were worn for about four to five hours. They go on at 10,000 feet. At 24,000 they are worn, and the face is really a bit sore. But without them we would never make it. We made our first mission with damage to the plane, but nobody got hurt. Our pilot and co-pilot did a wonderful job.

Mission #2: February 3, 1945
Target: Berlin, Germany

We flew *Lady Satan*, our newly-assigned B-17F. She had been on eighty-four combat missions. We saw no enemy fighters, but enemy flak was heavy and accurate. We almost lost our ball turret gunner, Morrie Kuhns, whose oxygen mask had frozen. Harold Chartrand and I cranked him up and revived him. He complained about cold feet so we put him in a British heated "suit" which looked like blue long john underwear, but after 15-20 minutes Morrie complained over the intercom that smoke was coming off the heated suit and it was hot—it had a short circuit in

Bombers in flight.

it. So we pulled off the "blue underwear" and pitched it out of the side door near the back of the plane. Unfortunately the suit hung up on the horizontal part of the tail - smoldering, but without flames. Soon, someone in another plane broke radio silence with *"Lady Satan's* on fire." What next? But our pilot, Bill Robinson, was able to "slip slide" it off. We were on oxygen for five of our eight hours and fifty minutes in the air.

The bomb group celebrated its 200th Combat Mission on February 14, shutting down for two days with parties on the base.

Mission #7: February 22, 1945
Target: Marshalling Yards/Targets of Opportunity

This was supposed to have been at ME (Maximum Effort by all the planes of the 8th Air Force). Bad weather forced us to break up the formations and drop bombs on targets of opportunity. We dropped on Ulm. Others in our group went to Frieburg. We flew plane #802 and were in the air 9 hours 10 minutes.

We took a flak burst in the cockpit and the wing tanks. Probably because we got in later than other planes our damage was not reported, so the official report said, "No air craft reported any battle damage." No one was hurt, but the gas gauges were shot out, so Bill Robinson decided to play it safe and we homed in on an emergency landing field near Lille, France, which had been a German fighter base during the occupation of France. The Melville Emergency Field had been badly bombed and strafed, but we got our gasoline and took off across the Channel for Deopham Green.

Eugene Enderson served as Technical Sergeant in the Air Force 452nd Bomb Group flying the B-17 Flying Fortress Lady in Waiting.

We were challenged by P-51s and Spitfires as we were returning late and without the proper radio ID codes for that hour, but Bill convinced them we were on the same side and continued back to the base after a long day.

Mission #11: March 10, 1945
Target: Frankfort Marshalling Yards

We flew plane #879, *Satan's Sister*, and were in the air 7 hours 30 minutes. Heavy flak was encountered and *Satan's Sister* is no longer a virgin. She had the dubious honor of being the 452nd's most shot up plane today. A five-inch piece of flak hit the fuselage near Bill Robinson's head. One shell went through our left wing tank but did not explode, but the left wing did have sixteen holes. All together we received forty-three holes in our plane. Anyhow, no one was hurt, but *Satan's Sister* had to have a replacement left wing (an old olive drab color). Twenty-one of our planes received damage including three with major damage.

Mission #24: April 11, 1945
Target: Bridge Near Munich at Donaworth

It seems the 8th Air Force has become a tactical Air Force, rather than strategic, by working with the infantry advance led by General George Patton. We were in the air 7 hours 50 minutes, flying plane #989. Hey, no flak, nor fighters!

Mission #25: April 14, 1945
Target: Royan, Near Bordeaux, France—Tank Traps

We were assigned a brand new plane (#326) and flew eight hours this day. We carried fragmentation bombs—twelve pounds each, wired in clusters of 25 or 50. Ten or twelve hung up or were on the catwalk in the bomb bay. Our radio operator hauled these errant frag bombs into the radio room and indicated he would train them out of the camera well in the radio room. We checked with navigator Bob Davis for any "restricted areas" on his maps. So, apparently, no anticipated problems, we trained the bombs out one by one as we approached the Bay of Biscay, north of the city of Bordeaux. We dropped the last bomb and followed it down directly on one of the "concrete islands." Our bombardier said over the intercom, "Direct hit," and we slammed the camera well door down to emphasize the announcement.

Wham, wham, wham, wham, and a battery of four 88s filled the sky around us with flak. We were only at 10,000 feet of altitude, expecting no trouble that day, but we soon were on our right side, sliding down to about 3, 4, or 5,000 feet. And I recalled how brown and cold the Bay of Biscay had looked when we trained those little bombs.

In the excitement and fear, I had pulled off my intercom line to reach for my parachute pack. Plugging back in I heard "Bailout"—and started to crawl back to the waist position. We leveled off, but no one was bailing out. I plugged into a waist position intercom line and got my answer, "Don't bail out."

We had 287 holes that day, and our brand new plane was christened *Flak Shy Lady*. A couple of new men who had moved into our hut when Bishop's crew went down early in the month had come down to the flight line to wish us good luck, saying, "Hope you get you're a—-shot off, today." Kind of like show people saying, "Break a leg!"

Mission #26: April 15, 1945
Target: Further Destruction of German Occupation Sites, Gun Emplacements Around Bordeaux

On our way to drop Napalm bombs on Bordeaux we flew over Paris at 6,000 feet, over the Eiffel Tower, down the Champs Elysees, and over the Arc de Triomphe. We dropped on the target and took some inaccurate flak. Coming back along the French coast we flew over the famous Mont St. Michel and Cherbourg, where our troops landed on "D" Day. We had a real "Cook's tour." We flew plane #326, *Flak Shy Lady*, eight hours today.

Mission #28: April 17, 1945
Target: Dresden—Heavy Troop Concentration in the City

We flew *Flak Shy Lady* for nine hours in the air today. Thousands of troops and civilians were killed. A real shame as far as I was concerned on this day—a feeling shared by many at briefing. Very little flak over the target. Five planes received minor damage.

Mission #30: April 21, 1945
Target: Munich Was Our Primary Target, but We Bombed the Marshalling Yard at Ingolstadt

The weather was too thick and soupy to allow us to get to Munich, so we had to go to our target of last resort. Neither flak nor fighters encountered because of weather. We flew plane *Flak Shy Lady* for this, our last combat mission. Germany was about to collapse. The 452nd had flown 250 combat missions.

Service Flag notation: Great record. S/Sgt Eugene F. Endrzejewski of Tapco, top-turret gunner and engineer of the B-17 Flying Fortress *Lady in Waiting*, has completed more than 225 combat hours, traversed approximately 30,000 miles, and helped his bomber fight its way through severe enemy opposition to drop more than 125,000 pounds of high explosives on Nazi industrial and military installations prior to V-E Day. Sgt. Endrzejewski has been awarded the Air Medal with four Oak Leaf Clusters for "meritorious achievement" in aerial combat.

"THE FLORENCE OF THE NORTH": MY SPIRITUAL RETURN

by Kilulu Von Prince

I was sixteen years old and my mother, younger sister, and I were in a train filled to capacity with other German refugees and wounded German soldiers heading into Dresden the night the city was bombed. It was February 13th and 14th, wondering if we would be attacked because it seemed like they focused their bombing along the railroad main station fifteen minutes away from where we were. The train had just stopped outside of Dresden when the bombing began shortly after 9 P.M. It saved our lives!

We could hear the drowning noise of several hundred airplanes flying over us in the sky, hearing the explosions of thousands of bombs that were dropped, and then seeing within a few minutes the huge fire ball over the city. It held all of us in total shock. The night sky lit up under the firestorm and lit up the train, which had been in a mantle of total darkness until then. Now we could see our faces, and we could feel the heat as we sat in shock in our tight sitting space whereas before we had felt the freezing, icy cold winter air that had surrounded us in the unheated train.

It was uncomfortably warm with all the human bodies in the train. People cried for the windows to be opened for air. Others were panic-stricken and wanted to get out of the train, but the doors were locked. Some tried to crawl out of the windows, but others pulled them back and tried to calm them down. People needed to go to the toilet, but they were occupied by wounded soldiers. Most everyone had to use containers, bags, or any papers they had in order to relieve themselves, or for throwing up. The air thickened with terrible odors. Children were crying, women were screaming, and many were praying. It felt like we were in a hellhole from which we could only escape through the windows into the flaming inferno outside a few miles where the train had stopped. The air coming from the open windows smelled awful. It was the smell of burning flesh.

We learned later that the smell was generated from the burning of the thousands of human bodies in the demolished Dresden. The first attack lasted a half-hour. Once it stopped we could hear the continuous explosions as the firestorm roared through the city. I remember that my mother, sister and I held each other's

A 1943 aerial photo of Dresden, Germany, prior to the air attacks by the allied forces. Von Prince was on the outskirts of Dresden and saw the devastation.

hands! We wondered if the fire would reach us in the train. After a little while a second raid occurred. It seemed that there were many, many more bombers returning with more massive loads of incendiary bombs. The explosions shook our train and people were shrieking, trying again to jump through the windows but couldn't because other people stood in the way. The sky glowed a fiercely bright orange, and the heat of the fire intensified. We all began to sweat. We tried to get more windows opened to cool the train but the outside air was too hot from the huge fire over the city. Hell could not have been worse.

We drank what water we had between the three of us to quench our thirst. We had to do it without getting anyone else's attention for the fear that our precious water supply would be taken from us. This was survival of the fittest in the truest sense where one did not think about caring about anyone else but yourself and your family. The air raid was finally over, but it took several hours before the word was given that we had to take a detour with the train. The detour took us through Leipzig via Berlin to our final destination, Ahrensburg, near Hamburg. We had to transfer in Berlin, which was also severely bombed out. We were able to have a room in the house of our aunt, which was to become our home for the next several years.

Years later I saw Dresden in photographs. The city looked like a ghost town, a totally demolished city. 174,000 homes, 20 churches, 40 hospitals, 68 cultural centers, and 35 schools were partially or totally destroyed. The numbers of death and injuries have not been given a final determination because no one had an account of the thousands of refugees fleeing the eastern front line that had flooded into Dresden. They could only identify 35,000 people because other casualties had been totally incinerated beyond recognition. Some assumptions were made

Dresden after the bombing, February 1945.

Dresden after the bombing, February 1945.

that anywhere between 200,000-600,000 had been killed. The military publications of the British and American air forces have much lower numbers. They might have omitted the many refugees that were killed, stalled at the Dresden main train station, waiting to connect with trains going west at the time of the bombing.

I am so glad that I had made the decision to see Dresden sixty years after that horrible night. The memories of that experience were wiped away as I entered Dresden by train. I was very impressed, despite the many areas of renovation and reconstruction that were still happening around the city. I was amazed how much had been and was being rebuilt to the city's old image with modern techniques and improved interiors. The picture of the destroyed city I had in my mind disappeared before my eyes as I walked through the old part of Dresden.

I went to the Kreuzkirche (Church of the Cross) and participated in their Sunday services. This church was a symbol of and gathering point for the democratic movement in 1989 when the "Wall" between East and West Germany came down and Germany unified. Candles and white roses were carried by many thousands of Germans in the city of Dresden, and over 3,000 people came to the Kreuzkirche to reconcile, sending the messages of forgiveness and praying for prevailing peace world wide.

THE STRAWBERRY BLONDE
by George Kastner

I'm a third generation Californian. I was born and raised in Clovis, California. My mother, Georgia Bell Kastner, died four days after I was born. My aunt and uncle, Mr. and Mrs. J. Wise Brown, raised me. I graduated from Clovis High School in 1937 and went on to graduate from Fresno State College in 1941.

I enlisted in the Army Air Corps in the weeks following the attack on Pearl Harbor. I received my wings and commission in August of 1942 and went to combat in September of 1942. I became a pilot in the 86th Fighter Bomber Group in the 12th Air Force. I named my A-36 *The Strawberry Blonde* after my wife Thelma, who was a redhead. I flew from North Africa, Sicily, and Italy and went to combat over the cities of Lengenya , Acena, Solano, and Naples.

I remember one mission in particular, near the end of my service. I had the task of organizing a mission to bomb a 16-inch gun that retracted from Angio Tunnel during the day and fired upon Naples during the night. I decided to let my Clovis buddy Bob Thomas lead the mission, and I followed with two other guys. We dropped two 500-pound bombs with delayed action. I was able to drop my bombs, but the *Strawberry Blonde* received heavy fire. I was headed down the mountain away from Angio Tunnel when the engine in my plane came to a sudden stop. I tried to open the canopy to parachute out but I was too low. I even tried to find somewhere to make an emergency landing, but there was no place to land, so I tried something drastic. I cut off the fuel to the engine and then turned it back on again causing the engine to back fire. Lucky for me the engine started again. I flew over the Mediterranean Sea back to Naples.

You don't think much during the first ten to fifteen missions because you have never been in battle before. But after about fifteen missions, when you start losing pilots, you wonder if you might be next; we (the 86th Fighter Bomber Group) lost over a hundred and seventy-four pilots. They were here one day and gone the next. When a member of the 86th was shot down, the other pilots and I would drink a cup of water and make a toast to our fallen comrade. I would spend a lot of time thinking about them that night, but the next day I had to stop thinking about them all together. In war you can't go into combat thinking about all the other pilots who have been shot down. You just have to put it out of your mind and move on the best that you can.

I was one of the lucky ones. Out of the eighty-three missions I flew, my bomber group never made a toast in my honor. During the war the *Strawberry Blonde* carried me through all of those missions; this was the record at the time. I received a certificate of valor from the 12th Air Force, and when I returned to the United States after the war I became a base commander at Lafayette Air Force Base in Louisiana. I stayed there in the Air Force Reserve and retired a full Colonel in 1959.

Thelma and I have been blessed with two sons, seven grandchildren, and two great-grandchildren. I started teaching American History at Clovis High School right after the war and eventually became Associate Superintendent for the Clovis Unified School District. After my retirement they named a middle school after me in Clovis. My wife and I make donations to Kastner Middle School to help the students there.

SERVING MY COUNTRY: FROM DEC. 1942–SEPT. 1945
by Fred Loring

I left school after WW II started. I was older than most of the students in my class and decided to go into the Army Air Corp. After basic training I went to aircraft school in Los Angeles and lived in a hotel. I enjoyed going to the Hollywood Canteen on weekends. After finishing school it was back to the old training at four other air bases, Nevada, Utah, North Carolina and Virginia.

In the summer of 1943 I was off to Tunis, North Africa. I was assigned to the 17th Bomber Group, which was flying B-26 Marauders Bombers. In November 1943 we moved to the Italian island of Sardinia. There in December 1943 I was shot in the right hip and was in the hospital six weeks.

In 1944 we moved to the French island of Corsica for the invasion of Southern France.

In October 1944 we moved to Dijon, France. I was an Engineer Gunner. While on a bombing mission December 17, 1944, our plane was shot up. Although one engine was on fire the pilot was able to keep it flying close enough to friendly lines that we could all parachute out and escape. After returning to our base in Dijon we went to Paris for ten days of R&R.

In March 1945 our plane crashed after taking off from the runway with a load of bombs. The plane broke in half and some of the bombs rolled from the plane. All crew members survived.

Fred Loring's plane crashed and broke in half after take-off in March 1945.

On April 26, 1945, while on a bombing mission over Bavaria, Germany, our flight was attacked by jet fighter planes. Three planes in our flight of six were shot down. The right wing of one of the planes hit the tail section of our plane as it went down. Our pilot was able to keep our plane under control, and we made it back to our base. Only two crewmembers from the three planes shot down survived. Our group doctor sent me to R&R in southern France. WW II ended while I was there.

I was stationed in Belgium for a short while before returning back to the United States and being stationed at Santa Ana Airbase. My first furlough I went back to Dos Palos. It was so good to be home. I didn't go anywhere for a few days.

A photo of Fred Loring taken at the end of the war in Belgium.

I went with some of the kids in our old neighborhood east of Dos Palos to the San Joaquin River for a swim party. While on our way home I heard over the radio that the war with Japan was over, and the celebration began.

Three weeks after the war ended I was discharged from the Air Corps. My first job was an airplane mechanic and flight engineer at the Stockton Air Base in Stockton, California. After two months my doctor suggested I stay away from airplanes for awhile. In 1946 I went to work for the Golden State Milk Co. in Los Banos. My job was testing milk in the lab, and that's when I started to remember what I had learned in Mr. Easter's Ag Class.

In 1946 I met my wife to be, Alta, and we married in December of that year. Our first daughter, Linda, was born in Los Banos in 1948. We moved to Fresno in 1949 and I went to work at the Veterans Hospital before it was opened for patients. Our son, Dennis, was born in 1951. After high school he enlisted in the Air Force for four years, then off to college. In 1961 our daughter, Roberta was born.

I retired from the Veterans Hospital in 1980. Alta and I have a small hobby farm east of Clovis where we have raised cows and sheep and a horse for about ten years. We now rent out our pasture so that we have more time for our volunteer work. We are both very active with the Clovis Veterans of Foreign Wars organization.

TWO ENGINES DOWN, TWO TO GO
by George Martin

I was born on March 17, 1919, in Fresno, California. My parents were Arthur W. and Gussie Welborn Martin. I was the seventh of nine children. There were five boys and four girls. My mother was a homemaker, and my father was a farmer, raising cotton, figs, corn and grapes.

I graduated as valedictorian from Roosevelt High School in 1937. I attended Fresno State College for two years and transferred to the University of California at Berkeley. After graduating from Berkeley I went to Los Angeles to celebrate my graduation. While at a hotel in Los Angeles, a bellboy came running up to me with a letter from Uncle Sam ordering me to report to the draft board in Oakland California at 12:00 p.m. the next day. Uncle Sam had not forgotten me. I enlisted in the U.S. Army Air Corps.

I arrived in Oakland just in time to board a train that took me to basic training at Lincoln Air Base in Lincoln, Nebraska. After basic training I was assigned as a flight officer on a B-24 Bomber. I went through training at the flight school. At the Army Air Base in Santa Ana, California, I was assigned co-pilot with a pilot named John Truer from Michigan. We organized the other eight members of the crew at March Field, in Riverside, California. We had more training at March Field before flying to Europe.

We were assigned to the 15th Air Force, 456th Bomb Group. We flew to Cerignola Airfield at Cerignola, Italy.

On our first mission over Germany we were flying at an altitude of 24,000 feet. We had just dropped our bombs on our target when we were immediately hit by German 88mm ground fire. One engine on the left side was hit and we had to turn it off. The engineer transferred the fuel from the damaged engine to the other three engines to enable us to fly home. Then an engine on the right side was hit and I turned it off. Both damaged engines were inboard.

We had gone from four working engines down to two. At this point we had to drop out of formation because we could not keep up with the rest of the group. We flew across the Alps at about 1,000 feet altitude, and then we proceeded across the Adriatic Sea. When we finally landed at Cerignola, Italy, we only had fifteen gallons of fuel left.

I flew thirty-six missions over Germany, France and Italy. Six of these missions, I flew as First Pilot. After the war ended I traveled for a week. I took a flight with an English bombing crew to southern Italy to see the country. I got a ride on a gondola to the Isle of Capri. I hitchhiked and walked back to Cerignola Italy just in time to join my crew to fly back home to the good old U.S.A.

Upon my return from the war in Europe, I met my wife Margie at the church I was ushering. Six months later we were married. Margie and I raised four great kids, two boys and two girls. We now have eight grandchildren, and I have made a good living in real estate.

I had some close calls during the war in Europe, but it was all worthwhile. I am proud to have served my country in its time of need.

THE GUNNERY GLIDER PILOT
by Glen McKinney

I was born in Tulare, California, on November 5, 1921, to Charles H. and Bertha McKinney. My dad, a carpenter, and my mom, a homemaker, had five children. We felt the effects of the Depression in many ways, one, especially, in that we had to put cardboard in our shoes to prevent the bottom of our feet from being punctured by the sticker veins common in the area. We grew chickens and had a vegetable garden, which helped to feed the family. I attended Roosevelt Elementary School, Central Grammar School, and Tulare Union High School, where I graduated in 1940. During my last two years in high school I worked weekends and summers at Lampe Lumber company where I applied my business education to reading blueprints, taking material lists from the blueprints, quoting costs, selling merchandise, and performing basic bookkeeping duties.

Three weeks after the attack on Pearl Harbor I enlisted in the Army Air Corp and was sent to Tucson, Arizona, where I was assigned to a headquarters squadron at Davis Munson Field. The squadron commander, knowing of my previous work experience, assigned me to a bookkeeping detail. I didn't want to be doing this. I wanted to fly.

While eating at the mess hall one day I became acquainted with some of the gunnery crew from the B17 squadron. They told me the crew was shorthanded and suggested that I transfer over. My squadron commanding officer said, "No!" I was later assigned duty in the school's office where I screened for qualifying personnel to be sent to the different schools. When I noticed that the quota for aerial gunnery school wasn't filled, I spoke with the captain at the school's office and volunteered to go, but he said that I would still need my squadron commanding officer's approval for release. My commanding officer remembered my having previously requested a change of duty, so he told the captain, "If he wants to go that bad, take him!" I left the next morning for Las Vegas and spent six weeks in flight training school as an aerial gunner. I later signed up for glider pilot training, which is what I wanted to be doing all along.

Flying gliders can be hazardous, especially when landing. The glider is towed into the air by another plane and then released and left to its pilot's devices. After the success of my first night landing in a cargo glider, it was my friend Alfred

Heren's turn to fly. He noticed that his wristwatch had stopped running and asked to borrow mine. I pulled it off, handed it to him, and said, "You'd better give it back to me in one piece!" Then I left. The next morning, I learned that he had crashed on landing, so I immediately went to see him at the hospital. The doctors had amputated his right leg, thus ending his career as a pilot. Although it was soon after surgery, and he was still out of it, he handed me pieces of metal and glass saying, "Here's your watch!" I still have my watch, in pieces, sixty years later.

In all I flew about twenty missions in Germany, France, Holland, England, Sicily, and North Africa with the 82nd Airborne and the 101st airborne units. I walked away from six crash landings, but somehow I was never wounded.

After serving in Africa, Italy, and Europe during WW II and experiencing combat, I was glad to receive my discharge as a First Lieutenant and return home. I married Dorothy Damron in 1946, and we had one son, Dennis. I moved my family to Modesto, California, and we were gone several years, but we returned to Tulare in 1984. My wife passed away in February 2003 after fifty-six years of marriage. In 1948 I became one of thirty charter members of the Captain Manuel Toledo AMVETS Post 56. Only three of the original members are living.

When I was in high school I learned the basics of business: honesty, diligence, consideration, and getting along with others. After entering the military, I made it a point to know the right officers and enlisted men and to get along with all of them. I believe that our academic and life experiences work together to provide us with a means for experiencing a full and successful life.

A SCOT WHO SERVED IN WORLD WAR II
by William Swinton McLeod, Jr.

I was born October 15, 1924, in Dallas, Texas. As a one-year old I resided in Sarasota, Florida, with my parents, leaving there for Dallas shortly after my father's business venture failed. With my family I lived in the Oak Cliff District of Dallas most of my early youth, except for short periods in Calvert, Texas, and Marshall, Texas. My father was buying cotton in those places and was able to have his family with him for short periods of time.

I graduated from Highland Park High School in 1941 and immediately went to a thirty-day R.O.T.C. Camp, located near Mineral Wells, Texas, called Camp Dallas. It was there that I met my future wife, Alice Joy Beiger, of New Orleans, LA. She had been visiting her aunt in Dallas and came with my family to visit and picnic one weekend at the camp.

That fall I enrolled at Texas A&M College in College Station, TX, majoring in Aero-Engineering. The following year my parents moved to Fresno, CA, just after visiting me at school, and again, bringing Alice Joy as a family guest. At that point I asked her for a picture, and she later responded favorably with one.

The United States had entered World War II by this time, and the nation was in a rush to mobilize both men and industry for the war effort. I volunteered for the Aviation Cadet program with the intent of becoming a pilot and flying airplanes. I enlisted as a private in the Enlisted Reserve Corps in December 1942, went back to school, and was later called to active duty in February 1943.

I entered active duty, completed all the requirements of ground and flying schools, and graduated on April 15, 1944, with my pilot's wings and a 2nd Lieutenant's Commission from Marfa AAF, Texas. I was selected for B-17 bomber pilot training and received my transition flying at Hobbs AAF, NM. Upon graduation at Hobbs, I was assigned a crew and sent to Drew Field in Tampa, Florida, for combat training.

Before starting this training, however, Alice Joy Beiger and I were married in the base chapel of McDill AAF, FL. I secured a 24-hour pass for my wedding and honeymoon before reporting to Drew Field.

My crew and I went overseas by ship after completing combat crew training, arriving in Scotland early in December 1944. We subsequently were assigned as a replacement crew to the 358th Bomb Squadron, 303rd Bomb Group, 8th Air Force located at Molesworth, England. My first completed combat mission was flown December 29, 1944, while my 36th and last mission was flown April 5, 1945. All missions were deep-penetration missions inside Nazi Germany.

During the war our two sons, William III and Murray, were born, Alice having returned to Fresno when pregnant with the second one. Resuming civilian life was not difficult for me, but some additional education and on-the-job training helped prepare me for the life of a purchasing agent, and later as a Financial Consultant for Merrill Lynch & Company. After twenty-seven years with Merrill Lynch I retired in 1987 and devoted my time to the pursuit of genealogy and Scottish studies. I helped form the Scottish Society of Central California and served as its first Chief. My genealogical research took me to Nassau, New Providence Island, Bahamas, Charleston, SC, and Savannah, GA in search of my roots.

Before retirement I had been appointed Regional Vice-President of The Clan MacLeod Society, USA, and Alice and I enjoyed traveling in the United States, Canada, and Scotland to participate in Clan meetings. In September 1992, while at a reunion in Boise, Idaho, I was elected President of the 303rd Bomb Group Association and served in that capacity for eighteen months.

REMEMBERING WW II
by Carl Nichols

I was twenty-five years old and a graduate of Fresno State when I joined the service, a civilian working as a training instructor and a coach. Six months after the war started, the government said they didn't want anymore civilians. I was the first one from Fresno to go to Officer Candidate School. There I met a base adjutant that happened to be from Hanford, who was married to a girl that I went to school with. He said, "Carl, I have a good job coming up, how would you like to go into the Intelligence Service?"

"How do I do that?" I asked.

"Well, I will put in orders for you and send you there."

I wound up in Harrisburg, Pennsylvania. It was one of those schools that if you went to O.C.S. and wanted to go into Intelligence, it was a prestige thing. If you graduated in the top ten they said they would send you anywhere you wanted. I came back to Hammer Field in Fresno for a few months after graduation, and I said I wanted to go to China. But I didn't get where I wanted to go. I was assigned to the 8th Air Force in England. I stayed in Intelligence the rest of the time.

I served under General LeMay who told us when I got my first star, "Put 'em on, you didn't deserve 'em, but you wear them." Then he told us that he wanted us all to go to the 100th Bomb group. He said, "There will be an alert tonight. It's top secret. Nobody knows about it yet. Since you are new here, tomorrow I want you to watch and listen to what they do, how they pull the targets out, give a number, pull a number out of the file. You go to the map board, and put it on the map."

He gave us the whole procedure of what we would do. We all went into the war room and there was this big map at the end of the room, all considered secret, why I don't know, because all the Germans knew exactly what we were going to do. They drew a coordinate on the map, and one of the guys that was to be the lead pilot in the squadron that day was Jack Swartout from Fresno. He was a Major at the time, and he said to me, "How the hell are you?" And we hugged each other and talked.

He said, "Well, I'm not going to fly today," and I said, "Jack, you mean you're quitting?" He said, "Well, you can do that when you've done twenty-five missions."

I was leading the group for the last mission we went on to Berlin. I'd done the briefing, and Jack and I had breakfast together. We hung around until the interrogation. Then we went outside to see the planes return. I looked up in the sky and saw two planes return. I said, "Jack, where are the rest of them?" Jack said, "Well, I guess they didn't make it." We had twenty-one that went out, and nineteen didn't come back. Actually, a few more survived, but they landed on other bases. Jack said, "Now you see why I'm a Major that's alive and not a Lt. Colonel that's dead. I'm going home."

Another Lt. Colonel deep wing commander who lived through the attacks was Billy Connely. I knew him as a cadet at Emmet Field. He lived near me, and I won-

Carl Nichols was assigned to Intelligence in the 8th Air Force.

dered how he earned his rank. I yelled at him, "How'd you do it so fast?" He said, "Easy, you just have to live through it."

The worst part of the war was in 1942—1943. You had to do twenty-five missions and half of the pilots made it. After we got over there to England, we (the 100th Bomb Group) were the only group that never lost a plane to enemy fire until one day the enemy came into our base. They shot four of our planes down. The other craft we later lost were due to anti-aircraft fire.

On V-Day we were on a late mission, about dusk, when an enemy plane, the night fighter, came in with our formation. He just tucked in with our planes and shot them down. He actually hit six planes, and four of them crashed.

Intelligence officers were not supposed to fly, even if we were pilots. One guy snuck out and flew a mission and was gunned down. General LeMay said, "If anyone does it again, you'll be fired. I don't want anybody from Intelligence flying these planes. That's all there is to it." We had two Intelligence officers in our group.

General LeMay signed for the main targets we had: a ball-bearing factory and an airplane factory. He was a Colonel then with one star. When we were in the war room you knew he was there. You might not see him, but you just had a feeling that the boss was around. We would get a report every day, very secret. The old man would read it and give us the co-ordinates of where the enemy airplanes were stationed.

We had one report that came in and no one knew where this was. It was called Operation Fury. We would load up a radio-controlled B24 with explosives and a bomb. Another plane would fly right beside it and guide it into a Nazi submarine.

What happened this particular day was that before the crew in the B24 could parachute out the bomb went off and the plane blew up. The next day we got an Intelligence report that a Navy Lieutenant was killed with a copilot and crew chief. It just so happened that the plane was carrying President Kennedy's brother. No one knew it was Joe Kennedy. I don't know if they named him in the report or not at first. At that time, no one knew who Kennedy was. After a later time, to put the report together, we did come up with Joe Kennedy's name, Jack Kennedy's brother. The plane was about five miles from us when it blew up. It was a terrific blast, and of course we knew everyone was killed.

When the war ended they said, "We don't know what to do with you guys. Go back and stay the night. We'll see what to do with you in the morning.

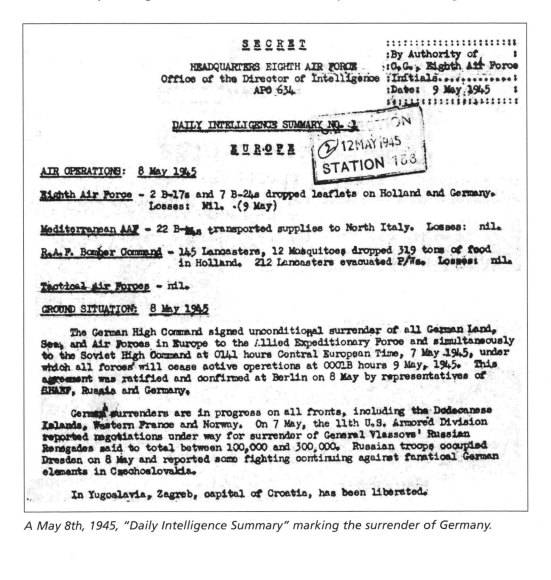

A May 8th, 1945, "Daily Intelligence Summary" marking the surrender of Germany.

VICTORY IN EUROPE

By the end of March 1945, with the crossing of the Rhine River, the Allies were surrounding the Germans on all fronts. On April 25, 1945, First Army patrols and Red Army units joined forces at Torgau, on the Elbe River. Meanwhile, Allied forces broke through the Gothic Line and began surrounding the German army in Italy. Mussolini was captured by Italian partisans and executed, and on April 30 Hitler and his wife, Eva Braun, committed suicide in Berlin. Germany's defeat became inevitable.

At 2:41 A.M., May 7th, 1945, in Rheims, France, Germany's Colonel General Alfred Jodl signed the terms of his country's unconditional surrender, and in the days following the free world celebrated. After five years, eight months, and seven days the European phase of World War II had ended.

A LOST BAR, AND AN UNLIKELY PRAYER
by John Costello

In November 1944, when still with C Company of the 398th Infantry Regiment, I'd hit the ground because of shelling by 88-millimeter artillery. I didn't have a good grip on my M-1. I started to move my hand to better grip the rifle when a voice said, "Don't move." When the shelling was over, I found shrapnel from the very last shell had destroyed the gas-powered return mechanism, ruining the rifle. It was where my hand would have been.

I was not always a BAR (Browning Automatic Rifle) man. I was made one when I was transferred from Company C to a newly formed Company A of the regiment. Since being reassigned, I'd been wounded in December 14, 1944, in the first assault on Fortress Bitche. I rejoined the company right after the first of the New Year.

It was now early February 1945. One night the company cooks provided us with a hot meal under very strict light security conditions. Flashlights held directly over each pan of hot food aided us in finding our way through the chow line.

A BAR is unwieldy. I was barely 5'8", and I'd done poorly firing it in basic training. The weapon weighs 16 pounds even without the accessory bi-pod and base plates. I couldn't keep the weapon up on my shoulder as I went though the chow line. I put it down outside, behind the mess tent. I got food, ate it and went back for my BAR. It wasn't where I'd left it. I was told later that the cost of the BAR would be taken out of my pay. No one believed I hadn't lost it on purpose.

February 7 dawned. For some time I'd had the premonition that February 7th would be special in some way. The hunch was right. Around 5 P.M., or a little earlier, I was sent to the rear to bring back K rations. I felt weak, half-sick, and not at all sure I had the strength to carry the rations up to the front line.

The trail was covered with slushy, half-melted snow. I got the box of rations up on my right shoulder and balanced it there precariously. At a very slippery place on the trail, I lost the rations trying to balance the load and keep my feet. The box went flying, and I found myself on my butt in the snow. In a split second, without thinking about it, I blurted aloud words I never should have thought, let alone said. "God damn it, I've had enough!"

I was sorry immediately. I didn't follow up with any sign of contrition. But I was genuinely sorry and shocked at myself. God will ignore it, I hoped.

But my eye caught sight of an unusual light 100 feet ahead, off slightly to the left of the path. It was about ten feet above ground and like no other light I've ever seen. It was an iridescent white, and seemed cold. It did not illuminate anything around it.

This light seemed to exist in a plane or dimension all its own. Somehow it appeared to pulsate to a predetermined beat. At each beat rays of light emanating from a center light disc would grow brighter, then dimmer. Each ray tilted toward me and then back, as each ray simultaneously grew brighter, then dimmer.

I was mesmerized and afraid of what might happen next. Abruptly the light was gone. Not more than fifty seconds elapsed from my first awareness of it until it vanished.

John Costello, in Army uniform, served in the A Company, 398th Regiment, February, 1945.

Still sitting in the icy snow, I was shaken and chastened. How had I had the guts to address God as I did? What I suspect is that the light was a presence. I cannot presume to say it was God, or came from God, or even why it came, but the connection seems inescapable. Maybe God would forget or ignore my utterance. I picked myself up, got the box of rations up on my shoulder again and delivered them.

At about nine that night, I found out God hadn't forgotten. It seemed innocent at first. I head the distinctive "wump" sound of a detonating mortar shell deep in the woods. Ours, I remember musing, as it exploded on what I felt sure was the German side of a very irregular front line.

A second mortar shell exploded much closer with a frightening roar. My terror was immediate. That was far too close! Mortar barrages come in sixes. Four more would be coming and much nearer. I had been lying on my back on blankets; a shelter-half tied to two huge trees was above me.

I might have only seconds to live, I thought.

No time to worry. Hope and pray. I flipped to my stomach; my hands flush by my sides.

The third mortar went off closer than the second. I tensed in aching dread. If death were coming it would be in the next shells. The deadly rain was in the air.

"Oh, God," I managed in desperation.

I heard no warning whistle before the fourth mortar fell, only a startlingly loud bang. I could hear its shrapnel whizzing by inches from me. Then in quick succession the fifth and sixth mortar shells exploded at greater distances to my immense relief.

Now, all was quiet. I was acutely aware of my body. I felt no pain. I moved my legs, then my toes. I then tried to move my arms. My right arm wouldn't move. I couldn't feel my right hand at all.

Then I felt a dull pain. I got up clumsily. Fearfully, I looked at my hand, then my arm. I still had both. The pain was in my arm, but at least I was whole.

In seconds the platoon was by me. No one else was wounded. Others who otherwise would have been hurt had been in an abandoned old German observation post. The acting C.O., a first lieutenant, apologized over and over for what he said were American mortars somehow misdirected.

I figured that already but only heard conflicting explanations from the Army. I was simply grateful I hadn't been killed. I had to sign an Army payroll before being evacuated in order to comply with an Army regulation. I scrawled the signature with my left hand.

My right arm healed in a little over three weeks, but I came down with hepatitis with pronounced jaundice at a replacement depot. I spent over six weeks at another Army general hospital. Finally the division could spare a six-by-six truck to pick me up from a second replacement depot. The day I rejoined A Company was May 8, 1945.

Germany surrendered that day which meant my petulant prayer to dignify the impromptu outburst by calling it that had been answered. This says more about God's mercy than I deserved.

A POW STORY

by Edward H. Daves

Pearl Harbor was bombed December 7th, 1941, and World War II was proclaimed. Reedley Jr. College offered a liaison pilot training program in Bishop, California, that I was very interested in. I was then called to Santa Ana, California, as an aviation cadet. I met my future wife, Edna, at Reedley College. She joined the WAVES (Navy) and was the first one called from Reedley.

My assignment was to the 401st Bomb Group and the 615th Bomb Squadron flying out of Deenethore, England. We landed in Liverpool, England, on D-Day. Our crew flew eight missions, and then on our ninth combat mission, flying a B-17, we were shot down over Magdeburg, Germany, with a crew of nine members on September 28, 1944.

We were returning after dropping our bomb load when the number two engine of *Little Moe* was hit by flak. This caused the engine to disintegrate and started a subsequent fire in the main fuel tank. A large hole was simultaneously blown into the left side of the bomb bay, and fire began shooting from the hole into the cabin burning through the flight control cable running along the side of the plane. Then the entire cabin started filling with smoke, funneled along through the defroster tubes at the base of the windshields, but since we had dropped our bomb load, we continued on in formation, away from Magdeburg. However, I knew that the aircraft was quickly losing power, and after confirmation from my tail gunner and ball turret gunner that large pieces of the plane were coming off, I knew it was time to give the entire crew the order to "Bail out."

As my crew left the *Little Moe* one-by-one, I stayed with her until I was reasonably sure they had all evacuated the airplane. Then I crawled back through the tip turret and opened the bomb bay doors to check the damage. It was then that I saw the full extent of the flak damage, and that the fire would soon reach the fuel tanks, which would destroy the aircraft.

I crawled back to the cockpit controls, which by now were completely gone. I continued crawling to the front escape hatch and parachuted out. We had been flying at 30,000 feet. As I jumped from the nose hatch the information that I received in B-17 flight crew training echoed in my mind—chances were that the person bailing out through the nose hatch would probably be hit by either the open bomb bay doors or one of the ball turret guns. Fortunately, I managed to get clear of the aircraft unscathed.

In the event it was necessary to parachute from a damaged aircraft, we were instructed to delay opening our chutes for as long as possible, as our chances of evading capture would be greater. I fell for several thousand feet through a complete undercast, and when I came out of the other side of the cloud cover opened my chute.

When the chute opened I started oscillating violently from side to side. I pulled up on the shroud lines which caused me to suddenly drop straight down. I was so close to the ground that I had to let the shroud lines go again to avoid serious injury or death, which started my pitching to and fro once again. Unfortunately, I let the shroud lines go too fast and I remember my feet just brushing the ground and then swinging up hard again. When I reached the high arc of the swing my chute collapsed onto the ground and I fell to earth, coming down on the back of my head. Needless to say, I was groggy from a lack of oxygen in high altitudes, and it seems that I was knocked unconscious.

When I came to I gathered my chute in a frantic evasion attempt, but it was too late as a German non-com and the local burgermeister were waiting for me. They took my chute and personal possessions, and then marched me back to town through a street thronged with civilians. The locals began throwing things, spitting at me, and yelling obscenities at me in German. After running this gauntlet my captors locked me up in a chicken coop.

I didn't know whether I would be taken to a German prison camp or Army or Air Force Base. It turned out to be Daek. Once at the base I was locked in a windowless room with no furnishings for a couple of days. At night they would take me out to be interrogated by a German Luftwaffe officer. He would sit behind a small table with two candles stuck into bottles behind him lighting him and an armed guard posted in the room. The effect was very eerie, and it had me at tremendous psychological disadvantage. After lengthy questioning, all he got out of me was my name, rank, and serial number. Since I was uncooperative I was returned to solitary confinement for days. Eventually I was given some ersatz brot (bread) and about six inches of blood sausage to eat.

This was all I was to have to eat until I was finally taken out and put aboard a German civilian passenger train to be transferred to the Frankfurt Dulag (a central processing area from which POWs were sent out to the various Stalags). I was not given a seat, but was made to stand in the aisle way with a "Jap" civilian sizing me up for most of the trip.

Along the route I was transferred to another train, and since it was awhile since I had eaten the guard who accompanied me offered me a bowl of unwashed potato soup. I gladly consumed it, although it did have quite a bit of dirt in it. When I finally arrived at the Dulag, night had fallen. I was once again placed in

A group photo of Edward Daves' unit of the 401st Bomb Group and the 615th Bomb Squadron, taken prior to their being shot down and captured (September 28th, 1944).

solitary confinement, and then extensively questioned. During the days following my initial arrival and confinement, a group of us POWs were brought into contact with an American Colonel and were fed a group of boiled prunes, raisins, and some other mixture that gave everyone a severe case of diarrhea. We were also given a small sack from the Red Cross that contained a bloc of tooth powder, a toothbrush, a safety razor, and a small bar of soap.

After this, some other POWs and I were loaded on to another train. Each time we passed through a town where bombing had occurred we were told to stay hidden, as the residents of the bombed area might try to kill us.

Eventually we reached Stalag Luft I at Barth (on the Baltic Sea) where we were questioned again, had our pictures taken, and were given an opportunity to send a note home to our families. I realized at the time that this might be a way of the Germans obtaining unauthorized information from the prisoners. Indeed my suspicions were confirmed upon arrival at home after V.E. Day, when I learned from my parents that the Germans used these letters home as a way to short wave propaganda to the East Coast of the United States.

After arriving at Stalag Luft I was given a long burlap sack and was told to put excelsior from a pile into the sack to serve as my mattress. I was then assigned to a room in one of the barracks with approximately twenty-seven other American flying officers. We had a heater-type stove which had been modified by the

German POW documentation for Edward Daves taken at Frankfurt Dulag, a central processing area from which POWs were sent out to the individual Stalags.

inmates with a firebox on top, just large enough to hold one galvanized bucket. Each room had two of these buckets, and with no running water in the barracks the bucket had to be used to carry and store water and wash our clothes, as well as cook our food. Besides potatoes, we were occasionally afforded some bug-infested rutabagas, ersatz coffee, black bread and cow or horsemeat.

The boredom of my seven-month stay in the camp was broken by our week-ly three-minute showers. However, the dull routine of the camp was disturbed one night. We were hustled into our barracks and confined there for a day and a night due to a massive American bomb raid to the east of Barth. Apparently, the Allies were pounding a German offensive missile conference in a neighboring town. We were able to see B-17s, B-27s, and some four-engine British bombers flying over the camp in formation silhouetted against the daylight. It was a glorious sight, and it filled us all with hope and pride!

Several days later a great deal of activity began in the German ranks. We later learned the neighboring camp had been bombed by the Americans and British, and the Germans were hastily packing up and leaving the area. When the Russian tanks and shock troops came into the Stalag we knew why "the krauts got the hell out of Dodge."

The Russians liberated our camp, and the next day a couple of my roommates and I walked into the town of Barth. But when we returned, we found the camp to be in total bedlam. At this point, three other Krieges (the German term for prisoner of war) and I decided to walk out of the Stalag.

We walked through woods, and eventually came to an inlet, where a couple of soused Russians had commandeered a rowboat. We talked them into taking us across the inlet, and hit the ground running on the other side until we reached a small village that another Russian unit had taken over. There we spent our first night of freedom. The next day we hitchhiked out of the village and kept on thumbing rides and walking until we reached Rostock and then hitched a ride on a truck on our way to Wisemar, which had been occupied by Canadian paratroop-ers. We gorged ourselves on a barrel of dill pickles we found on the truck. Unfortunately, this was the richest food we had had in some months, and we were all violently ill!

In Wisemar the Canadians put us on Lancasters back to Britain, and we were all shipped to an American military hospital in Braintree, England. When I was finally discharged by the hospital, after several days of quarantine, I was taken to London to await passage back to the States on a liberty ship that eventually docked in Newport News, VA. Although I was still numb from my POW experience, I practically sprinted off of the ship, I was so glad to be home.

ODYSSEY OF A "KRIEGIE"
by Charles D. (Mac) McMullen

I was assigned to the 106th Infantry Division in August of 1944 after I had completed ASTP. (ASTP was the Army Specialized Training Program, which sent people to college who would become officers after their two-year college program.)

We reported to the "Siegfried Line" in an area called the Schnee Eifel. There was a concrete bunker with metal bunks similar to those on a submarine (without mattresses). When we were not on duty we spent time in the bunker. At night for entertainment we listened to the "buzz bombs" clear our area a couple hundred feet in the air on their way to England. They had those loud noisy ramjet engines aimed at London.

I really don't remember "moving out." But I do remember seeing German troops 500-600 yards away crossing a big field. It was cloudy overhead, and there were P-51s trying to strafe them. They were going in a parallel direction to the road we were on.

Some time later, I remember being in a long column on the side of a long hill in the middle of a convoy. This is where they started to pick off the vehicles with their 88s. They were weird sounding. You heard woom, woom. One woom was the firing and the next was the shell exploding almost simultaneously.

We were captured in the village of Bleilf on December 19. Our situation was quite hopeless. We hadn't been fed for two days, we were out of contact with Division Headquarters, we had no idea where the Germans were, we were low on ammunition, and our long column of Jeeps and trucks was caught on a narrow road with no possibility of maneuver. At that point we ran into a German armored column and it was clear we could go no farther. Our company commander tried to find a way out by a side road but ran into a mine, and we decided that road was no good. We were surrendered by Capt. Foster of Regimental Headquarters.

The word came down that the column had been surrendered. This next incident is my remembrance that some of us were prepared to disable the gun and the truck; however, we were told not to do so. It is also my recollection that someone tried to break his rifle by hitting it on the truck and in doing so the rifle discharged and hit him in the thigh.

Then came confusion.

My next recollection was we were then marched to Limberg and Stalag XII-A, and then loaded into boxcars. I'm not sure how the walk actually started; however, I do remember the WALK. I never received Combat Boots (some problem with size or whatever) and along the walk I was unfortunate enough to get my feet wet. I was trying to get over a small stream that we thought we could jump. Both of my feet were frozen, the right more so than the left. I didn't lose any toes, but I did lose the toenails on two toes. Later I made little booties for my feet as they pained, and I tried to keep them warm when I slept.

I was never a big churchgoer, but I knew how to pray and I did every foot of the way. That spiritual help and the physical help from others in the group when it really got tough enabled me to make it.

A POW photo of Charles McMullen.

The next remembrance is being locked in the boxcars at Limburg during the December 23rd air raid. The boxcar ride to Stalag IV B took eight days. It was cold, especially so after we (the Americans) got approval to remove some of the horse manure from the car at a stop along the way. We city boys didn't realize how many BTU's there were in a pound of horse manure. I remember singing Xmas songs on Xmas evening along the way, and of course, "White Christmas" brought the tears.

My recollection is that we arrived at IVB late at night and that my ID picture was taken about midnight. I obtained this picture later on when the Russians took over at Stalag IIIA. Someone had obtained all of the ID pictures and passed them out. I still have it and my "Kriegie" dog tag. I posed as a non-com and was processed as a non-com and went to a non-com camp.

IVB gave me my first exposure to longtime POWs. The English, Aussies, Canadians, etc. had been prisoners, some for long times, and had learned to adapt and control the situation to the best of their ability. They put on a great New Year's show with music, some guys in drag singing and dancing.

The trip to IIIB is cloudy in my mind. I remember the SS loading us into cars, and I was hit on the head with a rifle butt because the people ahead of me were not moving in fast enough. At IIIB, I remember the dogs being let loose in the compound during air raids. I remember leaving IIIB in a hurry at night about the middle of February. The Russians had moved to the Oder River, and the Germans were going to try and make a stand there. I do remember one of the guards, who looked like "Schultsy" on the TV show. He was a Home Guard, about as old as my grandfather. He stood at the door with tears in his eyes and shook our hand as we left the barracks. I'm not sure if he was sorry to see us leave or that he was sorry he would have to fight the Russians the next day.

The trip to IIIA is also confusing in my mind. As near as I can tell this was a 100-mile walk. I know we walked, but I also seem to remember some time in a boxcar. I remember sleeping in a school one night, another night we slept in an enclosed farmyard and someone stole a glass egg from a chicken's nest. I thought someone was going to be shot over that damn egg. It reappeared, and we went on our way. I remember going through a small village and people lined the road. It was here some of the future German SS in their black Cub Scout uniforms threw sticks and rocks at us and occasionally spit. These were little Cub Scout age kids, the standard knife in their boot and all.

It was on this walk that we passed a column of Jewish prisoners in their flimsy black and white stripe pajama uniforms and wooden shoes, walking in the cold snow on the cobble stone road. The last man in the column would be hit on the back with a switch as they walked along. Since this would take its toll after a while, they exchanged places. A short time after we passed we heard a rifle shot and assumed that one of them had fallen out of line or something comparable.

Finally we got to IIIA, and they had a full house in the barracks. They put up some more wire and enclosed a tent area. They put up seven carnival or circus type tents side-by-side. I think there were 400 to a tent and seven tents. We slept

on the ground and each person had a space about 2' by 6' for his "condo." There was limited water available for the group at the end of the tents, all outdoors. The personal facilities were typical field latrines. This was home

A 1930s-era Polish boxcar from the Holocaust Museum in St. Petersburg, FL. 40 or more POWs would be transported in these vehicles, sometimes for days, usually forced to stand the entire time.

until the end of April. There were the usual potato, ersatz coffee, and a loaf of bread for five or six people. I got so upset one day over arguing which piece of bread was mine that from then on I took the last piece. It couldn't make that much difference, and I became upset with myself for becoming that unrestrained.

As the war progressed and the Allies went to 1000-plane daylight raids, we sat in the open picking lice and counting planes as they passed over. Things went the same each day. Lots of rumors. The Germans would ask, "What are you going to do when you meet the Russians?"

Finally the Russians did come. We went to sleep one night, and in the morning the Germans were gone and the Russians were in the towers.

Charles McMullen, Army 106th Infantry Division, 1944.

Naturally things were confused, and eventually we found out that the Russians would not shoot if you crossed the warning wire. There was no big exodus as we didn't know what was out there. They were feeding us, and there was some control. We heard all sorts of rumors. They were going to hold us hostage, and they were going to ship us to Odessa on the Black Sea, which was the wrong direction from where we wanted to head.

Finally we heard of a link up of Americans and Russians at Torgau. After some discussion, we decided to take off for Torgau. We bundled up our "ciggies" (cigarettes) and away we went. We got about fifteen miles away and were picked up at a Russian checkpoint, then returned to camp. We didn't relish going to Odessa, so we took off again. This time we hailed a 11/2-ton Russian truck, and with the aid of a few "ciggies" the driver let us climb up on top and lay on the canvas between the bows. Not only did we get through the checkpoint, the driver took us to his motor pool where we were fed and spent the night.

The next day we headed for Torgau. We were in our POW clothes, and I had made a "Mickey Mouse" U.S. flag from a handkerchief, red fingernail polish and black ink, and I put this on my arm. It was slow hitchhiking, so that left us to walking in Russian held German territory in a POW uniform looking for the American Army. I had grown a goatee and mustache, and I had lost about 40 pounds, which made my uniform look like it belonged to my big brother. About that time two Germans came along riding bicycles, and we proceeded to confis-cate them.

We rode on down the road and came to a town named Wittenberg where we were hailed by some non-Germans and non-Russians. They were two French couples that had been working in Germany as slave labor and were now trying to get to their home in France. They told us that there was also a link-up at Dessau, and it was supposed to be closer.

The next day in Dessau we saw a couple of GIs in a Jeep. We screamed and hollered and peddled like hell until they finally saw us. Their Colonel had crossed the river to meet with his Russian counter-part and was in a meeting. He finally showed up, and we were on our way home. This was an MP outfit, and they treat-ed us great. This was May 4, 1944. Big Day.

From here things started to move fast. They took us to Hildeschein and put us on C-47s and flew us to Nancy, France. Then the old boxcar trick to Le Harve with deluxe accommodations, only forty people to a boxcar. We spent some time in Camp Lucky Strike to try and put weight on us as fast as possible. I actually saw Gen. Eisenhower and a couple of Congressmen who told us they would get us home as soon as possible, but, "Don't gripe about the accommodations," they said.

I came home on a liberty ship. It took us eight days, and we arrived in the U.S. on June 12. After sixty days at home I reported to Ashville, N.C., at the Biltmore Estate for reassignment. The war in Japan ended while I was there, saving me a scheduled trip to Japan. I was on a tentative list to go as I was five points short of getting out of the Army.

From there to Fort Behaviour in Washington, then to Walter Reed Hospital as an MP until the 5th of December when I was discharged. I went back to Pittsburgh and onto West Virginia Wesleyan College for a BS in Chemistry. I married a great little co-ed fifty years ago in this May, and we have four children and three grandchildren.

WORLD WAR II AS I SAW IT
by Vernon Schmidt

One month from the day I said good-bye to my parents, sister, and girlfriend Dona, I was on the frontline in the infamous Siegfried Line in Germany. It was nighttime as we ferried across the New York harbor to board this huge troop ship. Due to wartime secrecy, we were not told where we were going or on what ship, but as we neared this huge ship I could make out the large letters *Queen Mary* painted on its bow. Rumors were flying as to where we were going, and because we were in our winter O.D's we felt we were headed for Europe. We were 15,000 troops aboard this ship, over five times as many people as lived in my hometown of Reedley, California.

The Atlantic crossing in January was very rough, and this huge ship was tossed like a bottle cork, hence many were seasick all six days. Landing in Glasgow, Scotland, was a relieving sight as land always looked good to me. We boarded a train and headed to Southampton, England, where we boarded another ship, this one being an American troop carrier, and sailed across the English Channel to the city of Le Havre, France. Due to the destruction of the harbor we anchored off shore and rappelled on ropes over the side to waiting landing craft each holding about fifty men. As we approached the beach the huge bow door opened forward and we headed out into the water and walked ashore. From there we went to a huge railroad center where we were fed. After dark we were marched to waiting boxcars, "40 x 8" they were called, from WW I, as those cars carried either forty men or eight horses. We had straw on the floor to help insulate against the cold winter nights, but we soon learned that the snow could sift through the cracks in the walls, so all huddled pretty close to each other.

The train ride to Metz, France, was not very eventful due to the extreme cold weather, and it seemed like we traveled so slow for three days. By the time we reached the replacement depot in Metz many of us were sick with colds and the shakes. At Metz they began to separate us into smaller groups, but we knew nothing and were told nothing. They issued us our weapons and ammunition. At dusk we mounted up on trucks and headed toward Luxembourg and then through Belgium where we crossed the border into Germany at the town of Habcheid. Several of us were lead into a bombed out church where we waited until dark. We could hear our artillery firing volleys overhead into enemy territory. The reality of being up on the front lines hadn't dawned on me until just then. I had just had my nineteenth birthday.

Suddenly some unshaved guy came up and said, "You three guys follow me." By then it was pitch black outside as we walked up the street and out to the edge of town. The guy behind me said, "Hey, I don't see you, where are you?" I told him to grab my belt and follow me as best he could. Our leader told us to be quiet and just follow him. It seemed like we were walking though a pasture as the ground was somewhat rough. Our leader suddenly stopped, and we heard him exchange passwords with a guard. A huge iron door slowly opened and he ushered us inside this German bunker commonly called a pillbox. We were introduced in this dimly lit room to Sgt. Mueller. He said, "Welcome, you are part of E Company, 358th regiment of the 90th infantry division serving under General Patton."

The next morning at 06:00 I learned we were not coming back to this pillbox unless the Germans drove us back. We had tank support our first day, and our objective was to advance through a series of bunkers making certain they were clear of Germans. The cold chilling mornings were fierce, and I recall running up behind one of our tanks to catch the hot exhaust from their big diesel engines. I learned later that tanks are a prime target of the enemy.

Resistance from the Germans was sporadic as we moved slowly eastward through the area of the pillboxes. The Krauts always seemed to know where we stopped for the night and managed to lob mortars into our positions. I recall an incident in early February as our squad was moving up a country road at dusk. Suddenly the clatter of machine guns rattled around us. We hit the dirt on each side of the road. After being pinned down for some time, our squad leader ordered us to move a short distance back into a wooded area and take cover.

We managed to find a number of fox holes, which the Germans had previously used. These usually had covers made from tree logs and covered with dirt, so they kept out the rain and snow but not the cold night air. We took turns being on guard, and no one talked above a whisper. As daylight came our squad formed up. We shook one another in our foxholes to be ready to move out. I don't recall how many GIs were in my foxhole, but one guy wouldn't wake up. Upon a closer check, we found this guy to be a dead German. History says the winter of 1944-1945 was one of the most severe ever. The roads were ankle deep in mud during the afternoons, and during the night would freeze into ruts so hard and rough that walking on them in the early mornings was almost impossible.

The 19th of February was a tragic day for our squad. We were ordered to take the high ground and then report our finding to the captain of E company. We took cover in some trees on the top of this hill. It was apparent the Germans had been here as they had made one fairly secure foxhole. Unknown to us, the Germans had us in perfect view for in just a few minutes they zeroed in on us with an 88 artillery gun and placed several tree bursts right on top of us. My buddy, Roper took a direct hit and was almost decapitated. Another buddy, Wigton, was hit by flying shrapnel over most of his body. He yelled for a medic but slumped over and never moved at all. Our machine gunner was also killed. Several others were injured quite severely. By this time the rest of us were somehow in this lone foxhole. I helped the medic as he tried to patch up one of our guys. A piece of shrapnel had taken part of the calf of his leg off and another piece had torn part of his boot and took the heel off his foot.

With three out of twelve guys killed and several wounded, we were down to a skeleton group to carry on. The sergeant told me to go back down the hill and get the captain. That really wasn't something I would volunteer for, but I crawled out of the foxhole and grabbed my M-1 and scurried down the side of this hill.

I hadn't gone very far when I heard one of those "Screaming Meemies" coming toward me. These were a series of six rockets that fired one after the other with a few seconds delay. We had learned by trial and error how to respect these. If the first rocket landed beyond you, the following five would keep landing beyond you, also. I heard the buzzing of the first as it passed over my head while I lay prone on the ground. Just to be sure, I heard the second one whiz by over my head, so I got brave in a hurry and ran down the hill as the remaining four kept coming. The siren sound of these are enough to terrorize you. I finally reached the captain who was waiting in a barn. I remember how he bawled me out because my M-1 was covered with mud. I never did like him after that incident and was happy the day we learned he was relieved of commanding E Co. Things got a little better as the month of February moved on.

We continued to move eastward, and by March we had pretty well broken through the Seigfried line. This barrier was built on Hitler's orders in 1939 and, according to him, this would be the western wall to keep the enemy out of his Fatherland. He failed to take into account the tenacity of the American G.I.

DACHAU
by Ellis Anderson

There is a side of life that is so vile that most people not only turn away from it but try resolutely to put it out of their minds and memories. Witness those misguided souls who claim that the Holocaust never happened except in some propagandist's mind. Sure, all that was sixty years ago now, before most people living today were born. Couple that with the fact that at the time the German government censored any mention of what went on in their concentration camps and conducted their actions in secrecy.

Of course, German officers and soldiers were seen herding Jews onto trains to be taken away, but the general impression was that they were simply being relocated as a result of the war effort. After all, this plus a desire not to become involved was a lot easier to accept than the admission that their government was engaged in anything as heinous as the extermination of a people—simply because they adhered to a different religion.

When our outfit entered Dachau, bodies were neatly stacked in piles like cordwood, poor devils who had starved to death. They were nothing but skeletons with skin stretched over the bones. From the remaining survivors we learned about what had been going on as our medics fed them sparingly on easily digested food (too much food in their shriveled up stomachs would kill them).

The gates to the notorious death camp stood wide open as we approached. And why not? Nobody inside was going anywhere. They were nothing but skin and bones. Army medics spoon-fed them with a nurturing gruel. Those who were able to walk were returned to their homes when possible.

To your left as you entered was a building with a small window in the end above a tractor-like seat. A series of knobs below the window provoked curiosity. Shortly we were approached by an individual who had no signs of starvation like the other inmates. He explained that because he had performed special duties as the furnace attendant, he was allowed a normal diet. How much truth there was to his story there was no way of telling, but when he offered to be our guide we readily accepted.

He took us first to that building on our left, which turned out to be an execution building. Newly-arrived people were brought to the building and told that they were to take a shower here. They were to disrobe and shower, and told that their clothes would be cleaned and pressed and returned to them. Huge hampers on wheels were provided in which the discarded clothing was to be placed. Indeed, in the ceiling, one could readily see the nozzles of the showers. What happened, of course, was that a guard, seated on the tractor-like seat on the outskirts of the building watched through the one-way window, and when everyone was properly washed the gas was turned on. When everyone was down, the gas was turned off, the ventilators turned on and, when it was safe, the doors opened and the bodies removed.

The next building we visited was the crematory. Our guide took us downstairs to the furnace. There it was with a zinc chute—like a coal chute—aimed at the door. He explained that bodies of deceased prisoners were placed on the chute and examined for items of value. Gold teeth were knocked out; rings were removed, if necessary by cutting off the finger. The body was then cremated. The ashes were added to the pile on the floor to the left of the furnace.

In order not to waste anything, if the deceased had any living relatives and the camp had a record of them, they would receive a "We regret to inform you" letter which would explain that the individual had passed away due to some innocuous disease or accident—never mentioning that he had been starved to death! The letter mentioned that the body had been cremated and if the relative wished, his ashes would be shipped to them upon payment of a certain amount. In the event that the money was paid, a shovel full was taken from that pile by the furnace and sent to the relative.

The survivors told us incredible stories: men having slim glass tubes inserted up their penis and then the penis squeezed to shatter the tube so that each time he urinated the acidic urine would cause excruciating pain. These sadistic German guards seemed preoccupied with the male sexual apparatus. Another pleasant game was to spread-eagle a naked man on a fence. One of the guards would then beat him around the genitals until he bled at which time a pair of specially trained dogs would be turned loose to tear and chew off his genitals.

No sooner had we entered the camp than some of the G.I.s (as they always did) went scrounging for souvenirs. In a desk drawer they found three negatives. A quick trip over to the photo recon outfit nearby and the photos were developed with enough copies so that everyone could have a set. The first of these pictures showed a man, obviously a prisoner, naked except for his socks, being conducted down a corridor by two uniformed guards.

The second picture showed him with his private parts tightly wound with tape and hanging from the ceiling by a chain with a hook through his genitals. The third picture showed him hanging there dead.

These pictures I eventually turned over to a Jewish organization here in Fresno. Unfortunately, they are not the people who need to be educated about these things.

STORIES
FROM THE
HOME FRONT

THE HOME FRONT

After the bombing of Pearl Harbor by Japan, Americans united in patriotism, volunteering for military service, creating various civic organizations to help the war effort, planting Victory Gardens, and willingly enduring the rationing of numerous items, including sugar, coffee, cigarettes, gasoline, nylon (for parachutes), and many other materials. Many volunteered for neighborhood and regional security efforts. Memorably, blue, silver, and gold stars placed strategically in windows communicated (respectively) that a family member served in the military, was wounded in action, or had paid the ultimate sacrifice in service to his country. These stars became a visual source of immense pride and shared sorrow.

On the industrial front, U.S. manufacturing plants and resources were converted to produce the tools of war. An astounding quantity of planes, ships, tanks, ordinance, and munitions were manufactured as America transformed into the "Arsenal of Democracy." Women played a critical role in the effort on the home front, flocking to industry as men left for war. "Rosie the Riveter's" hard work at home was integral to America's success on distant battlefields.

WAR AND DAD

by Maude Norris

My first nineteen-and-a-half years of life revolved around the military. I was raised a Navy brat for eighteen-and-a-half years; then I was married to a U.S. Marine for the next fourteen months until his hardship discharge from the corps. In those days a Navy officer's daughter marrying an enlisted Marine was considered a no-no.

When World War II broke out I was only eleven-and-a-half years old. December 7, 1941, the day the Japanese bombed Pearl Harbor, was a nice warm Sunday morning, and I was playing jacks on the front porch with a girlfriend of mine. Around twelve noon a group of Shore Patrolmen from the San Diego Naval Base and Military Policemen from the Marine Corps Depot (SP and MP as they were called) came up the streets telling us to have our fathers report to their duty stations as war had broken out with Japan. We were living in San Diego, right across from the Marine Corps Base. In 1941 it was known as Gate 3. I remember going into the house and telling Dad what the SPs had told us, and I came close to being punished because Dad thought I was joking. I told him to turn on the radio, and there it was telling about the sneak attack on Pearl Harbor, Hawaii. Dad reported to duty, and we didn't see him for over seventy-two hours. I wasn't sure where the Hawaiian Islands were at that time, nor did I really realize the implication of the attack.

Dad left for overseas duty in the Pacific on July 13, 1942. He came home once during the long period of 1942 to 1946, and that was during the Christmas holidays in December 1943. Even that was cut short as he was ordered back to the west coast to report for another overseas duty assignment. We did see him around 1944 when

Hubert Arnold Blankinship, Sr., in Navy uniform.

Maude Norris' father, Hubert Arnold Blankinship, Sr., on the USS Cheleb (far right).

his ship docked in Port Hueneme, California, but he did not come back home until June 1946.

A clear memory I have was on one day, after Dad came home from the war, we were sitting down to dinner in our home on Midvale Avenue, in West Los Angeles, and a car backfired outside our house. My father jumped from his chair at the head of the table and ducked under the table. Of course, we all laughed, but it wasn't funny to him. I know we upset him that day very much. That was one of the few times he did mention how he thought he would have to abandon his ship three different times due to Kamikaze attacks. I believe the name of the ship he was referring to was the USS *Cheleb*.

Dad was the paymaster for a large area when he was overseas. Somewhere I have a receipt for the amount of money he was responsible for. I think it was about

$6,000,000. He would fly to the different islands and board certain ships and pay the servicemen. I believe that is why he was on Espartos Santos for about thirteen or more months. I know he was supposed to have landed at Guadalcanal, but due to the battle going on at the time they diverted the ship to Espartos Santos. I heard Dad telling Mum about how he was in the outhouse one night, on the island of Espartos Santos, and he bent over to pick up the roll of toilet paper that had dropped to the floor when he heard a bullet wheeze over his head. If he hadn't bent down the bullet would have gotten him in the area of his throat.

Mum would get very upset when the mail was slow in getting to her. Years later Mum told me she always knew approximately the area where Dad was. Before Dad left, they had marked a global map into sections, and he would be able to tell her by that map what section he was in. In their early days of marriage Mum had taught Dad Pippin Shorthand. They stopped teaching it in the Massachusetts school in 1926, the year Mother graduated from high school. Dad was very proficient in Pippin, and he would scribble it on different sections of the paper. Mum was able to decipher by the number on the letter and scribbles in the letter approximately where he was. They would number the envelope so they could keep track of each other's letters. It never ceased to amaze me how Mum could write a specific question, and she would receive an answer to that question in Dad's next letter before he had received her letter with the question she was asking him. To the best of my knowledge, I don't think the censors ever caught on to what they were doing.

There were several more close calls that I heard him talking to Mum about, but he never talked to the five of us kids about anything that happened to him during the war. Of course, they did not know I was listening, and I would have been in deep trouble if they found out. The Armed Services now have realized that the men and women are under stress when they are fighting and each person reacts differently to a buddy's death, bombing of their ship, or an aircraft shot down. If the military had had Critical Incident Stress Disorder after World War II, maybe my parents might have stayed together. Both Mum and Dad could have used their services to talk out the problems they had while separated from one another.

Dad was an officer at the end of World War II, and if he had put himself into the hospital for war nerves his career in the U.S. Navy would have been over. I know Dad was very proud that he was a Mustanger in the Navy. A "Mustang" is someone who has come up the ranks as an enlisted man to become an officer.

I know it wasn't all bad from the stories he told about visiting USO entertainers and being able to see first-run movies. Dad wasn't any kind of a hero. He was just doing his job like many other servicemen, and all he wanted was to get home to his family. I did notice that when Dad came home for good he seemed more solemn and, to a degree, a bit more understanding of us with our problems of growing up.

ON THE HOME FRONT
by W.E. Burgstaller

The battle on the home front started before the cowardly attack on Pearl Harbor by Japan. The German invasion of Poland in September 1939 was the beginning of the heartbreak and worry for millions of people across the nation. Hitler started it. Then Great Britain, France, Australia, New Zealand and Canada pounced on him with guts, determination and staying power. That's when the worry started.

The war raged into the forties and was flashed on newsreels in every movie house. It seemed like every country in Europe was involved. When Pathe News showed the first shots of the air wars over Britain in July 1940, a fresh patriotic chord was struck among our youth. They volunteered by thousands to join the British Royal and the Canadian Royal Air Forces. Young men who didn't share their interest in flying joined the U.S. Army, Navy, Marine Corps and Merchant Marine.

In the grocery store where I worked as a delivery boy we could see the worry on the faces of mothers every day. Most didn't have any boys in the service yet, but they were of the age to join or be drafted, when and if needed.

In September the first draftee's number was selected from a goldfish bowl. The selection process started, and many young men in the neighborhood were affected. Suddenly they started to leave. Many were draftees. Jack, the nineteen-year-old National guardsman next door was called into the Army. Mr. Logsdon, my friend's father, suddenly appeared in a Navy Petty Officer's uniform. But only for a few days, then he was gone. James "Dick" Ward, a recent high school graduate, and Billy Welch, a senior in my sister's class, both joined the Navy along with many others in our small town. But it was happening thousands of times across the nation.

Some of the sources of relief and entertainment were local sporting events. The games, festivities, marching bands and roaring crowds were a welcome respite every Sunday afternoon from September to December.

It was a good year for the Irish, our football team, that adopted Notre Dame's fight song. This was going to be the last game of the year. It was a bright, sunny day, but a cold breeze whipped through the stadium, chilled ears and cheeks, and forced spectators to turn up their collars. The band played a rousing fight song, and the crowd was excited about leading more than half way through the fourth quarter.

Suddenly, an announcement boomed over the public address system: "Ladies and gentlemen! Ladies and gentlemen, your attention, please." Another repeat finally quieted the crowd. "We have just received a news bulletin that the Japanese attacked Pearl Harbor! I repeat. We have just received a bulletin that the Japanese attacked our fleet at Pearl Harbor!"

Stillness blanketed the stadium like a sudden fog.

Whistling wind suddenly became apparent as voices dropped to whispers of disbelief. They stood in shock even though most did not know where Pearl Harbor was located. After a long break, the game was restarted. But the enthusiasm had evaporated, and some spectators slowly departed the stadium. Cheers of victory and the usual applause didn't materialize when the game ended. The stadium emptied quickly as the crowd rushed home to hear the news on their radios.

The next day, President Roosevelt addressed the nation with his "Day of Infamy" speech to rally the country. Then Germany declared war on the United States.

Within several days casualty lists started to arrive. Billy Welch was on the sunken *Arizona*, Dick Ward was aboard the sunken *Oklahoma*. Our first casualties. Cousin Freddie was aboard the cruiser *Helena* when it was badly damaged. He survived the attack and traveled with the ship back to drydock in the United States.

Factories were retooled for wartime around-the-clock production. Male workers gradually started to leave for military assignments. Women stepped forward and filled the worker void. Grandmothers filled in as babysitters for daughters on production lines. Buses and streetcars were busy twenty-four hours a day and always crowded at transfer points. Restaurants were busy all night to accommodate shift workers and members of the military who started arriving and departing at all hours of the day and night.

Shortages resulted in rationing. Everybody needed ration booklets to purchase foods and things that we had forever taken for granted. Meat, fatty foods, fish, dairy products, cigarettes, coffee, fuel oil, gasoline, sugar and chocolate were some of the rationed items. Anything made of metal, nylon, or rubber made the list, plus hundreds of other items that were not rationed but were always in short supply.

Parents hung small cloth banners with stars in their front windows to show they had a son or daughter in the service. A blue star indicated a service person, a silver meant one was missing in action or taken prisoner, and gold for one killed in action. Mothers' stars were a sign of pride and respect. Some homes had them at first, then many, then almost all of them. They changed often, too often, as more stars were added, and some were changed to silver or gold. Both Billy

Welch's and Dick Ward's stars were changed to gold after Pearl Harbor. Dick was awarded the Medal of Honor posthumously for remaining in his turret and guiding other crewmembers to safety with a flashlight.

Families had a very difficult time, but I thought mothers suffered the most. Maybe it was because I saw them more often in the grocery stores and talked to them when making deliveries. It bothered me when I'd deliver to a home and see the banner now displayed a gold or silver star, or the number of stars increased to two, three, or four. I knew one family with five stars in the window, and two of them were later changed to silver and gold.

The Western Union Telegraph boy became a dreaded sight in a neighborhood, delivering the fateful message that someone had been killed, wounded or was missing in action. They were becoming more numerous around the city as they whizzed down streets to deliver the shocking news. Sometimes at night they'd have to ring their bell for a pedestrian or a stray dog or cat to get out of their way. Many people were startled by the sound, but greatly relieved when their doorbell did not ring.

Our staff of five clerks started to decrease immediately after Pearl Harbor and were replaced by older women. The younger ones were desperately needed in defense plants. By 1943 the manager, a deferred family man who ran the meat department, and I were the only male employees left. The four women and I ran the grocery department. They were very nice ladies who had sons, daughters, in-laws or husbands away in the war.

At the urging of a neighbor boy who worked the late shift in a defense plant, I applied for work there. They wanted me to start working that night, but I declined in order to give the store manager time to hire a replacement. I started the next Monday as a janitor in one of the many machine shops.

There were more than 2,000 employees in two buildings that operated around-the-clock. With a few exceptions, most of them were women. The rest were men either too young or too old for the service. I was impressed with everybody's friendliness and attitude. Almost everyone had worries about the raging conflicts that involved their loved ones.

There were ten lathes in my area of responsibility, operated by women wearing aprons over slacks, bandanas, goggles and gloves. All were very sharp, reliable, dedicated individuals who worked as hard as anybody in the factory.

My job was to sweep up the metal shavings and haul them to another area for salvage.

In three weeks, I was switched to trucker, someone who trucks components to the lathes in huge bins, then trucks them away after the lathing process had been completed. A month later I became a stock chaser, a person who locates the various components, completes the necessary paper work, then directs the trucker where to deliver them.

This job spread my work area over several departments where women performed every job. They were welders, furnace tenders, assemblers, wirers, inspectors and dozens of various machine operators. They hunched over benches, loaded furnaces, operated machines and kept assembly lines moving.

The shift bell rang at 11:30 P.M. Hundreds of workers emptied into the streets like ants, then patiently waited for seats on buses vacated by incoming workers. The factory continued to hum throughout the night with a new shift, as workers on my shift returned to their homes. They were always tired and eager to get home but worried about what news awaited them and the thought of hearing that dreaded bicycle bell during the night.

I stayed on for three more months and joined the service the week of my seventeenth birthday. The depot was filled to capacity with men and women in uniform, departing and arriving among a throng of people who came to see someone off or to welcome someone back. My group of enlistees looked out of place. Mostly my age, a few friends and acquaintances in an array of civilian clothing, whiskered or baby-faced, with long hair and looks of apprehension. We were en route to Cincinnati for swearing in, then off to boot camp in South Carolina.

But we shared a good feeling, and were thankful that the home front was in such capable hands.

THE WAR YEARS
by Nina York Coon

I always had a job from the time I was thirteen years old. I worked as a "mother's helper" in the home of a Jewish family. I baby-sat with the children three days after school and every other Sunday, and on Saturdays helped with the housework for $10.00 a month. At the age of fifteen I worked part-time at the Boys Market in the candy department and then later at the Farmers Market in the produce department. By that time the war had started, and all the men had joined the service, so the women had to do all the work, including heavy lifting. I went with a soldier whose uncles owned the Boys Market. I also dated a sailor, and when I graduated from high school, my boyfriend was a marine. He gave me a watch for graduation, and he was so handsome in his dress marine uniform. I think all the girls were in love with the uniforms.

During the War the hotels in Pasadena were used as command headquarters and for a convalescent hospital, and the Rose Bowl was used to house servicemen. Cal Tech and the Jet Propulsion Laboratory became the focal points for research and development. I remember when the Pasadena Freeway was built in 1940, the

first freeway in the West. By that time my mother had remarried and my brother and sister came to live with us. My brother soon found a job at the shipyards while he was going to high school. Everyone wanted to help with the war effort, so even my mother worked in a defense factory, pulling cells off tires, which was very hard work. She suffered with arthritis in her hands years later.

I found a job at a defense factory, the D.B. Milliken Company, a supplier of aeronautical parts. We inspected rivets

Nina Coon as a young girl in Pasadena, California.

which were swept up off the floors of all the airplane factories across the country, such as Boeing, Douglas, and Lockheed. We were the only company in the country that did this sort of work. As the rivets came down on two wires they were upright, and we would take out the damaged ones and push along the good ones. We were required to work fast as we were on a production line, and that is the only job I had ever had where I had to punch a time clock. The good rivets were washed and dried, and the bad ones were washed, melted down and made into new ones. Then they were all sent back to the airplane factories and to Rosie the Riveter. We didn't waste anything in those days, and we recycled what we could. I started wearing glasses when I worked there because of eyestrain from such close work.

I thought about joining the service and realized that I was too young, but I think I helped the war effort in other ways. My brother also wanted to join, but he was classified 4-F due to a hernia. After the war he had surgery, joined the Army, and was in the medical corps. He was stationed at Hudson Bay, Canada. He was "Sergeant York," but not that famous one from World War I.

During the war there was rationing of many items such as gasoline, fuel oil, meat, sugar and butter. Since I worked at grocery stores I was usually able to purchase anything I wanted. I even sent many items such as tea bags, candy, chewing gum, soap, etc., to my penpal in Bristol, England, since it was even more difficult for the British to acquire such items. My penpal and I have been writing to each other since 1942, and I finally met her in person in 1995 on a tour of Great Britain.

I was in Dallas during V-J Day, August 14, 1945, so I rode the streetcar to downtown Dallas, the same route my father used when he worked at the First National Bank. I was in the midst of all the laughter, excitement and elation because the war had ended. All the servicemen were kissing and hugging all the girls, and we were all filled with ecstasy.

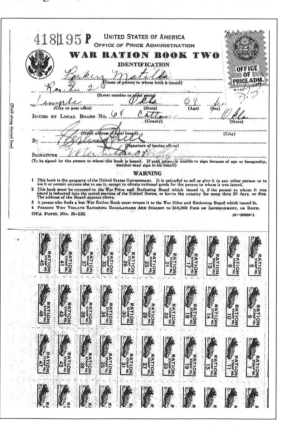

War rations certificate and coupons used to buy food, gasoline and other goods.

SHIPYARDS

by Thelma Wyman

During World War II, Henry J. Kaiser opened three shipyards in Richmond, California. He contracted to build Liberty Ships and rushed to complete them on schedule.

My husband Claude and a friend, Fats Reeves, met in Tulsa, Oklahoma, while training to be machinists. They completed the course and received their first nickel pay increase. They now earned 55 cents an hour.

They heard a rumor workers were needed in California and beginner's pay was 90 cents an hour. Fats said he would drive his 1938 Dodge sedan if Claude would go with him and share expenses. They planned to find work and send for their families. Judy and I moved home with our parents and waited to hear from them. I was expecting our second baby and didn't think I would be able to travel.

They found work right away in Richmond, California, at Kaiser Shipyard Number Two. Barracks-type buildings were erected to provide housing. A commuter train transported workers down Cutting Boulevard from San Francisco to Point Richmond. Claude rented a three-room furnished apartment for $34 a month from the Richmond housing authority.

I arrived by train with our seventeen-month-old daughter, Claudette, one month before I gave birth to another little girl. She was born in Richmond Hospital October, 1942. We named her Rita Darlene Pritchett. I breast-fed my baby for nine months. Soon after I weaned her, some neighbor women met in the laundry room and told of going to a hiring hall at Ninth and Nevin, in downtown Richmond. My next-door neighbor got a job as a welder.

She told me, "Thelma, why don't you go down? I'm sure you can get on." I was twenty-one years old and had never worked outside of my home. They were hiring laborers to push a broom, and I had done tons of that.

An elderly neighbor offered to come in and baby-sit for me. When Claude came home from work, I was excited when I told him what I wanted to do. He didn't want me to work a graveyard shift or in the double bottoms, but if I could get on days and work under decent conditions, he wouldn't object.

Monday morning I stood in line at the hiring hall. When my turn came, the Personnel Manager told me they were hiring twenty women as an experiment for the Pipefitting Department. I would work for a crew as Material Expediter. My pay would be 90 cents an hour, on day shift, in Shipyard Number Three. They required me to wear sensible shoes, long pants, and my hair tied in a bandana or hairnet under a hard hat.

The next morning, I walked two blocks to a train stop. A crowd gathered around a snack bar. I bought me a cup of coffee and stood shivering in the early morning air. When the train pulled up, I rushed to get on board. It was packed, standing room only. I grabbed for a leather strap overhead and held on. I carried a sack lunch and reported at the main gate to have my picture made for a pass. Then I was sent to the Pipefitting Department to be assigned to a crew.

A superintendent named Bill Walsh looked us over and picked me for his crew. He had one foreman, three leader men, and a crew of thirty men. I went with him to a change shack on the outfitting dock. He showed me how to keep the time cards, requisition slips for materials, and how to check out safety equipment for the men. One of the men told me why Bill Walsh picked me for this job. He was twenty-eight years old, a blond red-faced Mormon from Salt Lake City, Utah. I wore the least make-up and had a clean-cut look. Our crew ran the copper tubing to the mechanical cow (which mixed the powdered milk), connected air to the whistle, and put in all of the handrails.

At the Transportation Department I checked out a flat bed truck and driver, rode with him to the pipe yard, and picked up needed handrails. If the crane operator was tied up, a forklift unloaded the pipe on the doc, and it could lay there for two days. I made a friend of the rigger. When he saw me, he lifted my pipe from the truck bed right up on deck. Seldom did the men in my crew stand around waiting for materials.

At the welders' shack men waited to be assigned needed welders until nine o'clock sometimes. When the foreman saw me, he said, "How many do you need today, Thelma?"

I said, "Three." Our crews started to work at eight o'clock.

In the bathroom one Friday morning several expediters gathered together and shared their bad news. They each held layoff slips. They asked if I had got mine, and I told them, "No." They said, "Well, you will because they closed down the whole department." It was experimental and didn't work out.

Bill stopped me on the dock and asked how I liked my job and if I was thinking about quitting. I said, "No, I want to work." His boss was out of town, and he had my layoff slip. He took it on himself to hold it until Monday morning. He asked to have me transferred into his crew. I joined the union and became a card-carrying pipe fitter. I received my pay raises and soon made $1.20 an hour.

One morning, Bill and I stopped on the dock to look over the time book. I held the book with one hand, and he took hold of the other page. A seagull flew over and made a deposit that splattered my thumb. Bill turned beet red in the face, turned and walked away.

I loved to hear a good joke and have told a few. Everybody told "Okie" jokes. My sister-in-law told me, "Thelma, don't you know they're laughing at you?" I said, "No, they aren't. They are laughing with me." If the truth be known, they couldn't have built those ships without the "Okies," "Arkies," and women.

LIFE ON THE HOME FRONT—WORLD WAR II
by Aileen Bos

Aileen Wells Bos in Kingsburg, California.

My parents, four brothers, sister, and I lived in the Riverbend area just three and one-half miles southwest of Kingsburg, California. I was thirteen, and Gerald was fifteen on that fateful day of Sunday, December 7, 1941, when the Japanese attacked Pearl Harbor. We were riding horses at my Uncle Davis' place in the country. As we returned to the barn, parked in the yard was a car with radio blaring full blast. Family members were gathered around, listening intently to the excited voice of the speaker. Their faces were grim, and some looked incredulous. It was the following day when the full impact settled in as we heard President Franklin D. Roosevelt announce, "We are at war, this is a date that will live in infamy."

Our family meals were usually filled with conversation and laughter, but now my parents sat stoned-faced, and we all listened for the noise of aircraft overhead. My father was adamant about protecting his family, and volunteered after long working hours in the fields to act as an air warden on watch at the makeshift lookout in the evenings. Sometimes he took my brothers and me along, and we all studied the charts, noting the outlines of American and enemy aircraft.

On January 14th President Roosevelt authorized the transfer of more than 10,000 Japanese-Americans living in the coastal Pacific to internment camps in various inland areas, resulting in many losing their homes and property. Several of the farmers in the Riverbend area watched after their Japanese neighbors' farms for the duration. My two best school friends were Pearl Kubota and Michiko Shiine. We waved a tearful farewell to them at the Kingsburg Legion Hall as they boarded the buses with their families to go we knew not where.

Concern for helping the cause, plus the nagging fear of his four sons being drawn into the war, were prime factors in my parents' decision to move to Carmichael, outside of Sacramento. They began work in the Sacramento Air Depot at McClellan Field. Dad worked with the crew who cleaned motors and parts of aircraft by dropping them into large vats of cleaning solvent. Mom was a

"Rosie the Riveter," actually working on the fuselage and outer surfaces of the planes. They worked the swing shift. Therefore, being the oldest girl, I was responsible for getting everyone up and ready for school.

My brother and I belonged to a teenage church group in Carmichael. We pooled our resources, and luckily one member was of age to drive us in his car to a turkey hatchery nearby where we worked in the evenings candling eggs. Occasionally we had an evening at the roller rink in North Sacramento. The war was always on our minds as we observed the rationing of gasoline, butter, Crisco, and nylons, saving the green stamps and walking to spare the driving when possible. Stark realism to our teenage world occurred when members of our group left for service. Then, we learned about V-mails.

On February 7, 1943, shoe rationing began limiting civilians to three pairs of leather shoes per year, and meat rationing allowing 28 ounces per week. Then fats, canned goods, and cheese were rationed. We shared fresh tomatoes and vegetables with our neighbors from our "Victory Garden," and took advantage of leftover harvest in the fields, gleaning the fruit for canning. The May 29, 1943, cover of the *Saturday Evening Post* featured Norman Rockwell's interpretation of "Rosie the Riveter" as an American icon. Anti-black race riots broke out in Detroit, then later in Harlem and New York City. Gold star banners began to appear in windows, noting the lives of loved ones lost in the battles.

One day Mom returned home from work alone, announcing that Dad was in the hospital. The fumes from the cleaning vats had overcome him, and his already weak lungs could not handle the pressure. His job was through.

We moved back to the Central Valley to Reedley. Dad hoped that a farm venture might delay Gerald's entry into the service. We were juniors at Reedley High in 1943-44. Zealous Reedley High students met weekly for bond rallies. Only two or three young men attended Reedley College meetings on the high school campus, for most of the eligible young men had gone to war.

In the summer of 1944, brother Gerald was drafted into the Army, leaving for training at Camp Roberts, then assigned to Fort Bragg, North Carolina, for artillery training.

In April 1945 my brother's unit gathered at Fort Ord in California to ship out. Shortly after his nineteenth birthday in July, Gerald boarded the USS *C.G. Morton* troop ship with his 222nd Field Artillery Battalion, 40th Division. It took a month zigzagging across the water to avoid submarine attacks. They unloaded prisoners overnight in New Guinea, and then proceeded to Panay in the Philippines.

Because he knew how to type, he was assigned to the clerk's office. Not liking the desk job, he volunteered for bodyguard duty. He recalls the maneuver with the Marine Division for a diversionary invasion four or five days before the actual scheduled invasion of Japan. They were told eighty-percent casualties of American troops were expected. He was dressed in full gear climbing down the nets to the LST to head for the shore, when they received word Japan had surrendered.

On August 14, 1945, after Japan surrendered, shrill whistles blew, horns honked and voices filled the air with shouts. We wept with joy. President Truman declared August 14th V-J Day.

Besides my brother Gerald, my younger brothers each served in three separate branches of the military: Air Force, Coast Guard, and National Guard. My first husband was a Navy man, and our eldest son served with the Air Force 72nd Air Refueling Squadron in Desert Storm. My husband, Gene Bos, was a Navy man. He was discharged as an Electricians Mate, Third Class on October 6, 1947.

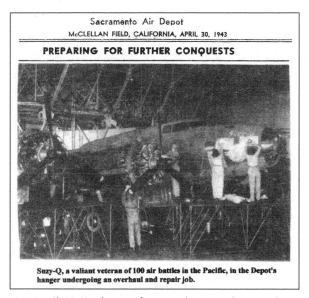

Sacramento Air Depot
McCLELLAN FIELD, CALIFORNIA, APRIL 30, 1943

PREPARING FOR FURTHER CONQUESTS

Suzy-Q, a valiant veteran of 100 air battles in the Pacific, in the Depot's hanger undergoing an overhaul and repair job.

An April 1943 photo of a warplane under repair at the Sacramento Air Depot, McClellan Field, CA.

JAPANESE-AMERICANS AND THE WAR

In 1942, with war tensions running high, President Franklin D. Roosevelt authorized the internment of some 90,000 people of Japanese ancestry with Executive Order 9066. With their lands and belongings confiscated, they were moved to interments camps throughout the country. Most were eventually released in 1944 and 1945.

Ironically, during this time several thousand Japanese-Americans went to war in the distinguished 442nd Infantry Regimental Combat Team, consisting at first of volunteers from the United States mainland and Hawaii. This unit became the most-decorated in the U.S. Army's history for its size. 18,000 total awards were earned, including 9,500 Purple Hearts, fifty-two Distinguished Service Crosses, seven Distinguished Unit Citations, and twenty-two Congressional Medals of Honor.

MY HERO

by Carolyn Tanaka
(excerpts from Katherine Baishiki/ George T. Ohama)

My cousin Abraham Ohama was a member of the famed F Company, 442nd Regimental Combat Team, who was killed in action in the bitter fighting along the French/Italian border. Abraham Jiro Ohama was born on June 1, 1916, in Guadalupe, California, to Kunzo and Hanako Ohama. Abraham's family moved to Sanger, California, where Abe graduated from Sanger High in 1935. After graduation Abraham worked for Round Mountain Citrus Company for two years and then worked for Guadalupe Produce Co. in Guadalupe until the second round of drafts, during which time he was inducted into the Army (Serial No. 39 227 865) on February 23, 1941, at Los Angeles. He received his basic training at Fort Lewis, Washington.

On the morning of December 7, 1941, Japan bombed Pearl Harbor, and things changed. Abraham's family was sent to Poston Camp in Arizona. Abraham wrote letters to his brother George in which he said, "Let's pray for peace and victory." Abraham was eventually sent to Camp Crowder, Missouri. After training for a month at Camp Crowder, Abraham was selected to train new recruits. From there Abraham was sent to Camp Shelby in Mississippi. He was given a furlough to be the best man at his brother George's wedding. It was during this visit to the Poston Camp that he told the group, "All of us can't stay in these camps until the end of the war. Some of us have to go to the front. The record on the battlefields will determine when we will get to go home. I don't know if I'll make it back." Then he went back to Camp Shelby for more training and soon to go overseas with the 442nd.

He was a great inspiration to his men of F Company, and often exposed himself to danger. Abe, in his calm manner, would walk up and down the foxholes talking to his men. One of their many exploits was the rescue of the lost Texas battalion in the Vosges Mountains. Placing his men under cover, he crawled to within twenty yards of the enemy and threw two hand grenades, which neutralized a machine gun nest. When another machine gun opened fire on him he momentarily silenced it with his machine gun, and then completely put it out with hand grenades.

Subsequently, when a comrade was wounded and left exposed to further injury, he disregarded enemy sniper fire to go to his aid, and as he reached the fallen man's side was himself mortally wounded. When news of how their leader had given his life reached the men of his company, they launched an attack, stormed the slopes and overran the top, killing 125 of the enemy and capturing twenty. Through Abe's efforts, the rifle company captured Hill 503, and later were credited with stabilizing the entire battalion sector east of Bruyeres, France.

Abe knew he was going to his death, so he told his Sergeant, Jack Wakamatsu, "I'm not coming out of this mission alive, so I want you to promise me that when the war is over, you will write a book about what we are doing here in Europe because it is an important part of America's history." Jack wrote the book *Silent Warriors*, and cousin Abraham Ohama is mentioned throughout it.

Abe was sort of a hero before he went off to war. Once he came across an automobile accident on Highway 99. He extricated the driver from the blazing auto and saved his life. He is the reason all my able-bodied cousins, my three brothers, and I served in the military in a war.

T/Sgt Abraham Ohama was killed in action on October 20, 1944, during the Battle of Bruyeres and was awarded the Purple Heart, Silver Star, and Combat Infantryman's Badge. He is buried at Centerville Cemetery in Sanger, California.

INTERNMENT

by Carolyn Tanaka

I remember being boarded on a train almost in the middle of the night, like cattle going to slaughter. We were packed like sardines in a can to standing room
only capacity. The train stopped in the middle of the desert. We were allowed to
disembark under the watchful eyes of the guards to stretch our cramped legs, use
the restroom, and be given salt tablets to endure the heat of the desert. When we
arrived in Parker, Arizona, we were transferred to Army buses for the next leg to
Poston, Camp III, still in the middle of the night. We saw barbed wired fences all
around the camp, and MPs with rifles watching our every move. We were told we
were going to the camp for our protection. Then why were the rifles pointed
inward in our direction, rather than outward at our perimeter?

Upon arriving at our block, 307, everyone's belongings were piled in a heap in
the middle of the block. We had to go, flashlights in hand, in search of our pieces
of luggage. When we finally got to our room in Building 3, Room C, a tar-
papered barrack, we found dust everywhere, straw to stuff our mattresses, and
army cots on which to sleep. Six of us lived in a room about 20x30 feet with no
provisions for privacy. There were no fans or coolers, only a pot bellied wood
burning stove in the middle of the room for the cold desert nights. Our address
for the next three years would be 307, 3-C, Poston, Arizona.

Mom did the best she could and strung sheets up to provide some semblance
of privacy. Even in those desperate times, the community pulled together.
Everyone's talent was put to use. A block manager form of government evolved
within this community. Schools were built. Anyone with teaching experience
became our teachers. My teacher in the second grade was Mr. Carl Yoshimine. He
was tall and lanky, and very handsome. Only one person was better looking, I
thought. That was the student sitting next to me. His name was Akira. I think I
fell in love at first sight.

One hot day I decided to raise the upper case window in the classroom. Being
the tomboy that I was, I climbed up on the back of my chair to reach the window.
It was stuck so I gave it a jerk. In so doing, I fell off my perch. I landed straddling
the back of the chair. I got a big bruise and started bleeding from my labia. We
had no doctors in Camp III, so mother took me by Army vehicle to Camp I, cross-

ing Camp II to get there. I don't know how many miles we traveled. That injury gave me a left inguinal hernia which I kept until I joined the Army in 1966.

Since there was no farming in Poston, Dad got a job in construction to help build the schools. He was good with tools. One day, however, he got his index finger in the way of a power saw and whacked the tip of it off. The injury ended his carpentry job. Prior to his injury, Dad brought home pieces of scrap lumber and made bunk beds for the two older boys. That saved needed floor space.

During our last year in camp, Dad went in search of work. He traveled as far as Chicago on the train, passing himself off as a Mexican to avoid being spat upon and called a Jap. He was dark skinned and spoke fluent Spanish, so he had no problems traveling. Unable to find work, he invested what savings we had left and planted a crop of lettuce on the Texas-New Mexico border. No one had ever grown anything there before in that desert. He siphoned water from the Rio Grande River to irrigate his crop. He grew a beautiful crop of lettuce. The day before harvest, a hailstorm left the entire field a slimy mess.

When the 100th Infantry Battalion 442nd Regimental Combat Team was formed in Hawaii of all Japanese-Americans willing to give their lives to prove their loyalty, the young men in camp were ready to join them. This unit was transferred to Camp Shelby, Mississippi. My cousin, Abraham Omaha, and his brothers went to join this unit. Their family lived in Camp I. Abe was sent to Europe, where he died a hero trying to save his buddy who was trapped behind enemy lines. He was awarded the Silver Star for his heroism and the Purple Heart for his mortal wounds.

The "Go for Broke" unit became the most decorated until in American history for its size, and I am proud of cousin Abe and his brothers for their contributions. I am equally proud of all my able-bodied male cousins and brothers who have served their country during subsequent wars.

The war ended, and we were allowed to go home. Home for us had been burned to the ground by Jap haters. Dad did not have the resources to return to Guadalupe to start farming again on a large scale. He moved the family to Fresno, mother's birthplace. We stayed at the Buddhist church until Dad could find us a home to rent.

Our parents decided we should have American names, so they gave us a new name. Hitoshi became Frank. I became Carolyn, and poor Kaysho got stuck with Hubert. He hated that name and went by Kay instead. We entered school in Fresno under our new names.

THE IRONY OF WARTIME ADULTHOOD:
A TWIST OF FATE
by William Tokumoto

On that fateful day of December 7, 1941, which President Franklin Delano Roosevelt declared as a "Day of Infamy," both of my uncles' lives would be altered significantly in different ways for the duration of the Second World War.

My Uncle Hisashi Fukuhara was born in Japan in 1897. At the age of nineteen, in 1916, he left Japan by ship to be with his father who had migrated earlier to Hawaii in 1904. In 1924, after serving as an apprentice to a local barber for three months, he purchased a barbershop and started his own business. In 1925, at the age of twenty-eight, he married Mitsue Nakata, both operating the shop in Honokaa. During his spare time he was often asked to write or read letters for those who were illiterate. He continued to assist others throughout the years and was honored when selected to do expatriation work for those with dual American/Japanese citizenship or children born to alien parents. To become a full-fledged American citizen, a release was necessary from the government of Japan. Because of this, Uncle Hisashi was in constant contact with the Consulate General of Japan in Honolulu to whom he applied for the releases.

On the morning of December 8, 1941, Hisashi, by a twist of fate, was one of many who were gathered and interned at the Kilauea Military Camp, Volcano, Hawaii, and later shipped to the mainland to be placed in internment camps in New Mexico, Arizona and Oklahoma. In 1946, after five long and hard years, Uncle Hisashi was released from the camps in the United States and returned home to Honokaa, Hawaii, to his wife, and to the very same barbershop, which sustained the family through the difficult war years.

In the same year of his return he studied hard to become an American citizen and was finally naturalized in 1954. This was one of his and his family's proudest moments. He retired in 1963 after which he dedicated most of his time as a writer and instructor in the art of Haiku. Many beautiful award-winning haikus written under his pen name "Getsugaku" expressed his love for the islands and America. In April of 1978 he was granted the Emperor's 6th Order of the Sacred Treasure Award for prestigious community service, another memorable achievement.

As an affirmation and further testament to Hisashi's loyalty to the United States, his only son Paul, born a U.S. citizen on April 2, 1930, volunteered into the U.S. Army in November of 1948 at age eighteen; he served through the Korean and Vietnam wars. This was another proud moment for Hisashi, a first generation naturalized Japanese-American. Hisashi passed away on May 2nd, 1985 at the age of 87.

On the other hand, my uncle Tsukasa Muramoto by a twist of fate followed an entirely different path after witnessing the planes that attacked Pearl Harbor. The day after, Tsukasa went to Schofield Barracks and volunteered to be placed back on active duty. Initially he served with the 298th and 299th Battalions, which later would become the 100th Battalion. They were retrained in Schofield before being sent to Honolulu Harbor by train, then to Oakland, California, on the SS *Maui*. From Oakland, the 100th traveled by train to Camp McCoy, Wisconsin, continuing their training as a unit for another six months before going to Camp Shelby, Mississippi, for their final maneuvers. They adopted the phrase "Remember Pearl Harbor" as their motto.

In 1943 the War Department, in need of manpower, reversed itself and sent recruiters to the relocation camps asking for volunteers to form a new Japanese-American combat unit, the 442nd Regimental Combat Team. Volunteers were also accepted from Hawaii. The Nisei volunteers were combined with Japanese-Americans already serving in the military and were sent to Camp Shelby for combat training. The 442nd chose "Go for Broke," a Hawaiian slang term from the dice game craps. "Go for Broke" meant to risk everything, give everything you have—all or nothing!

While the 442nd was being formed and trained the 1,432 men of the 100th Battalion had entered combat in Italy, September 26, 1943. The Italian campaign bloodied the 100th Battalion, and it suffered heavy casualties, earning the nickname "Purple Heart Battalion" as it was depleted down to 521 men by 1944. Replacements came from men who had finished training with the 442nd at Camp Shelby.

On June 2nd, 1944, the 442nd landed at Naples, Italy, and pushed their way to the beaches at Anzio. On June 15th, the 100th and the 442nd were merged into a single unit. Their heroics at Belvedere, Luciana, Ilivorno, Bruyeres and the Vosages are well-documented.

The 100th and 442nd suffered an unprecedented casualty rate of 314% and received over 18,000 individual decorations, including 9,486 Purple Hearts. The 442nd Combat Infantry group emerged as the most decorated combat unit of its size in the history of the United States Army. For its service in eight major campaigns in Italy and France, it earned eight Presidential Unit Citations.

My Uncle Tsukasa was shipped back to the United States in July 1944 to recuperate from injuries sustained in battle. Three months later he was honorably discharged from the Army after being awarded the Purple Heart, Bronze Star, Combat Infantry Badge, and the Distinguished Unit Badge. He died on March 23, 2004 at the age of 89.

An irony of wartime adulthood: one uncle returned home after a nation's victory at war, a recognized hero; another uncle returned home after a nation's unjust and shameful action caused the loss of his freedom during the war, but not his pride and faith, all because of a twist of fate.

An Air Force photo of William Tokumoto, who continued his family's tradition of military service by serving in the Air Force's Intelligence and Photo Reconnaissance section during the Korean War.

LETTER TO NOREEN

by June Yamasaki

5/19/99

Dear Noreen:

Memorial Day is only a week away. I've heard from Aunt Grace who now lives in a retirement center in Fairfield, California, saying she is going to Washington, D.C., to visit Uncle Saige's grave in Arlington National Cemetery and that she will also visit your father's grave. There's only one grave between them as they were buried only a month apart.

When she was there on Memorial Day in 1994, she sent a picture and it looked like flowers were strewn all over. When I was there in April of 1996, and left flowers at both graves, it was all green lawn. I can't believe it's been almost ten years since we were there for your father's military burial, and I think you had good foresight to have a photographer videotape the service. You can show it to

Tor when he is older, and he can gain some knowledge of his grandfather.

Have you seen the video *Honor Bound*? It is the story of Sgt. Howard Hanamura's march through war and racial turmoil as he revisits and traces his experiences in the European Theater of operations with his journalist daughter. It is a documentary, and although your father is not in it he was in Company L, the same unit as Sgt. Hanamura. Some of the names of places in the film have a familiar ring as I had read and also heard a few stories from

The gravestone in Arlington Cemetery of Harold H. Fujita, June Yamasaki's brother, who served in the 442nd Regimental Combat unit.

your father, although he never really talked much about his war experiences. The 442nd Regimental Combat team lost 500 men rescuing 200 Texans lost in the Vosges Mountains in Italy.

I once asked him if he was aware whether he actually killed a German soldier, and he said, "Sis, in close combat, it's kill or be killed!" I guess he considered himself lucky to be alive after being wounded twice for which he received the Purple Heart with Oak Leaf Cluster medal.

In the book *Go for Broke*, a pictorial history of the 442nd, one of the soldiers is quoted as saying, "Outside Bruyeres, we were there almost two weeks in the cold. It wasn't freezing, but it was very close to it. It was raining all of the time. After a while every muscle of your body starts to tremble. I think that's a way of your body trying to heat yourself. You see the muscles quivering under the skin. You're cold and you're sopping wet, and you've been sopping wet from the very first day. Yet under those conditions, nobody got sick, nobody got ill, nobody got pneumonia. On top of the physical hardships there was the constant terror of death, of people getting killed, mangled, or wounded. Again, I say it was sheer willpower. When you come down to it, combat is really sheer willpower."

Years ago, before you were born, Noreen, Memorial Day was called Decoration Day as all the cemeteries were filled with flowers decorating the graves. Veterans Day to remember veterans of all the wars, observed on November 11, was called Armistice Day until after WW II. It originally commemorated the end of WW I in 1917, and your grandfather was not conscripted because I was born in June.

I'm planning to visit Washington, D.C., next year to attend the dedication of the National Japanese-American Memorial to Patriotism. It will also be the tenth anniversary of your father's burial in Arlington National Cemetery. How about joining me?

MY LIFE IN INTERNMENT CAMPS DURING WORLD WAR II

by Hitoshi Yamada

One of the fond memories I have as a child was going to the Los Angeles County Fair. I was fascinated with the different produce and farm equipment displayed and the smell of food sold by the different vendors. I never dreamed one day I would be living on the parking lot of that fair.

December 7, 1941, changed everything. I was eight years old when Japanese warplanes bombed Pearl Harbor and destroyed a lot of the warships that were anchored and killed military personnel. When President Roosevelt signed Executive Order 9066, all people of Japanese ancestry were ordered out of the West Coast. We were given only a short notice to move, so many had to sell their possessions at giveaway prices. My mother burned a lot of Japanese books. The wind-up phonograph player was also burned. I took the remains of the phonograph player in a gunnysack and threw it into a ditch on the far side of the farm. Dad turned in the fold-up Kodak camera to the authorities. The government gave us a family ID number 5562, and Dad painted it on all the furniture he left behind. The government stored it for the duration of the war. We were allowed to take only what we could carry. With no information as to where we were going we could not prepare for the future. I was the oldest of five children. The youngest child was only six months old.

We were ordered to go to a section of Baldwin Park, a place I remembered going to on family outings. Dad drove us there in our family Plymouth sedan. We had to get out of the car with the baggage. It was loaded on trucks while we boarded a bus. Our car was impounded and sold cheap. When we arrived at the gate, armed soldiers with rifles were everywhere. The parking lot was now surrounded by barbwire and chain link fence.

Our barracks were near the entrance to the fairgrounds. It was divided into three rooms with a family living in each room. I remember that the boards dividing the room had about a half-inch of space between them. Dad happened to have a large canvas that he brought along. He put it up, and it covered most of the wall.

In the beginning, the mess hall was not well organized and food was scarce. Food was served on round metal pans with a handle that folded over. It was what the soldiers used in the war zone.

Over 5000 people were packed into this small camp. Every night about 10:00 to 11:00 p.m., men came around with flashlights counting heads to make sure no one was missing. Small children would awaken and cry at the loud knock having their sleep interrupted.

As the hot summer wore on, the dust in the camp grew deeper until the government began moving us out 500 a time in August to more permanent facilities at Heart Mountain Relocation Campsite in Cody, Wyoming. We lived there from August 1942 to October 30, 1945. Long lines were marched to the railroad tracks near the fairgrounds where old drab passenger cars waited. The trip was tiring and long. We saw mostly barren lands, deserts, mountains and small towns. We were ordered to put down our shades as we passed through towns. Apparently, rocks were thrown at the previous trains when some townspeople found out that Japanese were being transported. With the outbreak of World War II and all the war hysteria that the news media aimed against the Japanese in America, it was no surprise that we were classified as enemy aliens.

The train finally came to a stop on a plateau and we saw our future home in the distance. Tarpaper-covered barracks seemed to be everywhere. We were directed to a health inspection room where we were briefly checked out and then taken to the camp about a mile away.

Later at the onset of the harsh winter, many were found without adequate clothing. Those who were able ordered winter clothing from the Sears and Roebuck catalog. Others stood in line to receive used GI socks, long underwear, coats and wool pants. Some of the clothing had large patches over the holes and torn parts. Though battle-scarred and mended, my parents were thankful to have warm clothing.

Each block had twenty-four barracks that were divided into six rooms, one for each family. There was a potbelly stove on one side of the room. Each one was given two army blankets and a cot with cotton-stuffed mattress. Each half a block had a laundry-bathroom building and a mess hall, which had large coal-burning cook stoves.

Since Dad was hired as a cook, and our family had only young children, volunteers came and insulated our barracks. The laundry and bathroom building had a huge coal-burning boiler used for heating water for the laundry rooms and the showers. Men skilled in woodworking made square wooden "ofuros" (Japanese booths), where we soaked after our showers. One part was usually hotter than the other. I enjoyed soaking in the hot tub. It took away the chill in my bones during the cold winter months. Three shifts of men were on duty twenty-four hours a day just to keep the boilers fed with coal. Some of the pipes froze and burst during the cold winter.

By 1943, while still incarcerated, we were given permission to go outside the barbwire fence. One of the first things my friends and I did was to go down to the

Shoshone River about a mile away. On our hike we came upon a huge canal filled with water, so we could not get to the river. Then we noticed people in the deep ravine walking under the canal. We followed them through a large drainage pipe to the river. Other children were already wading in the water. We made many treks to the river to catch minnows or mud suckers for our gallon bottle aquarium.

The internees were offered small plots of land on the north side beyond the barbwire fence for "Victory Gardens." My dad received a plot and planted cucumbers, cantaloupe, melons and other vegetables. For fertilizer he borrowed a rusty wheelbarrow and together we looked in the nearby hills for rabbit dung, plentiful under the sagebrushes. In 1944 there was danger of an early frost that would freeze the melons. I remember Dad picking green ones and taking them to the mess hall. He salted them down to make pickles (tsukemono). It was a nice addition to the menu.

When it became known that we would be leaving camp to face the real world, I wanted to show my almost four years old brother, Harry, the Shoshone River. In August 1945, I was eleven years old and carried him most of the way to see the river that I had visited so often.

These and other memories welled up in my mind after visiting the campsite fifty-seven years later. It was good revisiting the place where I had lived during the war years, and seeing it again was like a proper closure to that part of my life. Heart Mountain still stands changeless through the years like a sentinel on duty watching over the territory that was once my home in captivity.

JUST AS RED
by Ike Ikeda

My name is Fubio Ike Ikeda. I was born in San Jose, California, but moved to Clovis when I was a year old, so I consider myself a native of Clovis. My dad's name was Ben Ikeda, and my mom's name was Suge Ikeda. Both were native-born Japanese. I also had one sister and one brother.

Growing up I had a carefree life that moved at a much slower pace than life today. My family and most of the families around me were farmers. We lived near the San Joaquin River. It was only a few miles away, and in the back of where we lived was the Enterprise Canal, so we spent a lot of time either swimming or fishing in the river or swimming in the canal.

I went to Clovis High School and graduated in 1938. I enlisted in the service before the attack on Pearl Harbor in November of 1941. My brother Hiye was classified as a 1A, who was someone ready for drafting. But talking things out with my brother, we decided that if I enlisted, then he would get a 3A agriculture deferment because the war hadn't started at that time. That was the way we preferred because personally I didn't want to stay home and run the ranch anyhow. We talked to our friend who was on the draft board and he came back about a week later and pointed to me and said, "You go," and pointed to my brother and said, "You can stay." So that worked out for the best.

I was in basic training in Camp Roberts down in Paso Robles when I heard that the Japanese attacked Pearl Harbor. I knew that America would be going to war, but I didn't think how it would affect Japanese-Americans such as myself.

I was never in hand-to-hand combat in my tour of duty, but I still feel I played an important part in the war. I was transferred into the Army's Military Intelligence Division as a Staff Sergeant. I was then shipped out to Asia where my job was to translate documents, interrogate prisoners, and interpret for American officers. I was doing what was called the "tight service" and was assigned to several different companies and groups. I was mainly assigned to the China Combat Command where I worked with Chinese troops and their fight against the Japanese. Our duty was to help the Chinese army keep the Japanese troops occupied in China so that they wouldn't be siphoned off and sent out to the South Pacific where the bigger war was being fought.

I never experienced any racial discrimination when I was in the service. Our commander was a fair minded man and he prohibited discrimination against any race in our company. He said if any one was going to be a racist, then they would have to answer to him. Those words must have worked because I never felt out of place.

My family back in the United States wasn't as fortunate. In 1942, after the attack on Pearl Harbor, all Japanese-Americans on the West Coast, citizens or illegal aliens, were evacuated to relocation centers. These relocation centers were more like concentration camps because it was fenced all around. They had gun towers and people could not go in and out as they pleased. More importantly, the people were sent there without a fair trial. General DeWitt was in charge of the Western Defense Command, and he decided that this needed to be done. His attitude was a Jap was a Jap. That was that. He couldn't see that Japanese-Americans were loyal to the United States.

When I was younger I didn't really think too much of the racism that we experienced. But as I get older, I reflect on this period of my life more often and it really makes me sad and angry. The discrimination and relocation that Japanese-Americans experienced during World War II was wrong. The internment that took place overrode the rights given to us in the Constitution. I feel that we must give our citizens the rights guaranteed to them in the Constitution, if this country is truly worth fighting for.

I served for four years and one month to defend America and that Constitution that makes this country so great. The American government eventually apologized for the relocation camps, which is what some countries would never own up to. I still believe that America is the greatest country in the world, and I hold my head high as an American citizen and also as a veteran of the United States Army. I think they found out that our blood, when we are shot or when we are killed, is just as red as the next guy's.

A FALL DAY

by June Yamasaki

It was in October of 1945 that I returned to Fresno from Washington, D.C., where, after three months of intensified training in Denver, Colorado, I had worked translating intercepted enemy broadcasts for the federal government.

The broadcasts in Japanese were being transmitted from Tokyo for domestic and overseas consumption. The United States had broke their code early on and were intercepting them in Portland, Oregon, where the voice broadcasts were translated. The "kana" and "romaji" broadcasts were decoded in Portland and sent by direct teletype to our office in Washington where eight of us did the translating.

Earlier in the war, the head of the Portland office had come to Denver to meet with us and go over our translations. He asked me to listen to a tape I had worked on, and said, "Isn't he saying 'nyikki' instead of 'sanjikski'?" I listened and found I could hear it either way I wanted to. Perhaps my being tone deaf may have had something to do with it, but I realized translating voice broadcasts was not for me. He still wanted me in Portland, but I told him I was really waiting for WAC induction and didn't think I'd be with them too much longer. I later learned he had contacted WAC headquarters and told them I was more valuable to the war effort at the State Department, so I was sent to Washington, D.C.

Tokyo was thirteen hours ahead of us so I worked the night shift mostly as that was when the bulk of the broadcasts came in. Later on we put in ten-hour shifts so we could rotate once a month without having to go directly from one shift to the other.

We knew from the broadcasts long before V.J. Day that Japan could not possibly continue fighting through the coming winter. There was neither food nor fuel to do so. Then we got repeated broadcasts for several days alerting the people to wait for an important radio announcement at a set hour on a set day. When the time came, it was the Emperor himself telling his subjects of the surrender.

It was a short broadcast, but an unprecedented event in the history of Japan. I was asked to translate it, and I did. The next day, my editor/boss came in jubilant saying the translation I had done was carried word for word in that morning's *New York Times*, which was something to really be proud of from a newspaperman's point of view.

For the eight of us working for the Foreign Broadcast Intelligence Service Section of the State Department, Japan's surrender meant the elimination of our jobs. All my co-workers were transferred to other departments, or found other work on their own. I was the only one returning to California, but I had no choice then as I was faced with an escheat suit: The People of the State of California vs. Fujita et al, regarding the prohibition of aliens ineligible for citizenship from owning real property. The first U.S. Naturalization Act of 1790 allowed only "free white persons" to become American citizens. After the Civil War, the Naturalization Act of 1870 extended the right to "person of African nativity and descent." The Chinese Exclusion Act was passed in 1882 and the Supreme Court extended the denial to Japanese immigrants, ruling that they were neither black nor white; therefore Asians were ineligible.

But as times change, Congress also changed over the years, so that Native Americans were allowed citizenship in 1924, Latin Americans in 1940, Chinese in 1943, Filipinos and Asian Indians in 1946. It wasn't until 1952 that Japanese and Koreans were finally eligible. Section 9 of the Alien Land Law (called the Presumption Clause) stated specifically that if any part of the consideration (this meant the compensation or payment) was provided for the property by an ineligible alien, such action was presumed to have been with intent to evade the Alien Land Law; therefore the property escheated to the State of California and title did not vest in the citizen in whose name it had been placed.

Because both my parents were in their forties when I was born, they thought it prudent to provide for a baby girl should anything happen to them. This was in 1917 and I was only six months old. The law allowed alien parents to act as guardians of underage citizen children's properties, although for the first several years a Caucasian neighbor whose son and daughter-in-law were both attorneys served as my guardian and it was she who wrote me in Washington, D.C., about the lawsuit.

On my return I was informed that it was possible to make a compromise settlement with the State by paying half of the then-appraised value of the property. If I did the suit would be dropped and I would retain title. I learned there were a number of Japanese-Americans who had done so. But poor me—I had no such funds. Even if I had, I don't know if I would have. It didn't seem at all right. The place had been paid for, why was it necessary to pay again?

STATESIDE SERVICE

Many American veterans of World War II served all or most of the war stateside, filling a variety of important capacities such as design engineers, flight instructors, test pilots, and trainers. Like their comrades overseas, they fulfilled their duty honorably and did everything in their power to help the war effort succeed.

LEAVING HOME TO GO TO WAR
by George Kerber

The most difficult part of growing up during World War II was to be called into the military service and forced to leave home. At age eighteen I was drafted and ordered to active duty in the Navy. Up to that time, I had never been away from home and my family or ever traveled outside of California. My family was devastated, especially my mother, who took my call to active duty very hard. Then, one year later, my younger brother Leroy was called into military service and was trained as a military police officer in the Army.

My mother was adamantly opposed to her sons going to war and would not permit us to volunteer for the service like my cousins, Eddie and Herman, who both joined the Marines, or Rueben, who joined the Navy. In addition, my mother's two brothers, Alex and George, were in the Army and Air Force.

I was sent to boot camp in Farragut, Idaho, a new Naval training center established by President Roosevelt in honor of Admiral Farragut from Civil War fame. Remember the statement, "Damn the torpedoes, full steam ahead!"? That was Farragut's order.

At the conclusion of my boot camp training, I was then ordered to the Engineering Service School at the Great Lakes Naval Training Center on Lake Michigan, north of the city of Chicago, Illinois. The Navy had decided, because of my background in science and engineering, that I should be trained as a steam engineer. But after my graduation from Service School I was assigned to the Amphibian Naval Base in Norfolk, Virginia, where I was designated to serve as a diesel engineer on landing boats. So after having spent three months in training as a steam engineer I was assigned to perform duties as a diesel engineer on landing craft. I was confused and annoyed by this assignment. But I was ordered to never question a direct order or assignment. I was expected to perform these duties without question.

Fortunately, there were a number of older and more experienced men at the base who took me under their wing and helped me through this very frustrating period. They taught me about diesel engines and how to repair and maintain this engine and its reverse gear transmission. They could tell I was a lonely kid who had never been away from home, especially three thousand miles away, and missed my family and mother.

I had nothing to give back for this help and support except for my friendship and loyalty, and my ration of cigarettes, which I disliked and was glad to give away to my comrades. Within a short time I became an accomplished diesel mechanic and was promoted to Machinist Mate Second Class and assigned to supervise a new team of servicemen.

I was away from home and in the service for three years, but I never got over the desire and yearning to go home. During that period of active duty I was able to get home only once. To keep myself busy on my free time, in addition to writing letters to my folks, I took a correspondence course in college physics, regularly visited the local public library and museum, and traveled to Washington, D.C., and toured our nation's capital. Occasionally, I would be invited to go home with one of the older married men who lived near the base, and share the weekend with his family. Those visits helped me to overcome my homesickness.

But to this day, I will never forget my mother's great mental pain and anguish that she suffered, and her crying, as I boarded the bus to report for active duty. That scene will haunt me forever. It's obvious that families, especially mothers, always suffer the most in war. I know what happened to my mother and eternally shared her extreme pain and distress.

THE PURSUIT OF FLIGHT
by Chris Christensen

I must have been born with a model airplane in my mouth. I was born on August 25, 1921, near Oshkosh, Nebraska, to Chris and Emma Christensen. I have one brother, Roland. He and I did everything together as we grew up. As children, we were obsessed with flight. I never lost the desire to fly. My brother and I were famous in our town for building kites, model airplanes, and pretty much anything that flew.

During the Great Depression my father lost the lease on the land we farmed, forcing him to sell our equipment and move us to the city. I vividly remember cutting cardboard to put into my shoes every morning, but I never considered my family poor. When I was fourteen years old I began working in a local grocery store. Ironically, years later, my father helped my brother and me to buy that same grocery store.

Like many patriotic mid-western young men of my time, the Japanese attack on Pearl Harbor changed my life's course. I decided to serve my country and fulfill my dreams at the same time by enlisting in the Army Air Corps. My father and I journeyed to the nearest army recruiter in Sterling, Colorado, and as fate would have it, the Army recruiter's extended lunch break lost the Air Corps a pilot. The Naval recruiter noticed us waiting; he mentioned that the Navy also had pilots—Naval Aviators. I signed up, and I soon received a letter of approval in the mail.

The desire to fly and the passion for it drove a young kid who had never left home before to travel from one end of the country to the other. After Sterling, I traveled to Denver to make up the two years of college I was lacking in three days of tests. Next, I went to San Francisco for the flight physical. The doctor told me I was underweight; I was sent back to Nebraska. Two weeks later, I was back to San Francisco, and I was still too light at 130 pounds, so the doctor instructed me to visit the local café and fill up on milk and bananas. Well, I was determined to fly, so I ate a lot of bananas and drank a lot of milk, but to this day, I look at eating a banana with little enthusiasm.

While back home, I received orders to Fort Collins, Colorado, and later Boulder for Civil Pilot Training. I spent time in San Luis Obispo and Del Monte, California; Hutchison, Kansas; Corpus Christi, Texas; New Orleans, Louisiana;

Ottumwa, Iowa; and Pensacola, Florida. Through all the travels I persevered, and I finally got to fly.

I will never forget the day my flight instructor hopped out of the plane after a few hours of instruction and told me to take off, fly, and land solo. The exhilaration of tearing through the sky in that open-cockpit Stearman was something I will never forget. Fortunately, the roar of the engine drowned out my whoops and hollers of joy. My solo flight made everything I endured, and was still to endure during training, worth it.

I met my lovely wife, Betty Munson, on a blind date while we were in high school. We were married on April 16, 1944, and had two children, a son and a daughter. We now have six grandchildren and two great-grandchildren. My

Chris Christensen flew the open-cockpit Stearman as a Naval Aviator.

two great-grandsons have followed their great-grandfather's passion for building model airplanes.

From my early flight days and when I became an instructor, I learned a man could do anything he sets his mind to do, no matter what is stacked against him. I also saw the power of teamwork—how well men can work together when they have a common purpose. Some say my generation saved the world. Maybe we did, but the world needs saving every day. Keep your eyes on whatever it is you want to accomplish in life and strive to fulfill your dreams.

MYTH OR TRUTH
by Harold Comstock

On November 12, 1942, my flight commander, Lieutenant Roger Dyer, and I were given the task to evaluate antennas on the new P47-C. As test pilots, we were flying the first of the Thunderbolts off the Republic Aviation assembly line. We had previously been flying the B for Baker model. We had just gotten the C-1 model, which was about two feet longer because the B model tail kept breaking off, resulting in a number of pilots getting killed.

The B model also had a very old oxygen system. The C model had a brand new type of oxygen system called the supply and demand system. We had been breaking off the radio antennas in the B models, as well, and the C models had a new type of antennae. Lt. Dyer and I had been picked to take the C model up and run it at high speed to see if the new antennae would hang on. We took off scheduled to fly three minutes at full military power every 5,000 feet until we got up to 40,000 feet. At 40,000 feet we were to do full military power every three minutes every 1,000 feet. We parted company, Roger went his way, I went my way.

At 40,000 feet I couldn't see him. It's reasonable to say I did leave it at full military power, kept checking oil and head temperature and kept reaching for height at the end of the three-minute run. I just climbed to the next 1,000 feet without losing that air speed. I got that plane up to 49,600 feet, which a lot of people challenge on the fact that the oxygen system wouldn't support that altitude. I later on talked to the outstanding physiologist on high altitude Dr. Sears, from San Antonio, Texas, and he said, "Yes, you could, but you couldn't stay there very long. You could stay there long enough, and I will support your claim of 49,600 feet."

At any event, when I reached 49,600 feet I turned the airplane over and started down when something weird happened. The airplane stalled out at 45,000 feet when I pulled the throttle back. I recovered probably at about 35,000 feet, and I brought the airplane in. This airplane had no weapons or ammunition. I was down to about thirty gallons of fuel. The public relations people published a report in the newspaper a couple days later stating that the aircraft had reached compressibility, which it did. The compressibility made for an erroneous airspeed indication on the recorders of 760 miles per hour. But a lot of people misinterpret that by saying the pilots claimed they had gone supersonic. At that time I had never even heard of the term "supersonic." Let me tell you right now. No, I never did, didn't then, haven't since. The first man to do so was probably a man of the name of George Welch, two days before Chuck Yeager did.

About six years ago a writer wrote a book, and in the first two pages he claims I went supersonic. Let me set the record straight. I never have. This is a myth that has been going on for almost 63 years that two pilots claimed to have gone supersonic. I certainly would like to have this on record that the Thunderbolt flyers never claimed to go supersonic. I wish that myth would die.

Later five of us had been sent down to Ryker Island in East River in New York to be trained on this new oxygen system for the C-47. It was a very tight fitting mask. In passing, these masks did not go with us to England. When we got to England, we used British masks for about six months until production caught up and then they sent us the same masks that we had been using in Bridgeport, Connecticut.

As the pressure and the altitude reduced, this mask would automatically feed you the proper amount of oxygen. One could say at 49,600 it was still pumping oxygen; however, it was not enough oxygen, as Dr. Sears wrote me, "You were losing oxygen in your blood system rapidly. You could get there, but you couldn't stay there very long." I didn't stay there very long, not more than two or three seconds.

As any aviator will tell you, you know when the airplane is finished flying. I had everything forward. I was drawing 52 inches of mercury and 27 hundred RPM, everything the airplane had, and that was as far as it would go, and as far as I know that's about as high as anybody ever put a World War II fighter. But it was a great airplane.

A pencil drawing of Harold Comstock, who flew Thunderbolts as a test pilot in 1942 for the Army Air Force.

207

JULY FLYING OVER FLORIDA
by James Warwick

I was drafted into military service during World War II in July 1943 while I was an undergraduate student of math, physics, and astronomy. The induction station was near my home in Toledo, Ohio. Long lines of soon-to-be military persons, young, nervous, and very uncertain of the future, went through the usual but still to us unfamiliar indignities of physical exams.

The Air Corps noted that my eyes were 20/20 and wondered whether I would like to become a flying cadet. I signed up as fast as I could and walked straight past the infantry without a single look back.

I had just ten hours of stick time in a tiny J3 trainer airplane. I was ready to solo, but never did. Instead, the Air Corps trained me to be a bombardier. I was commissioned in December 1944, and sent to Boca Raton Army Air Base, between Miami and Palm Beach, Florida, for training on the AN/APQ-13 bomb-laying radar. This devise had a television-like screen upon which was "painted" a map of the ground and ocean below the airplane.

Our training missions frequently took us out from Florida eastward over the Atlantic Ocean. This included specifically the area known as the Bermuda Triangle. We made flights all over the state and down south over the Caribbean Sea to Cuba and other islands.

By early May my radar-training days at Boca Raton were finished and I departed to aircrew training on Super Fortress B-29s at MacDill Army Air Base on a peninsula of land jutting into Tampa Bay just south of Tampa, Florida. The idea of this new training was to bring together a complete bomber crew—gunners, bombardiers, navigators, flight engineer, co-pilot, and pilot—aboard the kind of airplane they would fly in combat.

Only one of the ten of us, our first pilot and aircraft commander, J.J. O'Brien, had ever been in combat. From England he had flown Eighth Air Force B-17s over Germany. For him as for the rest of us, the B-29 was a novelty, although it had been dropping bombs on the home islands of Japan since before Saipan Island was secured in 1944. It was a huge aircraft, capable of delivering a bomb load of ten tons from the Marianas Islands to Japan on a round trip of fifteen hours and more than three thousand miles.

This was oceanic flying and required endurance. To accomplish a flight of this duration during mostly daylight hours, you rise at three in the morning, fly all day, and return home near sunset. Our training at MacDill involved long flights over the ocean and so continued over the Caribbean to Cuba and Puerto Rico.

When because of an undercast of clouds our visual bombardier, Charley Calhoun, couldn't see to line up the airplane, I, the radar bombardier, came into action. Radar showed the target, whether or not there were clouds. I would set the approach course of the aircraft and release the bombs at the exact instant required for them to hit the bull's eye.

The reality of these training missions was that the weather over the Caribbean was almost always beautiful, with only a few puffy cumulus clouds around. They concealed virtually nothing. As a result I had nothing to do but watch the radar go round and round or go to sleep in the rear compartment of the B-29.

One day in July we took off at dawn and set our course southeastward on a route passing near Lake Okeechobee and leaving land at the east coast near Palm Beach. The day warmed up and the fair weather cumulus clouds, far below us near the surface, began to grow vertically into small towers.

At our altitude we could see clouds above other Caribbean islands as remote as 150 miles. We practiced our bomb runs over San Juan and turned back towards Florida and home across the Florida peninsula on its west coast. And I went to sleep in my cozy corner alongside the radar unit.

Several hours later, about the time we crossed onto the Florida peninsula over its east coast, I was awakened by air bumps. I moved up to the left scanner's bubble to see what was happening. There wasn't much to see, however, only clouds, clouds, clouds. We were flying through turbulent rainstorms. The Florida peninsula was now covered by towering structures.

What had started out as a fun ride through the air above the Caribbean Sea was ending as a precarious journey though towering clouds evolving, even as we flew, into massive thunderstorms up to fifty or sixty thousand feet high. Our return home was blocked by picket lines of thunderstorms.

Even jet aircraft aren't able to surmount that high an obstacle. The preferred option is to detour around it. The B-29, capable though it was, had an effective ceiling somewhere between thirty and forty thousand feet, far below the peaks of these clouds. For us, it wasn't even clear whether we had an option to circumnavigate the clouds. Florida dips far south of where we had to fly. A detour may not have been practical given the limitations of our fuel reserves after an eleven-hour flight. We found ourselves surrounded by thunderstorms, any of them powerful enough to tear our aircraft apart wing from wing.

From the blister nothing could be seen except foggy swirls of cloudy convection. But the radar screen was splotched by echoes from the precipitation cores of the thunderstorms. Whether this information could save us was unclear to me, but

I called up J.J. to tell him about it anyway. He said I should give him a course heading out of the mess. I eyeballed the gaps between the clouds as they appeared on the screen and gave him a new heading. Each time I'd give him a course, he'd pull the B-29 around, but after a few minutes of relatively clear sailing, there'd be another thunderstorm confronting us. And so we continued, zigzagging but always trying to edge towards Tampa. Finally, J.J. announced, "I've got MacDill's landing lights!", and we were home.

A SAILOR IN THE DIRT NAVY

by Gene Bos

I was born August 22, 1926, in the Hollywood Hospital, to John and Lillian Bos. My dad was a U.S. Postal Mail Carrier in Los Angeles, California. I was pictured on my third birthday in a sailor suit, destined even then to join the U.S. Navy.

That Sunday morning, December 7, 1941, I had just completed my paper deliveries and was playing the pinball machine at Poncho's Mexican Restaurant on Blackstone Avenue in Fresno, where my mother worked. Almost sixteen and hearing the unbelievable news of Japan's attack on Pearl Harbor, even then I wondered if I could join the U.S. Navy when I became of age. The day after my seventeenth birthday, August 23, 1943, my dad consented, and signed for me to join the U.S. Navy. I had eight weeks of boot camp at Farragut, Idaho, in Company 714, Camp Hill, before becoming Seaman 2/C.

Assignments took me to Chicago, Illinois, Philadelphia, Virginia, back to California, Oxnard, and Twenty Nine Palms, all "dirt navy" assignments. Later our unit became ACORN 52 (code name for standard advanced naval base units), training for naval airbase occupation. We provided shore logistics for aviation, including assembly of airplanes ashore, ground combat, live fire, and combined arms training at the Marine base in Twenty-Nine Palms.

Carrying 782 gear, we boarded the troop ship USAT *Mormacsea* on May 31st, 1945, and waved good-bye as we left the San Francisco Bay. I was finally at sea.

My letter home was heavily censored, written on both sides of the pages, and arriving home full of holes, for I had described our South Pacific convoy route. Our convoy was routed through Pearl Harbor, Hawaii, Eniwetok, Marshall Islands, Ulithi, Leyte, Cebu, and Samar. On the 7th of July, 1945,

Gene Bos joined the Navy a day after his 17th birthday, August 23, 1943.

we landed on the shoreline of Mochlan Island on Palawan of the Philippine Islands, where we began base operations.

I recalled reading a story about American prisoners on Palawan dated December 1944. One hundred and fifty men as POWs suffered atrocities while building the airstrip at Puerto Princesa by pick and shovel and other crude methods. They were undernourished and subjected to extreme cruelty, and eventually were herded into makeshift bomb shelters and set on fire with aviation fuel. The escaping prisoners were machine-gunned or hacked with sabers and bayonets. Only eleven men survived. Never did I imagine I would be based on this same island, which had since been secured. We were warned to look out for Japanese soldiers coming out of hiding places in the hills. Some had been discovered waiting in our own chow lines!

I was on Palawan on August 6, 1945, when the first atom bomb was dropped on Hiroshima, Japan, and also on August 9 when the second bomb was dropped on Nagasaki. America celebrated as President Truman declared August 14th V-J Day. General MacArthur signed an unconditional surrender in Tokyo Bay aboard the USS *Missouri* on December 2, 1945.

It seemed that I was destined to stay in the dirt navy forever, until I spied an opening on the bulletin board on Palawan for Fireman 1/C and applied. In August I was flown from Palawan to San Jose, Mindoro, and on August 12 signed on board the USS *Half Moon* AVP26 in Mangarin Bay. Our duty was in the Lingayen Gulf for maintenance and refueling PBY seaplanes.

After taking on supplies, we left Subic Bay for Okinawa on August 30, 1945. The sea was fairly calm, only quiet ripples. Within twenty hours, a raging sea was tossing my ship unmercifully. As the typhoon progressed for twenty-seven hours with sixty-foot waves, 120-knot winds rolled the *Half Moon* at fifty-eight degrees maximum, creating structural damage and causing leaking in the octane fuel tanks, bent lifelines and lost lifeboats. Bottles of acetylene, oxygen, and carbon dioxide rolled from port to starboard bulkheads, along with other miscellaneous gear, and equipment washed into the sea. A huge freezer below deck bounced from bulkhead to bulkhead as they tried to contain it. Men on the bridge complained of aching eardrums, due to low atmospheric pressure, and the men at the master throttle control required bridles of manila line to maintain their positions. During the storm our ship became separated from the convoy, arriving in Okinawa a day late, on September 3rd. It was a miracle our ship and men survived!

The typhoon damage was mostly repaired before the *Half Moon* left Okinawa. From that point we were on duty in the Cavite and Linguyan Gulf area of the Philippines. On the 8th of November, 1945, we headed back to the good 'ole U.S.A., stopping off at Eniwetok in the Marshall Islands and Pearl Harbor, Hawaii. Our ship arrived December 1st in Seattle, Washington, anchoring in Winslow Harbor on Bainbridge Island, scheduled for pre-inactivation overhaul.

I became Electrician 3/C Petty Officer on December 7th, and was formally discharged. The offer of a thirty-day leave and extra pay influenced my decision to re-enlist in the regular Navy for two more years. I operated the movie projector, often driving a jeep into Seattle for film, and ran the ice-cream machine aboard ship. On April 9th, the *Half Moon* left Seattle for Alameda, then San Diego, California. She was placed on inactive status within the San Diego Group Pacific Reserve Fleet, then decommissioned on September 4, 1946.

I was assigned to COM Alameda Naval Group, 19th Fleet, for the mothballing operation, sealing compartments and installing dehydration systems on decommissioned ships. A large repair barge tied on the docks next to the airbase was our quarters. Here I was, in the dirt navy again! I lived there for thirteen months before my discharge.

Mothballing seaplane tenders NAS Alameda, CA.

Bos EM 3/c CA 1946

Although much of his service was in the "dirt navy," Bos served on the USS Half Moon *AVP26, shown here in mothball operations in Alameda, CA.*

DEPARTURE FROM ICELAND
by Russell H. Hinds

Early in 1945 the war in Europe was coming to an end but there was still intense fighting with Japan in the Pacific Theater. On March 16, 1945, I was sent back to the United States for a furlough and temporary reassignment to Ft. George G. Meade in Laurel, Maryland, only a few miles from my home in College Park. Shortly after my departure, and with help from the American Embassy in Reykjavik, Iceland, my war bride, Thora, and three-month old baby, Margret, Thora's family, and my commanding officer, were placed on a U.S. Navy Hospital ship and sent to the United States in April 1945. The ship began its voyage in England and was quite full with wounded soldiers along with ten British war brides when it arrived in Iceland to pick up Thora, five other war brides, and additional military personnel.

The trip from Reykjavik to New York took nine days during which the weather was good, and they did not encounter a North Atlantic storm. However, Thora recalls they were followed by three German submarines from the time they left Iceland until they reached Newfoundland. Four U.S. Navy destroyers accompanied the hospital ship for protection, but fortunately there were no encounters with the enemy submarines. At that stage of the war Allied victory was certain and the hopeless situation for submarine captains on patrol probably resulted in their decision not to engage the U.S. destroyers or torpedo a helpless hospital ship. Even so, everyone had to wear life preservers, there were several lifeboat drills during the voyage, and the ship was on continuous alert. Thora was very apprehensive, fearing for her own life and that of Margret. She recalls praying a lot during the entire trip.

The ship arrived safely in New York where Thora disembarked at Ellis Island with preferred immigration status as an Army War Bride. She passed through immigration quickly, and with help from The American Red Cross was placed on a train to Baltimore in just a few hours. Full of doubts and fear, she stepped off the train with one suitcase, a young baby, and a featherbed. I had been notified of her arrival and was waiting at the station. After many hugs and kisses, we were on our way to College Park where my loving family waited with open arms.

I commuted eleven miles daily via the Baltimore and Ohio Railroad from College Park to Ft. Meade since I was allowed to live off the base during this temporary assignment. A friendly and patriotic conductor was on the train daily and collected my ticket as I boarded in College Park. Then on arrival at Ft. Meade each day, much to my surprise, he would return the ticket when I left the train as a gesture of appreciation to all servicemen who were serving their country. On one occasion, the conductor even held the train when I was late, and he could see me running for the station.

Russell Hinds with his Icelandic war bride Thora.

During the next several months many important events occurred. Victory in Europe was declared, and World War II was officially over in Europe. Finally, President Harry Truman made the decision to try and end the war quickly with Japan by ordering the use of atom bombs. This resulted in the unconditional surrender of Japan. On September 2, 1945, Japan signed the formal surrender on board the U.S. battleship *Missouri* in Tokyo Bay.

With the war over, many changes took place throughout the U.S. Military. Troops were being brought home and a large number of discharges began based on a point system for length and type of military service. Ft. Meade, where I was stationed, became a major Army separation center, and I became part of the discharge activities while operating a motor pool. On November 1st the necessary point score for discharge was reduced to 65, and that was the exact number I had earned during almost three years of domestic and overseas service. On November 4, 1945, I was given an honorable discharge from the U.S. Army, mustering out pay of $328.76, and a $2.50 railroad ticket for the eleven-mile trip from Laurel to College Park, Maryland. My wartime experience in the Army had ended, and I was safely home with my family.

I applied for an obtained education benefits under the GI Bill and returned to the University of Maryland for the 1946 spring semester to complete my education. Meanwhile, Thora spent her time improving her English language abilities, learning the ways of her new environment, raising her daughter, and being a good wife. She attended naturalization classes and after passing both written and oral examinations was awarded U.S. Citizenship in a formal ceremony at the Frederick County Circuit Court on September 18, 1951. Much to our surprise, however, our daughter Margret did not automatically attain U.S. citizenship because of an oversight in the immigration statues that did not specifically give citizenship to children

A watercolor painting of Skalholt, the home in southwestern Iceland where Russell and Thora Hinds' daughter Margret was born. The three birds flying toward the rainbow depict the Hinds family's journey to their new home in the United States.

born overseas to U. S. soldiers under twenty-one years of age. Fortunately, a friend and member of St. Paul's Church in Washington was a House of Representatives staff member on the Congressional Immigration and Naturalization Committee. She had special wording added as an amendment to the existing law that granted citizenship to children like Margret whose servicemen fathers were not yet twenty-one years old at the time they were born overseas.

In 1983, after a return visit to Iceland, Thora's nephew, Skuli, painted a watercolor showing the house in Iceland where our daughter, Margret Ora, named after her maternal grandmothers, was born on January 3, 1945. It's located in the town of Gadar on the remote southwestern tip of Iceland. All of these houses in this area are given names instead of street addresses. Each house is equipped with a windmill type generator for electric power and a bank of wet-celled storage batteries in the basement for those few days when the wind does not blow. The house, named Skalholt, is the home of Thora's brother Oskar, father of the artist, Skuli Oskarson. The painting shows three birds above the house on the left side depicting Thora, Margret and me leaving Iceland to follow the rainbow westward to a new home in the United States.

WOMEN IN THE MILITARY

The women who served in the military as WACs (Women's Army Corp), WASPs (Women Airforce Service Pilots), WAVES (Women Accepted for Volunteer Emergency Service, a unit of the U.S. Naval Reserve), and "Women Marines" deserve recognition and appreciation for their military service. These women veterans of WW II physically trained, endured barracks life, and learned military arts much as their male counterparts, but were given neither the same benefits nor appreciation. In addition to the myriad clerical and nursing positions filled by military women, many women worked in specialized services such as cartography, air traffic control, flight training, translation and radio operation.

The women who served in WW II are unsung heroines because they not only distinguished themselves in service, but also blazed the trail for future women's military service.

THE WW II STORY OF SEAMAN PENNY MIRIGIAN
by Penny Mirigian-Emerzian

My life has been influenced by my growing up in the Great Depression in Fowler, California, home of the world's best raisins. We learned a moral code of behavior through example by observing our elders. I was a sophomore at Fresno State College when the Japanese attacked Pearl Harbor. My reasons for being in school didn't seem important anymore. My country was at war. I finished my junior year and wondered why I was still in school when most of my friends were involved in the war effort.

During my senior year of college, recruiters for the WACs and WAVES came to our campus. Many girls signed up to serve their country. I felt an obligation to my parents and family, yet, I felt I should be doing something for my country, too. My grandfather's words filled my thoughts. He said, "Take care of this country; it is all we Armenians have. The Turks have destroyed Armenia. We will never have our country back. Take care of America!"

Reluctantly, I stayed in school and graduated from Fresno State in June 1943, with my bachelor's degree in business, speech, and psychology. In October I enlisted in the Navy. I kept my enlistment secret from my parents. Each time I was scheduled to deploy, I was granted a deferment. On the way home from work one evening, I broke the news to my dad. Dad was easy to talk to, and we had an especially close father-daughter relationship. He sat quietly for what seemed like a very long time, and then asked if I had told my mother.

Penny Mirigian enlisted in the Navy WAVEs in October 1943.

"No!" I replied. I was too afraid of my mother to tell her first. I was hoping Dad would help cushion the news. In America in the 1940s, "good girls" did not join the military. The public general opinion was servicewomen were there to "service" the servicemen and were no better than prostitutes. When I broke the news at home, my mother was terribly upset and yelled, "You will turn into a street walker!" "No, I won't," I replied, but I'm not sure she was convinced.

There must have been fifty or sixty people on the railroad platform the morning I departed. The all-military train traveled through California and filled up with service personnel. The women and men were segregated in different railcars. I lead the singing in my car. My musical training came in handy. We spent several days traveling to the east coast, and my first train ride landed me in New York City.

I arrived for boot camp at Hunter College in the Bronx and vividly recall a room with a stage at one end and a piano. I was asked if I could sing. A sheet of music was pushed into my hand and I was asked to read the music. My training in piano and Glee Club came in very handy. I had no idea what they were looking for, until someone designated me as qualified for the "singing platoon."

At Hunter College we learned to march and drill in the Armory. We went through the "Daisy Chain," where each WAVE received a thorough physical exam and a series of shots and inoculations. Many of the girls fainted and were just not physically strong enough to serve their country. The family values and work ethic I learned at home held me in good stead during my military career.

During hearing tests at boot camp I discovered I had rather acute hearing abilities—I could hear high frequencies over the encompassing sounds. This qualified me to go to radio school. We learned the Navy's pattern of sending coded messages and drilled hour after hour. Some of us went dit-dot happy. The training was hard on the nerves at times, and the repeated tapping sounds drove some off the deep end.

My next assignment was in the middle of the Puget Sound on Bainbridge Island in Seattle, Washington. I was shocked to discover I was one of 200 women chosen to participate in the elite cryptography group for the Navy. Before being chosen, I was investigated by the FBI. My first grade teacher, Edith Davis, was interviewed, and she promptly called my mother to ask what I was doing that the FBI would be interested. Small town gossip didn't change, even in wartime.

A group photo from Penny Mirigian's radio school in Ohio.

My job as a cryptographer was to spy on our Japanese enemy by listening to radio broadcasts. We were sworn to secrecy: loose lips sink ships. I spent hour after hour listening to the dots and dashes and learning the Japanese code. I was helping my country to win the war.

After completing code training in Washington, I was sent back to my home state and stationed on the Strand across the bay from San Diego. I worked eight-hour shifts—eight on and eight off—around the clock. The WAVES and sailors lined up along the walls at their stations, headphones on, typing away the messages they were intercepting. I wasn't able to tell my parents about my job but assured them it was important, and I loved my work. Because of the intercepted Japanese transmissions, we cryptographers knew the war with Japan was coming to a close, but we could not tell anyone.

After the war I returned home to Fowler and married a returning Army Air Force soldier. We had four children. For the next twenty-four years I taught high school in Fresno. When I attended the 50th reunion of my high school class, I met my present husband, George Emerzian.

Fifty years had transpired since I was discharged from the Navy. We were told we could not contact each other nor talk to anyone about our secret job. We maintained our silence. But still I often thought about my former shipmates. I listened to many stories about the Indian code talkers, but nothing was ever disclosed in the media about the part we women played in code talking.

In 1996 the ban of silence was lifted and I attended the US Naval Cryptologic Veterans Association reunion in Seattle, Washington, and was reunited with my former roommates and friends. My Navy hitch lasted two-and-one-half years. Our silence lasted fifty-plus years.

DUTY CALLS

by Dorothy Dormandy

When my friend Charlie Curran of New Jersey died in his P-38 over Tunisia in May 1943, I wanted to help win the war for Charlie. I applied to Jackie Cochran's WASP program to learn to fly military planes. I joined the WASPs on November 2, 1943, and studied Morse code, meteorology, navigation, aircraft engines, and flying. But in February 1944 I washed out of cadet school. I was simply not a pilot. I joined the Navy to become a control tower operator at one of their airfields.

However, the Navy sent me to Link Instructor School to teach a refresher course in instrument flying to Navy and Marine pilots. At Camp Kearney Naval Air Station, San Diego, I helped pilots locate their aircraft carriers.

I remember when it all started.

At 1700 hours on a Friday in October of 1944, Pat Byrd and I, with our new Specialist Teacher, Third Class stripes on our sleeves, reported to the Administration Building at the Naval Air Station in San Diego for our assignment to Camp Kearney, eager to help win the war, especially if the base to which we'd been assigned was full of officers.

In a screech of tires a Jeep pulled up and a Marine sergeant yelled out our names. We climbed aboard with the gear we'd been sitting on for half an hour. Two big girls also in blue uniforms with Sp(T) on their sleeves moved over a bit, and we managed to squeeze in. "We're gunnery instructors," one of them informed us.

"Link instructors," I said, trying to be friendly.

The Jeep raced through town, and once we'd passed paved roads and left civilization behind the sergeant fairly flew over the scrubby, chaparral-covered foothills. It was late on Sunday evening, and the last rays of sunlight stretched across the open sky. For fifteen minutes we bounced along, holding the sides of the Jeep, saying little over the rattle of the fenders.

We entered Camp Kearney's main gates, and the sergeant slowed slightly. I nudged Byrdie and our hopes soared as we passed rows of officers' quarters with green grass and trees, like an oasis in the desert—but he didn't stop. He made some snappy turns and raced at top speed across more open scrubby countryside.

Navy WASP Dorothy Dormandy was a Link Instructor for Navy and Marine pilots in 1944.

In the distance, silhouetted against the late evening sky, a two-story barracks building loomed, dark and forbidding, standing alone on a slight rise. "There's home, Toots," the sergeant called out.

"Cripes!" I said. "Why aren't there any lights in the place?"

"You're the first chicks there, Sweetheart. Never had girls stationed on the base before. We built it just for you."

The Jeep screeched to a stop at the front door of our lonely barracks. "The Taj Mahal of the Sahara Desert," he announced. Dust flew everywhere. Not too eagerly, we climbed out. "Don't forget your key, Sweetheart." Byrdie caught it as he sped away in another cloud of dust.

"Let's get inside," she said, unlocking the door. She switched on the light by the front desk marked Duty Station. "Who wants to be on duty?" she quipped. "Someone always mans the Duty Station. It's the law of the Navy."

"Don't ask us," the gunnery girls shrugged and started up the stairs. Since Byrdie and I didn't have orders to stay up all night and guard the place either, we hurried past the Duty Station, lugged our gear topside and down the long corridor. All four of us had to teach at 0800.

Byrdie and I hung up our uniforms and hit the showers. I scrubbed my hair to get the dust out and put it up in pin curls. We had time for a pillow fight before we hit the sack.

I was awakened by the distant sound of pounding. Sunlight streamed through the windows. "What's that?" Loud determined banging continued.

"It's the front door," I yelled. I grabbed a robe, raced the length of the building and took the stairs two at a time, dashed past the unmanned Duty Station and yanked open the front door. "Ah!" I gasped. "The Brass!"

Two officers glared at me from a Jeep parked in the dirt by the door. I started to salute but remembered the Navy manual. You must be in proper uniform when saluting.

A Marine lieutenant roared, "Don't you know what time it is, young lady?"

"No, Sir!"

"Who's on duty?"

"Nobody, Sir! Only four of us here, Sir!"

"Get over to the Mess Hall, young lady. On the double!"

"Where is it, Sir?" I couldn't see anything but dirt and hills.

The Colonel took charge. "Lieutenant, you can't throw these girls in with the men." He turned to the driver. "Sergeant, give these women twenty minutes and deliver them to the Officers' Mess."

That sounded pretty good to me. The Jeep whirled around to leave, stirring up the dust, but before it sped off, the Lieutenant shouted back, "Man the Duty Station!"

Before I had time to wonder who'd be the unlucky one, the Jeep screeched to a halt, and the Colonel shouted, "Lieutenant, these girls are teachers. They can't be up all night." While a conference took place in the back seat of the Jeep I waited, embarrassed and humble, in my bare feet and pin curls. Finally the Colonel sang out, "Sergeant, get these girls an alarm clock!"

I must have been grinning for the Jeep, with tires spinning, backed up to within inches of my bare feet, and the Colonel roared, "Damn it all, young lady. Don't you know there's a war on?"

"Yes, Sir!" Without thinking, I gave him my snappiest salute, considering the bathrobe, the pin curls, and the cloud of dust I was standing in.

As a young girl in Hollywood during World War II, dancing in films, as well as taking advantage of all those opportunities the war opened up for women, I had the time of my life. Yes, war is horrible and some of my friends died, but I also tell my children that our country was united as never before. Each one of us in our own way helped to win the war.

ON SERVING THE WAR EFFORT

by Edna Daves

When Pearl Harbor was attacked on December 7, 1941, I was a freshman at Fresno State College. Everything changed that day for my generation, and I, like so many other young Americans, knew that I would need to do my part to aid our country in winning the war.

Shortly after Pearl, I made the decision to leave Fresno State to attend Reedley Junior College and to live with my parents in Cutler, California. In my second year at Reedley J.C., Navy recruiters came to the college and I was impressed by their presentation. I made up my mind that I wanted to become a Navy WAVE, but I wanted to know my parents' feelings on the matter before I signed up. After speaking to them, they gave their blessing to my Naval career on the condition that I would not go overseas. This probably would not happen in this day and age, but I was respectful of my parents' wishes and wanted to make sure they approved.

Since the sign-ups for the Navy were taking place at Reedley Junior College, I enlisted along with several other recruits. After this, I made the trip to San Francisco for my induction into the Navy, and was sworn in May 1943. Since I would have been graduating with my Associate of Arts degree from Reedley during my induction, my mother received my degree for me. They were especially proud because I was the first person in my family to go to college and receive a degree, in addition to being the second member of my family in the service.

After my official induction in the WAVES I was sent to the prestigious Hunter College for boot camp. Needless to say, I hated boot camp! However, because I had taken an aeronautics course at Reedley J.C. they felt I was a good candidate for Control Tower Operator training. Thus, I was sent to Atlanta, Georgia, to attend the C.T. Operator training school for six weeks. After completing my training, I graduated with honors, and the Navy suggested that I remain in Atlanta, but being a native Californian, I wanted to go to Alameda Naval Air Station in Alameda, CA.

So my friend and fellow control Tower Operator graduate, Billie Baker, hopped on a train for California. Five rather uncomfortable days later, after sitting in a packed train and on our suitcases most of the trip, we arrived in Hanford.

Edna Daves (on the left) directing traffic in a control tower at Alameda Naval Air Station.

Billie and I both had a week's leave, so she headed for Monrovia, CA, to visit her family, and my mother picked me up at the train station for some family visit before I went to my post.

It was during my Reedley J.C. days that I met my future husband, Edward Daves, who had already enlisted in the Army Air Corp and was on his way to B-17 training in Roswell, N.M. He had no idea that I had joined the WAVES and completed all of my training in twelve weeks. Due to his training schedule we had been out of contact during my enlistment and training. Imagine his surprise when he saw a picture of his fiancée in Popular Mechanics Magazine showing her in uniform directing air traffic at Alameda Naval Air Station. He called me shortly after this to suggest we get married right away as he was being sent to England as a B-17 pilot. Unfortunately, I could not get leave, and he went off to the European theater. It was ironic that I had not seen him since a few days after our engagement early 1943, and did not see him again until the war was over and he returned from a POW camp.

During my time at Alameda the work of being a Control Tower Operator was exhilarating, but also stressful. The Naval Air Station was one of the largest on the Pacific coast, so we had lots of air traffic. However it was not all work, as we did

Edna and Ed Daves were engaged in early 1943 but unable to get married until the war ended. They married on July 28, 1945.

meet lots of interesting people coming through the Air Station. I met the movie star Tyrone Power, who came into the tower on my watch. I was told later that he asked some of the guys to, "Say 'hi' to that cute little WAVE in the tower." I was over the moon about this, being somewhat boy-crazy. I would not let anyone wash the coffee cup I served him for a month. The whole incident was pretty neat for a little gal from Cutler.

Unfortunately, I was notified in September 1944 that Ed was missing in action over in Europe, and that his B-17 had gone down somewhere over Germany. I was in shock for sometime, and despondency set in. I found out through his family that he had survived his plane being shot down by flak over Magdeburg, Germany, and was now a guest of the Third Reich, a prisoner of war. I went on with my daily life and sent him letters and parcels every week once we found what camp he was in.

When Germany surrendered in June of 1945, I had been at Alameda Naval Air Station for about a year and a half. Shortly before this, in May of 1945, my fiancé had been liberated from his German POW camp and had returned to the states. I was not even aware of this until the operations office downstairs in the Tower called and said, "Edna, there is someone here to see you," and imagine my surprise and joy at seeing his welcome face. There was a lot of "welcome home" kissing that day, I can tell you.

Shortly after Ed's return, I was given an honorable discharge from the Navy, since I was to marry an ex-POW. My actual discharge did not come through right away after his return, and I was officially discharged on May 27, 1945. Ed and I were married on July 28, 1945.

WAVES—WE DID OUR PART, TOO
by Betty Bragg Clark

Betty Clark in her Navy WAVE uniform.

On December 7, 1941, I volunteered to help in the "filter center," located in the basement of the Fresno Main Post Office on Van Ness Ave. The filter center was a place where a tracking system was set up to observe any and all aircraft flying around the area. The Center operated on a 24-hour-a-day basis. There was a large map on a table, which filled a considerable part of the room. The map reflected the area from San Francisco to below Bakersfield. Over 3,000 people known as "spotters" were located all around the valley.

The spotters were all civilian volunteers and had regular assigned stations and certain time periods to work. If they saw an airplane they placed a call to the filter center and, using a code name for their station to identify themselves, they passed the information on about the type of airplane, approximate altitude, speed and direction of travel. This information was then transferred to the large map. We used long sticks to push toy airplanes, resembling different types of aircraft, around the map to simulate their flight paths across the valley. This type of operation was needed because radar wasn't available at the time. I worked my regular job during the day, and at night I volunteered to track air traffic through the valley. I thought it was fun to work in the filter center, and I also felt I was helping the war effort.

A close friend, Helen Jane Hall (Caraway), had joined the Navy and was stationed at Corpus Christi, Texas. My cousins, Patty Nutt, and I decided that was just the thing to do, so we enlisted in the WAVES (Women Accepted for Voluntary Emergency Service). On July 9, 1944, we left Fresno on our first cross-country train trip headed to Hunter College in New York City, New York, for basic training. The trip was to take about five days and I had an upper berth in the

NERVE CENTER OF VALLEY'S AIR PROTECTIVE SERVICE

On December 7, 1941, Betty Clark volunteered to work in the Fresno filter center. (Photo from the Fresno Bee, *December 8th, 1941.)*

sleeper car. I woke up the first morning about 5:00 A.M. with some man calling out, "Hit the deck! Hit the deck!" I couldn't figure out what in the world he was yelling about, but I soon found out.

My father definitely was not too happy with my decision to enlist. He had sometimes worked near Fort Mason, California, and he had seen how some of the soldiers treated the WACS (Women's Army Corps). He did not want his little girl treated that way. I told him, "Oh, that wouldn't happen to us," and it didn't. Anytime it looked like I was in trouble of any kind there was a sailor around they would always stop us and ask, "May I help you?" or "Do you need my help?" I felt very safe. My dad also thought some of the WACs were not very refined, so he was apprehensive when I told him I had enlisted, but I hadn't told him until after I had joined, so there wasn't much anyone could do but make the best of it.

At basic training we studied the nomenclatures of ships and planes, and we did the usual calisthenics and marching. I loved the marching and the reviews. While we were at Hunter College the WAVES celebrated their third birthday. We had a great big to-do about that. We had all kinds of admirals and officers in attendance and New York City Mayor Fiorello LaGuardia was there. I thought it all was just wonderful, but it was very hot and the girls were dropping over like flies. They had warned us against standing with our knees stiff. If you keep your knees bent, you won't faint, but there were still a lot of mishaps.

The Navy had apartments for us in the Bronx, close to Hunter College. Our apartment had two bedrooms with one bathroom, with ten girls to share it. The only furnishings were bunk beds and a couple of chairs.

After another school session in Milledgeville, Georgia, to study to become a storekeeper, I was assigned back to San Francisco, California. My parents had sold their ranch outside of Fresno, and my father was working repairing ships at

General Engineering and Dry Dock in San Francisco. This proved to be very lucky for me because the Navy didn't have any barracks for women, and upon arrival we were told, "Go find a place to live." The YWCA was full, and housing was hard to find, so I was indeed fortunate to be able to move home with my parents.

I was attached to the 12th Naval District, and my office was at 3rd and Berry St. at the Overseas Transport Shipment Depot. Two sailors and two civilians co-workers went out everyday to the various freight yards and inspected all the shipments that were coming in and gave me reports. From those reports I had the typists type up the ocean bills of lading. I came to work at 8:00 A.M. and went home at 5:00 P.M. I enjoyed the work and my being there helped free up the men to do their work during the war.

On August 15, 1945, I was on the Southern Pacific "Daylight" headed toward Los Angeles for a few day's vacation when it was announced over the loud speakers that the war had ended in Japan. World War II was over! No one said a word. Everyone just sat there stunned. Nobody turned to his neighbor, shook hands, hugged or anything. There was just stone silence. We had gotten so used to having war that it seemed like it could go on forever and ever and ever. I don't think anything really went back to "normal" after that because things had changed so much. People were landing in different parts of the country, but it was wonderful to be able to look toward the future.

Betty Clark volunteered to enlist in the WAVES in July, 1944. The photo is of her graduation ceremony.

A CORPUS CHRISTI HURRICANE
by Helen Caraway

A storm warning came to Corpus Christi Naval Air Station. "A hurricane approaching," was announced over the squawk box in the women's barracks. It was around eleven in the morning, and the barracks were secured and had sand bags at the doors by that time.

"No personnel are to leave quarters," the squawk box announced.

By noon, many of the WAVES had gathered needlework and hurried toward the large recreation room in the barracks. Being with others seemed to be comforting. Some brought in books and magazines to read, but didn't.

I joined some of my co-workers near the window. I put my embroidery aside and looked outside. All I could see were small four-foot palm trees here and there on the flat, level ground. I turned to my friend Marion and said, "Oh, I'd sure like to see some trees with size to them. There's nothing around here that resembles a tree of any size. When I get leave and get back to California, I'm going to hug the first big tree I can. This place is so treeless, flat, hot and humid."

"Well, maybe it'll look different soon. You heard the announcement on the squawk box. I'm really afraid. I've never been in a hurricane before," Marion said. "Neither have I," I replied, as I restlessly moved away from the windows.

The room seemed exceptionally quiet, and a tenseness filled the air as if something serious was about to happen. It soon did. It started to rain, and the sky became dark. The wind was extremely strong and rattled the windows and blew things against the building. It was unreal. By noon heavy rains and wild winds struck harder.

Before long, ugly brown water was as high as the windowsills. The rain was coming down so hard and fast, one couldn't see anything outside the window. Around 3:00 P.M. the phones were still operating. A call came through from the commander of the Celestial Navigation Link Trainer building. The order was made: three of us WAVES SpTs were to leave the barracks and go secure the Celestial Navigation building which was approximately a mile and a half away.

It was an unbelievable order.

The WAVES' barracks were secured; no one was to leave the barracks. There was ugly water, waist-high, swirling around the door and windows. The winds were ferocious. The Watch Officer on duty made some telephone calls, but the commander's orders stood. Edie, Trudy, and I were told to leave the barracks as ordered. We were warned to be careful as the power lines were down in many places.

A last minute attempt was made by another officer to get the orders changed, but by that time the telephone lines were down, too. She was unsuccessful.

We donned our lined overcoats over our uniforms, put on our overseas caps and helped remove sand bags from inside. We stepped out into blackness, heavy rain, wild winds, and waist high flood waters. We grabbed the overcoat belt of our friend in front of us. We struggled in single file away from our well-wishers and the warmth of the barracks, each carrying a small useless flashlight, and headed out for the Link Trainer building.

Helen Caraway volunteered for the WAVES and survived a hurricane while stationed at Corpus Christi.

We had walked our way through the barracks grounds hundreds of times but never under conditions like this. After a little progress was made, the one in front felt her way back to the end position, and leadership changed positions. We continued this pattern periodically. All three hung on for dear life to one another, and not a word was exchanged.

It took a long, long time to get through the line of barracks. There were many stumbles and sometimes one or another would go completely under the flood waters. Each one knew there could be live electric wires down, but in the blackness and dark very little could be seen.

After finally leaving the barracks area we trudged, slopped and stumbled through the muddy water. It seemed like an eternity. We were cold, wet, and so terribly frightened. We became confused and numb but still kept moving, as if in a dream. The strong wind pushed us as if we were in a current, maybe we were. There's no logical explanation of how we ended up at the Celestial Navigation building. The power and guidance from above, our continued moving, the strength gained from one another and our own inner strength may have helped. Many unexplainable factors helped us arrive, only to learn that three sailors had secured the building earlier.

The earlier warning of the approaching hurricane had given the sailors of the crew enough time to be prepared. They had lanterns, strong flashlights, candles, food, blankets and coffee. The sailors welcomed three drenched, almost hysteri-cal WAVES. They gave us cups of hot Navy coffee, plenty of compassion, and cheered us with their jokes and banter. Tears of relief and hysteria were drowned in the coffee and stories began to sprout forth of the commander's attitude and ineptitude.

One of the sailors commented, "What do you expect from a commander that got his commission the way he did. You know he was a professor of astronomy at some little college in a hick town in the middle of California."

About that time Trudy spoke up, "I'll never forgive him for sending us out into that hurricane and fallen electrical wires to secure this darned building!" For quiet, proper little Trudy to speak up like that really impressed me. In fact, I felt very impressed and proud of everyone there at the time of the hurricane.

The hurricane eventually passed. We three WAVES survived, clean-up took place, and Navy life continued.

FOR THE CONVENIENCE OF THE GOVERNMENT

by Vera Thacker

I was born in Woodbury, New York, in January of 1923. My mother was a home-maker, and my father worked for the Long Island Railroad. We lived in Syosset in Long Island, New York. My father passed away when I was fifteen years old and my mother was left to support two children, remaining at home on her own. My personal hopes of acquiring a college education grew dim.

As I entered my high school years, America was on the verge of war. I can recall on one peaceful Sunday afternoon when my girlfriend and I came out of a matinee movie to hear the excitement brewing on the streets. We were both shocked to hear that Japan had attacked Pearl Harbor, Hawaii, earlier that day. It was December 7, 1941.

As I was completing my high school education, I experienced America at war on the home front, and even though we were now at war, I still felt secure in our home in Mountain Lakes, New Jersey, even after we were told to put up blackout curtains in our homes at night.

As time went by there were vital jobs in the community that were being vacated by men who were joining the war effort in growing numbers. Many women were now being called upon to fill in the vacu-um, and they willingly accepted jobs once traditionally available exclusively for men. The era of "Rosie the Riveter" was now in full swing. At the same time, more and more women began to appear in uniform. This trend surprised the recruiters. I thought that this might be my big chance to see the world outside New Jersey at last. As my college hopes were further

Vera Thacker enlisted in the US Marines, where she met and married a Marine.

A Marine recruiting poster targeting women.

dimmed by shadows of war, I decided to enlist in the military after high school.

After considering my choices, I decided that the title of U.S. Marine sounded the best to me. I kept my enlistment a secret until I needed my mother's signature freeing me to appear for boot camp. When my mother finally did find out about my plan, she was quite upset and really worried for me. But there was a war on, and I wanted to help out and maybe see some of the world outside New Jersey.

Not long afterward I reported for my Marine boot training at Camp Lejune, North Carolina. I was now considered government property. Boot camp in the U.S. Marines was about the toughest experience of my life. We were up at 6 A.M. for military training, close order drills, barracks' inspections and lots and lots of physical training. And I'll never forget all those shots, the push-ups and the nasty kick of an M-14 out on the rifle range. After what felt like a lifetime, I graduated from boot camp. I was now officially a United States Woman Marine.

After boot camp, I can recall my excitement when I was asked for my choice of possible duty station assignments. I requested a duty station in some far off, exotic place like California. I received my placement orders soon afterward, assigning me as a Marine escort/guard at a supply depot....in Philadelphia. I don't remember which was greater, my own disappointment or my Mother's relief.

After some time in duty at the supply depot, I met a handsome, young Marine by the name of Gordon Thacker. We fell in love and were later married in May of 1944. Soon afterward, my new husband was ordered to ship out for overseas duty. I had later learned that married Marines were not allowed to share the same duty assignment location.

Although our letters were heavily censored, my husband and I communicated with a little pre-established code system. I knew he was now stationed in Hawaii. I also knew, as many assumed, that the Marines were there to train for the inevitable invasion of Japan. Along with this unnerving news, I also was surprised to learn that I was expecting our first child.

Well, the U.S. military apparently had little need for a pregnant Marine corporal, and not long afterward I received an honorable discharge with the added clause "for the convenience of the government."

With my husband still overseas, our daughter was born; the total cost to us at that time was 54 cents in state tax. Uncle Sam picked up the tab for the hospital and doctor's bill.

Not long after our daughter's birth, President Truman ordered that the atomic bomb be dropped on Japan. A land invasion became unnecessary, and the war came to a speedy end. With my husband missing out on an active combat assignment, he lacked sufficient service points for an early discharge. By the time he was finally discharged, the job market at home had already reached the saturation point. Our daughter was now seven months old.

In spite of our financial hardships, we managed to survive and go on to contribute a second and third child, both boys, to the great baby boom generation of the early 50s.

In 1965, in the midst of the Vietnam War, our son, Gordon Jr., repeated my enlistment scheme and secretly enlisted in the U.S. Marines. He served a full tour of duty in Vietnam and completed a second tour stateside at the Lemoore Naval Air Station through the war's end. In my son's absence, I went through the same sense of fear, apprehension and eventual relief that my mother must have felt for me, many years earlier. But I can also assure you, that there were two ex-Marines in the family that were mighty proud of him.

EPILOGUE: VICTORY IN THE PACIFIC

On August 10th, 1945, the Japanese Empire, recognizing its imminent defeat, asked the Allies if unconditional surrender meant that Emperor Hirohito would have to give up his throne. The Allies responded that they would leave it to the Japanese to decide his fate. On August 14th the Allies received the message that Japan would lay down their arms.

On September 2, 1945, meeting on the deck of the battleship *Missouri* in Tokyo Bay, General MacArthur signed the terms of surrender for the Allies, with Admiral Nimitz signing for the United States. Foreign Minister Mamoru Shigemitsu signed for Japan. President Truman proclaimed September 2 as V-J Day (Victory over Japan Day).

World War II came to a close exactly three years, eight months, and twenty-two days after the Japanese bombed Pearl Harbor. When the war was over, lives returned to a new normal. Loved ones in the armed forces returned home, many suffering physical or psychological scars. The economy was robust, and a new era of prosperity emerged.

After World War II ended history books on the subject started appearing. The "whys" and the "why nots," the "should haves," the regrets, and the pain lingered, but a powerful sense of satisfaction in overcoming a tremendous worldwide evil remained a dominant theme in America for a long time to come.

Now, sixty years later, the veterans of the San Joaquin Valley have told their stories.

APPENDIX: CONTRIBUTORS' RANK AND SERVICE

Anderson, Ellis . . . . Colonel, Army Air Corp
Bestenheider, Louis . . . . Tech Sgt. Radio Operator, Army Air Corp
Begley, Bill . . . . Senior Master Sergeant B-2, Army Air Corp
Blankinship, Hubert Arnold . . . . Paymaster, Navy
Bos, Aileen . . . . Home front
Bos, Gene . . . . Electrician's Mate 3rd Class, Navy
Blumer, Albert Fred . . . . Gunners Mate 2nd Class, Navy
Brummer, Robert . . . . Merchant Marine
Burgstaller, W.E. . . . . Home front
Burgess, Troy . . . . Boatswain Mate 2nd Class, Navy
Caraway, Helen . . . . Specialist First Class, Navy
Cedillo, Juan . . . . 23rd Armored Infantry Division, E-5, Army
Christensen, Chris . . . . Lieutenant Junior Grade, Navy
Clark, Betty Bragg . . . . Storekeeper 2nd Class, Navy
Comstock, Harold . . . . Colonel, Army Air Corp/Air Force (WWII, Vietnam)
Coon, Harold . . . . Private First Class, Army
Coon, Nina York . . . . Home front
Costello, John . . . . Private First Class, Army
Creed, Frank J. . . . . Private First Class, Army
Daves, Edward H. . . . . Captain, Army Air Corp
Daves, Edna . . . . Specialist First Class, Navy
Day, Russell E. . . . . Gunners Mate 1st Class, Navy
Dormandy, Dorothy . . . . Specialist Teacher 3rd Class, Navy
Dumas, Jim . . . . Major, Army Air Corp
Dunbar, Robert . . . . 2nd Lieutenant, Army Air Corp
Dyer, Robert E. . . . . Staff Sergeant, Army Air Corp
Enderson, Eugene . . . . Technical Sergeant, Army Air Corp
Fisher, Jerry . . . . Home front
Frame, Leonard . . . . Lieutenant Colonel, Army Air Corp/USAF Reserve
Gilpin, Thomas . . . . Aviation Engineer, Army Air Corp
Harmon, Hubert B. "Doc" . . . . . Petty Officer 3rd Class, Navy
Hill, Art . . . . Captain, Army Combat Engineers
Hinds, Russell H. . . . . Corporal, Army
Horton, Lowell Ivan . . . . 1st Class Petty Officer, Navy Sea Bees
Ikeda, Ike . . . . Military Intelligence Staff Sergeant, Army
Jenks, LeRoy . . . . Captain, Army

Johnson, Richard Y. . . . . 1st Lieutenant, Army (WWII, Korea)

Johnston, Hugh . . . . Staff Sgt, Army Air Corp

Jones, Charles H. . . . . Private First Class, Army

Kastner, George . . . . Colonel, Army Air Corp (WWII, Korea)

Kerber, George . . . . Machinist Mate 2nd Class, Navy

Knight, Jack . . . . Staff Sergeant, Army Air Corp

Lee, Harold . . . . Private First Class, Army

Lindquist, Stan . . . . Medical Corp, Army

Loring, Fred . . . . Staff Sergeant, Army Air Corp

Lynch, Betty Jane . . . . Lieutenant Colonel, Army Nurse Corp

Martin, George . . . . Major, Army Air Corp

McKinney, Glen . . . . 1st Lieutenant, Army Air Corp

McLaughlin, Thomas . . . . Lieutenant, Navy

McLeod, William Swinton . . . . . Lieutenant Colonel, Army Air Corp/
Air Force Reserve

McMullen, Charles D. . . . . Military Police Sergeant, Army

Mirigian-Emerzian, Penny . . . . . Radioman 3rd Class, Navy

Middleton, George Delbert. . . . . Brigadier General, Army Air Corp/Air Force/
Air National Guard

Nicholson, Fred . . . . Gunner's Mate 3rd Class, Navy

Nichols, Carl . . . . Intelligence Officer, Army Air Corp

Norris, Maude . . . . Home front

Ohama, Abraham . . . . Technical Sergeant, Army

Owens, Robert . . . . Commander, Navy

Porter, R. Bruce . . . . Colonel, Marines

Rockwell, Leon . . . . Major, Army Air Corp

Roddy, Edward . . . . Colonel, Army Air Corp

Ruggles, Joseph A. . . . . Hospital Corpsman, Navy

Rye, Jay . . . . Master Sergeant, Army

Salazar, Jose Sanchez . . . . Medical Corp, Army

Schmidt, Vernon . . . . Master Sergeant, Army

Sidebottom, Alfred . . . . Chief Boatswain Mate, Navy

Smith, Victor . . . . Aviator Radar Tech 3rd Class, Navy

Spencer, Herbert . . . . Boatswain Mate, Navy

Stella, William . . . . Lieutenant 2nd Grade, Navy

Tanaka, Carolyn, ... Army Nurse Corp.

Thacker, Vera . . . . Corporal, Marines

Tokumoto, William . . . . Major, Army Air Corp

Toledo, Manuel . . . . Staff Sergeant, Army; Captain, National Guard

Von Prince, Kilulu . . . . Lieutenant Colonel, Army

Warwick, James . . . . First Lieutenant, Army Air Corp

Woodward, Jess . . . . Merchant Marine

Wyman, Thelma . . . . Home front

Yamada, Hitoshi. . . . . Home front

Yamasaki, June . . . . Translator, State Department

INDEX

Note: Names of aircraft and ships can be found under the heading for the type of craft, ie., entries for the B-17 Flying Fortress can be found under the heading "bombers."

ABOUT THE AUTHOR

Janice Stevens has an accomplished academic career, earning an MA from California State University Fresno in English Composition, and a BA from CSU Fresno in English Literature. Additionally, she holds a State of California Clear Teaching Credential in the designated subjects of Gerontology and Communications.

Janice was a former staff writer for the *Business Journal*, and a freelance writer for the *Fresno Bee* and other community newspapers. Much of her professional life has been in the classroom, teaching English and related courses at State Center Community College in Clovis, California, and memoir writing, literature and genealogy at Clovis Adult Education. She is also the co-owner of Gallery II, an art gallery shared with her colleague, water colorist Pat Hunter. Together the two co-authored Janice's first book, *Fresno's Architectural Past*, published in 2006 by Linden Publishing. Its sequel, *Fresno's Architectural Past, Vol. II*, will be published in the fall of 2007.